PENELOPE HOBHOUSE'S NATURAL PLANTING

PENELOPE HOBHOUSE'S
Natural Planting

PENELOPE HOBHOUSE

Photographs by Jerry Harpur

Henry Holt and Company

New York

Henry Holt and Company, Inc.
Publishers since 1866
115 West 18th Street
New York, New York 10011

Henry Holt® is a registered trademark of Henry Holt and Company, Inc.

Copyright © 1997 by Penelope Hobhouse
All photographs copyright © by Jerry Harpur
except: 129 © Philip Corell
130, 131TL,B © Galen Gates
114, 118, 142 © Marcus Harpur
120 © Nan Sinton
10L, R © Royal Horticultural Society, Lindley Library

Originally published in 1997 in Great Britain by Pavilion Books Ltd.

Library of Congress Cataloging in Publication Data is available on request.

ISBN 0-8050-4490-6

Henry Holt Books are available for special promotions and premiums.
For details contact: Director, Special Markets.

First American Edition – 1997

Printed and bound in Spain by Egedsa

All first editions are printed on acid-free paper ∞

10 9 8 7 6 5 4 3 2 1

AUTHOR'S ACKNOWLEDGEMENTS

I am so grateful to Pavilion for allowing me to write this book. I particularly enjoyed working with Anne Askwith and James Bennett. I have worked with Penny David on many books, and cannot sufficiently express my admiration for her skills, her grasp of the subject matter for each book in turn and for her rare editorial skill, which enables her to gather up my writing inadequacies and turn the book into an efficient text. I must also thank her for always being at the end of the telephone or fax machine ready with wise advice. Nan Sinton has been invaluable in correcting horticultural slips and guiding me through the American climatic extremes, as well as, in a more practical way, identifying plants. Dr Brent Elliott and his team at the Lindley Library were invaluable to my research.

Jerry Harpur's pictures speak for themselves. He has captured the essence of the gardens, their rare beauty and, above all, the 'natural' look which conveys the message of the book. In order to do this he has travelled extensively. Nothing would be possible without the kindness of the owners of the gardens who have allowed Jerry Harpur to take the pictures. The gardens, of course, have also inspired the book. It is the owners who work with nature who have encouraged me to discuss natural planting. I cannot name them all but amongst the modern gardeners who have most influenced me, and whose gardens help to illustrate the book, are those of John Brookes, Frank Cabot, Beth Chatto and Ton ter Linden.

PHOTOGRAPHER'S ACKNOWLEDGEMENTS

I would particularly like to thank all of the garden owners and designers in Great Britain, the United States, Canada, France, Germany, Italy, Holland, Australia, New Zealand and Chile who co-operated with the photography of this book. Without the enthusiasm of Susan Rowley, who edited all of the pictures, liaised with the author and the publisher and ensured that they arrived on schedule, none of these could have appeared and I am very grateful.

CONTENTS

Foreword 6

Chapter 1
THE NATURAL TRADITION 8

Chapter 2
PLANTING TO PLEASE PLANTS 36

Chapter 3
WOODLAND AND WOODLAND EDGE 64

Chapter 4
SHRUB BORDER AND SHRUBBERY 92

Chapter 5
OPEN GROUND 116

Chapter 6
WATER, ROCK AND GRAVEL 156

Bibliography 184
Index 186

FOREWORD

*I*N ANY WILD landscape, nature establishes natural plant communities which depend on the climate and aspect: heat and cold, soil, sun and shade, rain and moisture, altitude and latitude. In the best gardens, man-made communities of garden plants – many coming from different lands but with similar needs – live and thrive together in natural harmonies. When you first start to garden you see the plants only as tools to be used for composing pictures. Colours, shapes, forms and habits of plants are combined together to produce certain aesthetically pleasing results. In arranging the plants to make a beautiful garden the gardener needs to be an artist; but he also needs to know his plants and the individual plants' requirements in order to get them to grow well. Plants will only give a sustainable 'performance' if they are given the sort of growing conditions they enjoy. In appreciating garden planting it is worthwhile looking beyond the purely pictorial effects and thinking about whether the plant associations will work in the long term, with plants from similar habitats growing together in harmony. It is far more jarring to the eye and mind to see a garden where the wrong plants have been placed beside one another, plants which, in nature, have completely different requirements, than it is to feel that the wrong sorts of colour scheme have been used – a very subjective and unimportant judgement. The experienced gardener finds that plants have other characteristics besides their obvious and rather superficial colours and shapes. These may be nothing to do with their botanical characteristics. They have certain identifiable traits which can help identify their garden requirements, and give a hint as to the sort of habitats they will have come from. Just by looking at a plant, it is often possible to make a very good guess as to what sort of conditions it will enjoy. Grey-leaved plants generally come from countries with hot summers and will need a well-drained garden soil; lush thick-stemmed plants with large leaves come from wet regions, and they need moisture. A plant's appearance, or physiognomy, will reveal whether it thrives in dry stony ground and will endure hot sun, or comes from swampy marshy meadows and will need plenty of moisture, especially in its growing period in spring. Large soft exotic-shaped leaves which allow rain to run off will come from tropical regions and be too tender for most garden situations above a certain latitude or altitude.

More and more gardeners today want to garden in a natural way. They do not necessarily want to make gardening dull by growing only indigenous plants, but they want to make garden tasks less onerous, less labour-intensive, by growing plants together which will not require endless sorting out, dividing, and replanting. They also want to prevent pollution by using artificial fertilizers and pesticides as little as possible.

Planting in natural ways – that is 'planting to please plants' – can be done in different ways. Leaving out true native plant gardening – for which there may often be sound ecological arguments – the most obvious is to select only plants which are native to your region or come from regions which are almost identical in aspect. An example would be gardening in California with natives and Mediterranean-type plants. This should mean literally gardening with nature and, apart from design and aesthetic considerations, entails minimum preparation and amendment of the site, although there may well be frequent and quite skilful 'editing'. William Robinson recommended this sort of planting in his wild garden. The second natural approach involves using plants from all parts of the world and trying to re-create for each plant the garden conditions as similar as possible to those of their own habitat, and growing plants with similar needs together, so that they look comfortable and 'right' in association. Beth Chatto has been the great teacher in this context. Obviously this approach, while still 'natural', is less ecologically and environmentally orientated and more labour-intensive, but it does mean that the possible range of plants you can grow is extended. Soil can be amended, microclimatic pockets created and any other horticultural skills employed to 'improve' the site in a permanent way so that exotic plants from other regions will form their own artificial plant communities. The important point is that plants are given conditions to please them, and will reward you by thriving. This 'right association' theme can and should be extended to include emphasizing growing plants which not only look right together but look right in their landscape. In a country garden on chalk downs or alkaline clay (such as my own new garden in Dorset)

it would seem folly to try to make a rhododendron garden. And it would be unsuitable. John Brookes has reminded us how important it is to look at your own countryside and try to match seasonal colours to the landscape, fitting your garden into its surroundings. As a designer I want to consider all these things. First, to discover the nature of the landscape in which the garden you are about to work on is set, and then try to make an appropriate garden. Then in choosing the actual plants I need to know as much as possible about the terrain and climate of the original habitat of any exotics, and decide how they will mix with plants native to the region. In some circumstances, for conservation reasons or in order to keep an unspoiled landscape 'pure', it may be good to use only natives – especially where (as in North America) so much damage has been done by the spread of escaped aliens; originally introduced to gardens or planted to prevent erosion, these are now known as ecological bandits and prevent re-creation of vanished landscape features such as the Midwest prairies.

Professor's Hansen's book *Perennials and their Garden Habitats* has been a great source of inspiration. My own book, quite different in content and only exploratory, has been shaped around his definition of different garden environments, which helped me to decide on the themes of my chapters. For me, writing this book has proved not only an exploration of the natural planting movement but – by studying plant origins and needs in so much detail – a learning experience which enriches my whole gardening life.

Penelope Hobhouse

CHAPTER ONE

The NATURAL TRADITION

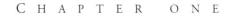

*T*HE TWENTIETH CENTURY has seen a significant development in approaches to gardening that can be described as 'natural'. This means capturing the essence of nature's intentions, and interpreting that by using plants appropriate to the environment – thus, incidentally, saving water and eliminating the need for fertilizers and pesticides. All over the world gardeners have found strong reasons for gardening in these new ecological ways and are succeeding in doing so effectively, without sacrificing aesthetic values, although as we learn from nature these values may change to allow new interpretations of beauty. This book sets out to explore the origins of the movement and how it is the legacy of one man in particular that has influenced such gardening today; to show why, both for ecological reasons and for the benefit of plants, gardeners should consider this approach; and to demonstrate, using examples of gardens from around the world, how natural gardening works and how it can be adopted in one's own garden.

(Left) Planting looks relaxed and naturalistic in the old gravel quarry at Weihenstephan in Munich, with plants establishing almost self-sustaining communities. This 'extensive' gardening works best in large areas. *Lobelia cardinalis* and *L. siphilitica*, cardinal flowers from eastern North America, and *Ligularia przewalskii* (from northern China) thrive in deep moist soil. Big, heavy grasses form the backdrop and a riot of nasturtiums (*Tropaeolum majus*) carpets the ground. The butterfly bush (*Buddleja davidii*) prefers poor waste ground where it will seed prolifically.

(Above) Papery Californian matilija poppies (romneyas) grow with *Lobelia tupa* from Chile in the Essex garden of Beth Chatto, one of the most influential naturalistic modern gardeners, who skilfully combines plants from the same sorts of habitat and with similar requirements. These two examples both need full sun and excellent drainage.

Chromolithographs of the garden at William Robinson's home, Gravetye Manor in Sussex, pictured in *What England Can Teach Us About Gardening* by Wilhelm Miller (Doubleday, Page and Co., 1911).

During William Robinson's working life – between approximately 1870, the date when his book *The Wild Garden* was published, and 1935, when he died – a new naturalistic mode of gardening adaptable for climates all over the world was established and encouraged. Robinson's literary output in books and magazines lasted from his first publication in 1859 almost to his death. It was through these prolific writings, rather than for designing gardens, that he exerted the great influence that has continued to inspire gardeners ever since. His primary aim, first expressed in *The Wild Garden*, had been to discourage the annual waste involved in bedding-out schemes where untold amounts of skill, energy and expense went into creating colourful patterns of tender exotics that would succumb to the first frosts, but the implications of his advocating using 'vast numbers of beautiful hardy plants from other countries which might be naturalised ... in many situations in our plantations, field and woods – a world of delightful plant beauty' goes far beyond this limited

viewpoint. Although other writers and gardeners had expressed similar ideas to this all through the period of the fashionable bedding system, what distinguished his approach was his insistence on using hardy plants, both native and exotic, in places where they would spread and thrive – especially in the outer garden, in woodland, on woodland edge and by natural water. He himself was careful to point out the difference between the 'wild garden' and the older (and strangely formal) idea of the 'wilderness' plantation: 'What it does mean is best explained by the winter Aconite flowering under a grove of naked trees in February; by the Snowflake, tall and numerous in meadows by the Thames side; by the blue Lupine dyeing an islet purple in a Scotch river; and by the blue Apennine Anemone staining an English wood blue before the coming of our blue bells. Multiply these instances a thousandfold, given by many types of plants, from countries colder than ours, and one may get a just idea of the "Wild Garden".' In 1870, a time when the fashionable grand gardens still indulged in all sorts of artificially produced planting schemes, Robinson's ideas seemed revolutionary. He encouraged working with nature rather than in contradiction to it, choosing plants suitable for a garden site rather than first choosing a style (or plants to suit a style) and then adapting the conditions and aspect to accommodate those plants. The development of this 'Robinsonian' way of planting (long before gardeners adopted the more scientific jargon of ecological gardening, habitats and plant communities), influenced the twentieth-century development of appropriate garden planting all over the world: gardening styles in which not only wild flowers but also exotic ornamentals are given conditions as similar as possible to those they enjoy in their native regions. Robinson did not insist on native planting only. The right plants for the natural garden were those – from any country – that would grow and spread in their new garden environment. With justification William Robinson can be named the 'grandfather' of the natural tradition and of the environmental movement.

Parts of his work reflect his bombastic style, his hostility to the role in the garden of the architect (or indeed of any preconceived pattern design; he referred to Victorian formality as 'the pastry-cook's garden'), and an emotional rather than a rational appeal to nature. Most of his thoughts were not original, but his great success was in putting his ideas across. Much of his best writing concentrates on the simple fact that plants will thrive if given the conditions they enjoy. It is Robinson's influence on plants and planting styles, on the essential role of knowledge in planning, planting and maintaining schemes, that are important. His advocation of observing nature and of using plants in natural ways, meaning that only plants, both native and exotic, suitable for a garden site would be used, mirrors modern ecological thought in garden practice and horticultural styles.

Although William Robinson's publication of *The Wild Garden* in 1870 was a landmark in its advocacy of using hardy plants in natural ways, his was not an original or indeed a sole voice condemning the artificiality of

excessive formality and of Victorian bedding-out extravagance. But in his descriptive detail he has had more influence on twentieth-century planting habits than perhaps any other writer or designer. His viewpoint, derived in part from Ruskin, and much in sympathy with views later expressed by William Morris and the whole Arts and Crafts movement, was as highly moral in tone as the native-plant enthusiasts of today. His works are still quoted in each continent, wherever 'natural gardening' is advocated.

William Robinson's thoughts echoed another, earlier gardening philosophy in which nature was invoked. The almost flowerless eighteenth-century naturalistic landscape evolved in England as an art form. The style was adopted and developed all over the globe, and is still in places revered as 'the English Garden', although its 'Englishness' lies mainly in its interpretation as such in the minds of historians of garden development in western civilization. The natural landscape garden, which

At the Edsell Ford Garden in Detroit, Robinsonian-type natural planting includes drifts of American woodland plants such as the Virginia bluebells or Virginia cowslip (*Mertensia virginica*, syn. *M. pulmonaroides*), planted in naturalistic sweeps in the acid soil under the light canopy of amelanchiers, also from northeast America. Mertensias go dormant during the summer and winter and flower briefly in the spring, colonizing with daffodils or other American woodlanders.

Putting Theory into Practice: Robinson at Gravetye

(Left) In the small walled garden beside the manor house, where Robinson originally experimented with carnations, aromatic-leaved sages from eastern and southern Europe grow with glaucous-leaved *Crambe maritima* in the flowerbeds under walls clothed with honeysuckle and roses. The common valerian (*Centhranthus ruber*), with long flowerheads of small pinkish-red blooms, seeds and spreads throughout – as Robinson says, valerian is 'often naturalized on walls, ruins, and on rocky and stony banks' – but also fits well into more formal schemes, providing a naturalistic touch to more stereotyped planting.

(Below) So-called Japanese anemones, many originating in China, and *Anemone hupehensis* – together with their many hybrids and cultivars – are very adaptable, but prefer moist, fertile, humus-rich soil. Well-mulched in winter, even in more continental-type climates, they are quite hardy, but will not tolerate waterlogged soil. They look their best when grown in great sweeps on the sunnier edges of woodland or at the backs of borders.

The garden at William Robinson's own home, Gravetye Manor in Sussex, has been meticulously restored by Peter Herbert since 1958, and the house with its grounds is now run as a luxury hotel. In the woods and fields – his 'wild garden' – bulbs planted in thousands by Robinson in the first thirty years of the twentieth century continue to multiply. It is for this style of natural gardening that he is best remembered; however, he also recognized the need for some formal features near the house, designing terracing and putting up pergolas to make a visual platform on which the building could rest comfortably and providing vertical accents to balance with its strong architectural lines. Although in this area much of the actual design is based on geometry, with stone paths parallel to the house intersecting at right angles, the planting reflects Robinson's – and Gertrude Jekyll's – natural style. Plants spill over walls, steps and terraces; shrubs suitable to the acid sandy soil are mixed in cottage-garden abandon with bulbs and summer-flowering perennials; climbers twine over the surrounding walls, and self-seeding plants volunteer to blur the more formal outlines of hardscape. Robinson sowed forget-me-nots and Iceland poppies between the rhizomes of German irises and encouraged common centranthus to seed into nooks and crannies where it could never be planted. 'The real flower garden near the house is for the ceaseless care and culture of many diverse things often tender and in need of protection in varied and artificial soils, staking, cleaning, trials of novelties, study of colour effects lasting many weeks, sowing and mowing at all seasons.'

Robinson recognized that all gardeners have to experiment with plants from many diverse origins before being certain of success in their particular ground – especially when planting out in the wilder areas of lower maintenance, where plants are expected to thrive and spread as they do in nature. Unless growing only native plants (the requirements of which can be studied at first hand), the natural gardener who uses exotics in the garden is often reliant on the accumulated experience of earlier gardeners who have experimented with new plants over years, or even centuries.

(Right) Robinson's garden at Gravetye is now a hundred years old, but recent restoration by Peter Herbert and his gardening team has ensured that the planting on the main terraces still has the Robinsonian look of tightly packed profusion. The view is dominated by a curtain of white wisteria – just beginning to fade – intermingling with a red rose. Edging the path, catmint (*Nepeta* 'Six Hills Giant') and *Iris pallida*, thriving in full sun and requiring well-drained stony soil, are enjoying the situation backed by the silver-leaved, pineapple-scented Moroccan broom (*Cytisus battandieri*), the latter introduced from Morocco only in 1922 but hardy enough in Sussex. The feathery *Aruncus dioicus* or goat's beard is an early-flowering perennial, thriving in any soil in sun and shade.

(Below right) Although William Robinson is remembered for his naturalistic planting, around the house he made formal terraces where planting was traditional, with straight-edged beds and paths at right angles. Among plants suitable for the well-drained soil is the spectactular *Eremurus robustus* from central Asia, a tufted perennial with strap-shaped leaves bearing pinkish-white flowers in early spring. It shares the open sunny site on the main terrace with flowering sages, hollyhocks and silver-leaved stachys.

The story of planting the garden at Gravetye, published in 1911 as *Gravetye Manor: or Twenty Years' Work round an Old Manor House*, describes the experimental nature of much of Robinson's early work in both the woods and the gardens around the house. In the original manuscript, as in his diary, he reveals not only successes but also failures and frustrations that are cheering to struggling gardeners today. Over the years Robinson planted hundreds of cyclamen, native bluebells (*Hyacinthoides non-scripta*), Apennine anemones and trilliums – although a note added that the ground was too dry and these had been 'much worried by slugs'. Aconites were planted but 'never did any good not liking soil'. The wild garden was for 'things that take care of themselves in the soil of the place ... Like narcissi on a rich orchard bottom, or blue anemones in a grove on the limestone soil'. Like most gardeners, Robinson wanted to grow everything possible, and was prepared to accept some failures with the successes. But his vision of the natural style provides the modern ecological gardener with an inspiring and idealistic example.

At Cetinale near Siena in Italy roses and the evergreen magnolia from Virginia (*Magnolia grandiflora*) grow below the more formal Italian garden, which dates to the seventeenth century. This English-type garden has distinct nuances of the cottage-style planting of Robinson and Jekyll, in which suitable plants scramble together creating natural-looking pictures inside quite a strong framework of walls and pathways. Roses, lavender and peonies all flower early in the summer before the hottest days.

changed the English countryside, imitated and idealized nature, copying nature's planting schemes with groves of trees rather than straight-lined avenues. Based on a naturalistic philosophy, influenced by romanticism in literature and painting, it permitted 'landscapers' to shape the countryside with trees and to mould land, lakes and rivers into new liquid shapes, imitating what they saw as nature. Not only were the 'old-fashioned' formal gardens featuring geometry and patterns inspired by Italian, French or Dutch models banned; indeed, the very countryside, currently being turned by newly enclosed fields into checkerboard patterns of hedgerows,

was also hidden from sight: replaced in grand estates by seamless views of pastoral parkland. The greatest practitioner of the new landscape movement, Lancelot 'Capability' Brown (1716–83), evolved a formula for creating artificial water features (their ends concealed by belts of trees), planting hanging woods, introducing trees in the middle distance and encircling the perimeter of an estate to bring parkland, grazed by sheep or deer, up to the windows of the house.

By the eighteenth century, when trees and shrubs hitherto unknown in Europe were flooding in to England (mainly from north-east America), the newly emerging naturalistic landscape style provided the perfect medium for experimenting with exotic arrivals. Indeed, it is possible that the existence and availability of the woody plants – English nurserymen were quick to start propagating and distributing – played a considerable part in directing the change in fashion from Italian and French garden formality, in which trees and shrubs of known predictability were clipped and shaped to make alleys and geometric patterns, to the more natural style, in which both native trees and new exotics would grow as free specimens in naturalistic groves. 'Capability' Brown himself was not primarily interested in new and rare trees (culture of which was still experimental), but he did include some of them as part of schemes in which he planted many hundreds of thousands of native oaks and developed trees from 'slips' taken from the hedgerows. However, many landowners – among them Lord Petre at Thorndon Hall in Essex, the Duke of Bedford at Woburn, the Duke of Richmond at Goodwood and Charles Hamilton at Painshill – assembled great collections of newly introduced trees and shrubs. As Thomas Whately remarked in *Observations on Modern Gardening* published in 1770, 'Gardening ... being released now from the restraints of regularity ... the most beautiful, the most simple, the most noble scenes of nature are all within its province.' Brown's schemes, designed to mature in two hundred years, involved planting 'nurse' trees calculated to shelter and promote growth of the more permanent specimens, designed as single landscape trees or part of a pleasing group.

Although it was the style that was naturalistic – an imitation, but not a copy of nature – much attention was given to providing the sort of conditions which both well-known and newly introduced trees, shrubs and plants required. Tree planting was the main ingredient of the great parks, but new shrubs and other plants found places in many experimental gardens and in more intimate areas of the pleasure grounds. At Whitton on Hounslow Heath in Middlesex the Duke of Argyll experimented with growing trees and shrubs from North America in his acid-type gravelly soil. Given these suitable conditions, andromedas and the small narrow-leaved shrubby *Kalmia angustifolia* from northern swamps spread rapidly to make thickets between American birch. In the acid soil at Painshill, Charles Hamilton grew American rhododendrons and azaleas. 'American Gardens', a newly coined term, had specially prepared acid soil to provide homes for trees and shrubs and small American woodlanders, which would even survive if given sites only approximating to their own native habitats. These gardens for calcifuges were not limited to American plants. So-called 'American Gardens' came to contain plants with similar requirements from other continents. Humphry Repton (1752–1818) laid out the American Garden at Woburn specifically for both American rhododendrons and Chinese plants such as hydrangeas, aucubas and *Camellia japonica*. Repton, a follower and admirer of Brown, improved his clients' grounds in practical ways, reinstating relatively formal gardens, terraces and balustrades near the house, while leaving the outer park to contain the elements of landscape in which nature should be manipulated to look as if 'art had never interfered'.

In the larger estates before the more formal box-edged layouts and hedged walks, and the great French-style avenues of the seventeenth century, had been swept away by the early 'landscapers', gardens for shrubs and flowers had developed along more naturalistic lines in what were known as 'wilderness' areas. At first these bosky regions were laid out with geometric walks; later, by the early eighteenth century, they included serpentine paths. Both Stephen Switzer (1682–1745) and Batty Langley in 1728 recommended an 'irregularity' in garden layouts. The wilderness served the need for seclusion, shelter and an element of surprise in the design of fashionable pleasure grounds. As early as 1700 Timothy Nourse in *Campania Foelix* seemed to pre-empt William Robinson by nearly two hundred years in his recommendations for planting naturalism. The evergreens were to be planted 'in some negligent Order', and 'Up and down let there be little Banks or Hillocks, planted with wild Thyme, Violets, Primroses, Cowslips, Daffadille, Lilies of the Valley, Blew-Bottles [*Centaurea cyanus*], Daisies, with all kinds of Flowers which grow wild in the Fields and Woods ... in a word let this be ... a real wilderness or Thicket ... to represent a perpetual Spring'. By the 1730s Philip Miller, curator of the Chelsea Physic Garden, in his *Gardener's Dictionary*, suggested planting 'next the walks and openings' of plantations (a naturalistic development of the geometric seventeenth-century wilderness), 'Roses, Honeysuckles, Spiraea frutex and other kinds of low flowering shrubs ... and at the foot of them, near the sides of the walks, may be planted primroses, Violets, daffodils and many sorts of wood flowers, to appear as a natural wood'. And again Joseph Spence, designing between 1736 and 1766, recommended that the 'best and lowest things should be scattered near the margins, the most pleasing wild flowers ... in the grove but particularly towards the walks and margins: primroses, violets, cowslips, wood strawberries', and beds were to be 'sow'd with grass seed ... intermix't with seeds of violets, cowslips, primroses and wild strawberries' to make a miniature meadow.

It is interesting to note the reiteration of old favourites, in spite of the fact that by this time many new woodland plants had been introduced. In his *ferme ornée* at Wooburn Farm, Philip Southcote grew beds of flowers between thickets of shrubs as described by Thomas

Whately in *Observations on Modern Gardening* (1770). At the front pinks served as edging, behind which in the first rank were bulbs – crocus, snowdrops, jonquils – succeeded by primroses. Stocks, sweet Williams, Canterbury bells, wallflowers, catchfly, carnations, lavender, scabious, marjoram and cotton lavender grew in the next line – all plants that cover the fading leaves of the spring flowers. Behind, taller lilies, hollyhocks, golden rod, columbine, starwort, honesty, crown imperials, sunflowers, peonies and evening primroses 'all replenished the air with their perfumes' and made 'every gale full of fragrancy'.

By the latter half of the eighteenth century the naturalistic contours of the English landscape were already being reinterpreted abroad, although not always successfully. The French *jardin anglais* or *anglo-chinois* with winding paths, bridges, follies and temples, often on quite a small scale, had little resemblance to the grandeur of the Brownian park: it merely lacked the formality that had earlier characterized French layouts (and that lack of symmetry reminded the French of the Chinese). A new English Garden was made in the 1780s for Queen Maria-Carolina of Naples at La Reggia, Caserta. As well as a pleasure garden laid out in the natural style, it was to be in part a botanic garden with schemes for experimental acclimatization of ornamentals and growing agricultural grasses. Those introducing foreign plants were already aware of climatic limitations.

The history of the landscape movement in the so-called English sense and its further development in other countries hardly concerns this book, but its philosophy is an important ingredient in the emergence of a distinctive way of natural planting, which, during the last hundred years, has been almost equally influential in garden development all over the world. Pioneers of natural gardening, although more concerned with plant detail, can, like Robinson, trace their inspiration to the landscape movement, and also to the more romantic and wilder notions contained in the advocation of the picturesque style by Uvedale Price in his *Essay on the*

Picturesque (1794) and by William Gilpin's *Tours* from 1787, in which Brown's serene lawns, quiet lakes and rounded clumps of trees could be replaced by the excitement of the jagged rocks, tumbling waters and windswept trees that were closer to a painter's idea of wild landscape. In some respects Gilpin anticipated Robinson in his naturalization of bulbs under trees and in the grass. 'Wild underwood may be an appendage of the grandest scene. It is a beautiful appendage. A bed of violets, or lillies may enamel the ground, with propriety, at the root of an oak; but if you introduce them artificially in a border, you introduce a trifling formality; and disgrace the noble object you wish to adorn' (*Observations on the River Wye*, 1782).

Humphry Repton's work in domesticating the gloomier aspects of the picturesque school while retaining the earlier naturalism was much appreciated by Prince Pückler-Muskau; later Repton's son helped with his designs. The prince experimented with his own landscape ideas along the river Neisse on the Polish-East German border and developed his version of the landscape park during the 1820s and '30s. He published his treatise on the subject *Andeutungen über Landschaftsgärtnerei* in 1834 (translated into English in 1917 as *Hints on Landscape Gardening*). Inspired in his youth by Goethe with an interest in nature, the prince

(Left) *Cycas revoluta*, the Japanese sago palm, growing in the dry gardens at Lotusland at Santa Barbara, California. Lotusland was made in the years 1941–84 by the opera singer Madame Ganna Walska, in what was originally an oak wood. The estate encompasses a series of gardens, each devoted to different plant collections suited to the favourable climatic possibilities, but each also having aesthetic appeal. Madame Walska established a fine collection of bromeliads, palms, cacti and euphorbias and her last creation, the Cycad Garden, was designed in association with Charles Glass in 1978–9. In this garden plants are distributed in geographical areas, cycads from Asia, Australia, Africa and Mexico in separate beds, the land contoured into gentle hollows and mounds. Frost-tender cycads are found on hot, stony slopes; they resemble palm trees, but are more closely related to pines, bearing cones rather than flowers.

(Right) In Santa Barbara the climate is particularly favourable. Mountains offer protection from winds to the north and east, for a wide range of temperate, tropical and subtropical plants, with water available to make conditions ideal for cultivation. At the entrance to the Blue Garden at Lotusland, developed in the 1960s, in which grow an extraordinary assembly of 'blue' foliaged plants, the succulent *Agave americana* has sculptural glaucous leaves, and flourishes on the edge beneath a blue Atlas cedar (*Cedrus atlantica glauca*) with surrounding groundcover of blue fescue (*Festuca ovina* var. *glauca*). Succulents store water in fleshy

leaves or stems in order to survive periods of drought and usually have a tough waxy skin to prevent transpiration. The agave dies after flowering, but may take a hundred years to complete its life cycle. Palms, among which are the Mexican blue palm (*Erythea armata*), allow shafts of sunlight to filter through to the ground below.

travelled to England and subsequently reorganized his park (retaining a village and an alum factory) on naturalistic lines: 'In the park I avail myself, as a rule, of native or thoroughly acclimated trees and shrubs, and avoid all foreign ornamental plants, for idealized Nature must still be true to the character of the country and climate to which it belongs so as to appear of spontaneous growth and not betray the artifice which may have been

used ... Such grounds should represent Nature, it is true, but Nature arranged for the use and comfort of man' (*Andeutungen*, 1834). He diverted the river with a new stream to convert the existing moat into a lake, and created a series of views of pastoral spaces with interconnected open meadows backed by forest plantings, to be viewed from a new system of roads, paths and bridges, creating a scene which seemed to beholders quintessentially English. The prince had an important influence on the development of the landscape park in Germany, with others such as the architect Karl Freidrich Schinkel and the landscape gardener Peter Josef Lenné further interpreting the style.

Meantime in North America both George Washington and Thomas Jefferson had, by the end of the eighteenth century, adapted some of the principles of naturalism on their estates, Washington introducing some serpentine walks in his gardens as well as planting native trees. Both were aware of the richness of nature in North America, and conscious of their responsibilities. 'How much more delightful to an undebauched mind is the task of making improvements on the earth to all the vain glory which can be acquired from ravaging it?' wrote George Washington to his friend Arthur Young in 1788.

Jefferson travelled extensively through England during the 1780s and introduced informal flowerbeds similar to those he had seen at Philip Southcote's Wooburn Farm in England around the gravel drives at Monticello. A passionate gardener, Jefferson was growing almost every flower available by the end of his life, and trying out trees and shrubs brought back from the Lewis and Clark expedition to western America in 1804–6.

Also in America, both Andrew Jackson Downing (1815–52), active in garden journalism in the early 1840s, and his disciple, the great landscape architect Frederick Law Olmsted (1822–98), were influenced by the naturalism of English parkland. Downing encouraged Americans to appreciate their own picturesque native landscape and to develop urban parks and cemeteries; although his writings contributed little in detail to American design, Downing did make Americans aware of the desirability of 'improving' their properties, and it was he, just before he drowned in an accident on the Hudson River, who led a campaign for a public park in New York. Olmsted and the English architect Calvert Vaux won the competition for the design of Central Park in New York in 1858. Their plan, entitled 'Greensward', owed much to the English landscape tradition, which by

now had been adopted throughout Europe, but also drew on American romanticism and the picturesque images of the Hudson River school of painting.

Olmsted's plan to make Central Park a pastoral retreat or haven for the workers of the city was inspired by a visit to Birkenhead Park in Liverpool in 1850, recently laid out by Joseph Paxton. Olmsted was influenced by Downing, especially in his appreciation of scenic beauty, rather than paying homage to the gardenesque school of John Claudius Loudon (1783–1843), in which plants were arranged for display rather than as part of a coherent design. Olmsted became the greatest of all American landscape designers in his actual layouts for city parks and suburbs and his use of native plants in many of his schemes as well as in his concern for the wider environment. Olmsted's landscape appreciation was further inspired by his readings of Virgil's *Georgics*, by Uvedale Price's *Essays on the Picturesque* and by William Gilpin's 'picturesque' tours of the British Isles, which put great stress on the restorative and moving qualities of natural scenery. He did not see plants as individuals but relied on them for their contribution to the scheme as a whole, objecting to much of the ostentatious planting of newly introduced exotics, which instead of allowing the old landscape style to prevail, emphasized botanical variety at the expense of a coherent design. Like Robinson, Olmsted deplored specimen planting in Loudon's gardenesque style, and disliked bedding-out, feeling that the plants' attention-seeking qualities often went against the true spirit of the place. In general he believed that non-native plants were only permissible as long as their exotic character was evident to none but experts; he considered that as a designer his own role was to work with and enhance nature.

In 1871 Robinson wrote to Olmsted encouraging him to plant English plants in Central Park: 'I have thought it would be very pleasing result of my Wild Garden if it led to the naturalization of some of the sweet wild flowers of England, primroses etc in your country.' In practice the primroses suggested by Robinson would not survive the New York winters; but in the event his ideas did exert a direct influence. By 1875, disappointed in the way native plants had been planted in 'The Ramble' in Central Park, Olmsted sent the superintendent, Mr Fischer, a copy of William Robinson's *The Wild Garden*, writing that the author expressed the 'views I have always had for the Ramble, the Winter Drive district and the more rocky and broken parts of the park. There can be no better place than the Ramble for the perfect realization of the wild garden and I want to stock it in that way as fully and as rapidly as possible.' In those parts of the park where (owing to shade or to the presence of rocky outcrops) a fine close turf would be out of character, liable to drought or very difficult to mow, Olmsted recommended a mixture of plants suitable for the site: thickets of low mountain shrubs such as broom, furze or heaths, or mats of trailing vines or herbaceous plants such as asters, gentians, lobelias, hepaticas, southernwoods, camomile, tansy, vervain, wild arum, wake-robin, epigaea, Solomon's seal, golden rod, lysimachia, lycopodium, convolvulus and vinca 'to be diligently introduced in patches and encouraged to completely cover the surface'. Instructing his planting superintendent for the lagoon section at the Columbian Exposition in Chicago in 1893, Olmsted directed that 'The vegetation must appear spontaneous and thoroughly wild (to all unlearned visitors)'. Throughout his life Olmsted was in the forefront of schemes for forestry conservation and the establishment of National Parks. In the San Francisco Bay area he advised on a prototypical water-conserving landscape for the American west. At the end of his working life he persuaded the Vanderbilts to dedicate acres of the Biltmore Estate in North Carolina as a centre for research in scientific forestry.

The native gardening movement in North America is generally considered to have originated with Jens Jensen (1860–1951), a contemporary of Robinson, in the Midwest. Like Robinson, Jensen, the great landscape architect of the early twentieth century, originally from Denmark, did not 'invent' these new ideas; they were

On an island off the coast of Maine, Mary Homans has made a naturalistic garden. Indigenous trees, judiciously thinned to provide more light, are underplanted with suitable woodland and rock-garden plants from all parts of the world, which will thrive in her conditions of acid soil and rocky outcrops. Although inland Maine has very cold winters, coastal gardens benefit from the mass of the adjacent ocean and do not have such low temperatures. Local birch (*Betula papyrifera*) and red maple (*Acer rubrum*) provide protection and some shade above hostas and hardy ferns, which will increase over the years.

part of an evolving process linked with a spreading antipathy to more artificial styles of gardening and an increasing awareness of vanishing landscapes, and the need to re-create them. Long before the environmental movement had got under way, Jensen, working in the Midwest, used nature as his theme. He was an advocate of using native plants to create landscapes in harmony with the regional environment. His development was stimulated by the work of O. C. Simmonds (1855–1931) and Simmonds's designs from 1881 (four years before Jensen emigrated to America) for Graceland Cemetery and other Midwestern projects. Perhaps neither man would have achieved such prominence without the

JENSEN: THE FIRST ENVIRONMENTALIST

Jens Jensen (1860–1951) was one of the first landscape gardeners to be thought of as a pioneering environmentalist and to preach the beauty and value of the Midwest's native plants and other natural elements such as rock and water – features rapidly disappearing as land was developed for agriculture and industry. After his arrival in the United States from Denmark in 1884, Jensen lived and worked mainly in Chicago. Working for the parks system there, he rose to become superintendent of landscape architecture. He was responsible for many of the city parks, including Garfield, Humboldt and Columbus. He also worked for private clients, including the Fords of Detroit.

With Frank Lloyd Wright, who built his houses with flowing horizontal lines as if they were an organic part of the landscape, Jensen helped establish the Prairie Style of landscape gardening. This strove to capture the spirit of the prairie on the one hand through conservation and restoration of native flora, and also in visual terms by exploiting the repetition of horizontal lines in landforms, stonework – symbolizing typical bluffs on the shores of Lake Michigan – and the natural branching habits of plants such as hawthorns (*Crataegus* species), which matched the prairie landscape and its broad horizons. Council Rings, inspired by the native American, were built to provide outdoor sites for gatherings, contemplation and readings.

Jensen's philosophy involved an admiration for native plants which, by their shapes and suitability, belonged to and enhanced the Midwestern landscape in a visual sense; at the same time he perceived the necessity of saving the prairie landscape and its indigenous plants.

One of his most memorable commissions was the Lincoln Memorial Garden in Springfield, Illinois, on the shores of Lake Springfield, where he was able to choose an unspoilt, unexploited site – he noted the 'gentle slopes and meadows, the little hills and valleys'. His first plans were produced in 1936. Many of the native trees and plants were unobtainable from nurseries, so Jensen encouraged garden clubs and schoolchildren to collect acorns and other seeds throughout the state, gathering plants from natural areas that were in the process of being destroyed. (It is only recently that nurseries in North America, in response to educated demand, have started to supply a wide range of native plants. In areas such as southern Europe it is still difficult to obtain native Mediterranean flora from local nurseries and growers, many of which have a wide range of exotics suitable to the climate but show no interest in natives, presumably illustrating a lack of specific pressure from the gardening public.) Jensen's design for the garden consisted of a series of open spaces or lanes surrounded by woodland, with each space a showcase for certain plants native to Illinois: small trees such as redbud (*Cercis canadensis*), flowering dogwood (*Cornus florida*) and grey dogwood (*C. racemosa*), hawthorns, sumach, plum and the prairie crab-apple (*Malus ioensis*), which were typical woodland-edge plants. The lower levels, along Lake Springfield, were to be filled with sun-loving flowers – asters, helianthus and liatris – and the uplands covered with 'trees native to the states in which Lincoln lived'. These larger trees were a mixture: buckeye, sassafras, *Magnolia acuminata*, maple, oak, hickory (*Carya*), tulip trees, Kentucky coffee tree (*Gymnocladus dioicus*), basswood (*Tilia americana*) and yellowwood (*Cladastris lutea*, now correctly *C. kentukia*). In his final version of the plans the lanes curved ever

(Left) Native redbuds (*Cercis canadensis*) flower in early spring before the leaves unfurl. Other natives used by Jensen for the lakeshore garden at Springfield include dogwoods and hawthorns. Sumach, plums and prairie crab (*Malus ioensis*), often obtained from sites under threat, were all part of the understorey. Curving rides through the woods were designed to reveal glimpses of the lake to the exploring visitor.

(Above) Under the tree canopy Jensen encouraged native wild flowers to spread in natural ways. *Trillium grandiflorum*, the wake robin of the north-eastern American woods (described by Robinson as 'one of the most beautiful hardy plants'), does well

here in the shade and deep leaf-litter. In the more open landscape on the lake shore at Springfield, Jensen used sun-loving natives such as the late-flowering daisy *Heliopsis helianthoides* with semi-double flowers and bright yellow centres. Jensen rarely located individual plants on his plans, instead showing massing plants in interlocking patterns, closely related to the way he had observed them growing in nature. He often arranged his own plants in natural compositions, finding that a 'blueprint' could hardly reflect the more haphazard way of planting that would occur in the wild. He also used the same plant again and again, or plants similar in texture and form, to create harmonies and unity in his design.

so slightly, creating a sense of mystery in which the lake became visible only at the last moment.

The Clearing in Wisconsin, his home and 'school of the soil', was founded in 1935 on a high bluff near Ellison Bay. Now run by an independent board, The Friends of the Clearing, it offers week-long courses in the study of nature, arts and the humanities. Jensen described the natural setting of about sixty acres/twenty-four hectares: 'Many beautiful flowers thrive along the path, like trilliums, dogtooth violets, bearberry ... nothing is cultivated. There are three clearings in the woodland ... they bring poetry and beauty into the woods; and you have to see them in the moonlight or in the autumn, when the forest is ablaze in all shades of scarlet and yellow.' In an article in a German magazine, Jensen emphasized how natural groupings establish their own plant communities: 'I note with great satisfaction how certain wild forms appear in inimitable groupings ... I find *Lilium philadelphicum* in full bloom, here and there along the trail. They appear like an easy-going social gathering, now loosely dispersed, now huddled together. Many of them stand away from the mass and form small groupings on their own. And now and then some solitary specimen glimmers in the darkness of the woods.'

promotion of the Prairie Style school of architecture in the writings, in *Country Life in America* and in *Garden Magazine*, of Professor Wilhelm Miller from the University of Illinois at Urbana, who recognized that Simmonds and Jensen were achieving for Midwestern landscape gardening what Frank Lloyd Wright (1867–1959) was doing for architecture: Wright felt that a house should grow out of and be an organic part of the landscape. Miller set out to publicize the Prairie School's love of the flat prairie landscape, and particularly its horizontal lines accentuated by native hawthorns and crab-apples (which became constant features in Jensen's designs, framing vistas, used as accents on lawns and, by association, reducing the apparent height of buildings that seemed too tall) and the stratified rocks found edging ravines and prairie rivers. After travelling in England in the early 1900s Miller published a series of articles on 'What England Can Teach Us About

In the foothills of the Blue Ridge Mountains in central Virginia, a garden by the American designers Oehme and van Sweden has a partly naturalistic style. Massed plants grow in situations they enjoy, but at the same time the scheme is so carefully planned and executed that there is no freedom to change, or for plants to overrun their positions as they would do in nature. In late summer a dense planting of *Sedum telephium* 'Autumn Joy' with *Pennisetum alopecuroides* and Russian sage (*Perovskia atriplicifolia*), black seedheads of rudbeckia and bright-flowered swamp mallow (*Hibiscus moscheutos*) interlock in smooth abstract-shaped blocks. Reed grass (*Calamagrostis* x *acutiflora*), from damp woodland and marshes, grows in the distance, linking garden and landscape.

Gardening' (1909–10), urging Americans not to copy English planting – often so unsuitable for the terrain – but to adapt the naturalistic mode of gardening by using native American plants to give similar effects. In an article devoted exclusively to the Midwest, he described the use by Simmonds and Jensen of native species transplanted from the countryside to man-made landscapes. In merging ideas taken from the English landscape school with the use of native indigenous plants, neither Simmonds nor Jensen recommended copying haphazard plant arrangements found in nature, but rather that, by observation, it was possible to translate nature's 'motives' into designed landscapes. Natural gardening is an illusion – 'it is the perfection of art to conceal art'. A modern American landscape architect, A. E. Bye, in his book *Art into Landscape, Landscape into Art* (1983), pays tribute to Jensen's influence on his work, and his admiration for Frank Lloyd Wright. One of Bye's earlier commissions was on a landscape for a Wright house, where, true to Wright's organic principles, he used only indigenous natives, thinning the existing forest to make a garden. Bye works on a grand scale, contouring pastures to give effects of light and shadow, ridiculing the use of 'tiresome exotics that line our streets and fill our parks'. Jensen's influence is also visible today with the re-establishment of prairie landscape throughout the Midwest. In 1934 Aldo Leopold, author of the *Sand County Almanac*, the classic reminiscence on native plant communities, re-established a planted prairie at the University of Wisconsin Arboretum in Madison (now known as the Curtis Prairie), the first of its kind.

With Robinson and Jensen the emphasis on naturalism thus began to shift from the design of romantic parks on a grand scale to more specific plants and plantings, and this, accompanied with a new environmental vocabulary, stimulated gardeners to think in terms of the site and its possible support for ecologically orientated plant communities. In other words, they began to consider allowing plants to become established in communities, appropriate to existing garden conditions.

Side by side with the development of naturalistic planting ideas in both Britain and the USA, planting in borders became freer in concept, although it often remained contained by formal straight lines. In Britain Edwardian gardening – today considered to represent a certain sort of 'Englishness' in its mixture of architectural formality and cottage-style planting – was partly inspired by Robinson's writings encouraging the use of hardy plants in natural ways. His ideas popularizing the woodland or 'wild' garden and the English flower garden and herbaceous border were successfully combined with the more formalized colour borders of his disciple Gertrude Jekyll, who often developed her flowerbeds within the framework given by strong architectural features, creating schemes with old cottage-garden plants in an apparently simple, but in fact artfully contrived, cottage-garden style. Her partnership with architects such as Edwin Lutyens, whom she met in 1889, combined her imaginative planting with his architectural 'bones' (which drew on local materials to make a design fit into its setting) and produced some of the finest gardens of the period. A 'Lutyens house with a Jekyll garden' – illustrated and described in magazines like *Country Life*, and visited by an increasingly mobile travelling public – that became the envy of and the model for gardeners all over the world. On the Riviera, in the American Midwest, and in countless other up-and-coming areas, wealthy home-owners commissioned their architects to build houses with 'old English' gardens in the newest fashion.

The origins of the Edwardian garden can be traced back well into the nineteenth century. By 1870 the revival of the old pre-eighteenth-century English garden, with clipped hedges, trellised walks and flowerbeds filled with 'old' English flowers, later to be best expressed (in Europe and North America as well as in England) as the Arts and Crafts movement extended to gardening, was well under way. Robinson had been much influenced by both John Ruskin and William Morris and agreed with many of the movement's ideals. Ruskin's conviction that the real quality in architecture and design was directly related to the degree in which the craftsman's imagination and creative powers were integrated into the 'product' – as opposed to the inhuman character of mass-produced factory goods – included looking to nature for aesthetic guidance. William Morris, the most important figure in the Arts and Crafts movement, also emphasized the importance of genuine craftsmanship – and expressed his abhorrence of the contemporary bedding system. Robinson quoted Morris in his frontispiece-epigraph to some editions of *The English Flower Garden* (first published in 1883): 'Another thing also much too commonly seen, is an aberration of the human mind, which otherwise I would have been ashamed to warn you of. It is technically called carpet-gardening. Need I explain it further? I had rather not, for when I think of it, even when I am quite alone, I blush with shame at the thought'.

The Arts and Crafts movement encouraged the use and preservation of traditional and regional crafts. As it developed, the Arts and Crafts garden in turn reflected the inspiration of both Robinson and Jekyll, in their insistence on learning from nature. The movement looked back towards the seventeenth century, before the more formal gardens were swept away to make room for the new landscape parks, while the main planting of trees and hedges – hedges were used to make enclosures instead of masonry walls – should be of traditional plants, mainly indigenous to the area, with a self-conscious avoidance of the exotic trees and plants favoured by the Victorians. Both house and garden should be constructed only of local materials. But Robinson disagreed profoundly with the role given to architects. Architects demanded an all-embracing plan, while Robinson felt 'gardeners' should design the garden and choose the plants. Although Robinson himself used many architectural features around his own home, Graveye Manor in Sussex, in much of his writing, he continued to condemn the role of the architect in the garden, preaching the naturalism of which he had

become the prime mover. Robinson's advocation of naturalistic planting and the dislike, so often expressed in his writings, of more architectural themes, became reconciled in much of Miss Jekyll's work. In Jekyll borders, it was the style that was naturalistic rather than the plants. Although in the outer garden Jekyll, like Robinson, would propose native plants in naturalistic drifts and as design features to link the garden with the countryside beyond, the plants she used in her theatrical borders were those that would enhance the scheme and extend its flowering periods. Instead of being in isolated blocks and regimented in heights graduated from the back to front, a mixture of hardy perennials, biennials, annuals and bulbs was woven together to make 'natural' cottage-garden pictures, in which flowers and leaves covered any bare earth between the bases of plants and flowed over the borders' edges.

The Arts and Crafts movement extended into Europe and North America. The German architect Hermann Muthesius studied architecture in England and published his *Landhaus und Garten* in 1907, insisting in it also 'that garden and house are a unit of which the main features must be thought out by the same genius'. In North America the Arts and Crafts movement stressed the importance of regional gardening and planting at a time when gardening styles were still apt to cling to old European formulae, with little attention being paid to suitability of planting over the vast climatic range.

Many, of course, among Robinson's contemporaries and those succeeding him have also played important roles in developing more natural gardening. Some, such as Jens Jensen, found their landscaping inspiration in native landscape and indigenous trees. Others have further developed Robinson's themes, translating his natural appreciation of well-associated plant groups in natural settings into more scientific ecological formulae of native planting. Some, such as Willy Lange in early twentieth-century Germany, have been landscape architects who turned the 'nature garden' into an almost 'design-less' entity based on political ideology. Others in

At Inverewe on the west coast of Scotland, brushed by the warm Gulf Stream, the Chusan palm (*Trachycarpus fortunei*), a single-stemmed evergreen palm from Asia with fan-shaped, dark green leaves, thrives by the shore. Frosts are seldom experienced at Inverewe but the Chusan palm is frost hardy to 23°F/-5°C, especially if protected from cold drying winds. An Australian cabbage palm (*Cordyline australis*), *Persicaria amplexicaule* and oriental poppies can be glimpsed in the foreground. The climate allows a very naturalistic type of planting with plants from many different habitats growing happily together.

Europe, such as Karl Foerster in Germany, J.P. Thijsse in Holland and more recently Professor Richard Hansen, have been plantsmen, designers and experimenters in using plants in gardens in natural ways.

Karl Foerster (1874–1970), perennial breeder and nurseryman, was influential in bringing herbaceous plants back into the landscape, using native perennials, ferns and grasses seldom found in gardens, as well as appropriate exotics in less geometric designs, not only in gardens but in public spaces such as along motorway verges. In Holland Dr Jacques P. Thijsse (1865–1945) encouraged more native-style landscaping, making use of existing natural features such as indigenous Dutch oaks, groves of alders, lake and river banks, sand dunes and heathland, extending his approach beyond the garden into the whole countryside. All the plants, trees, shrubs and flowers should positively encourage birds and insects. 'The ground should be entirely covered with flowering plants, mosses and ferns, in substantial masses and according to landscape type, so that they attract our attention,' he wrote in *Nature Conservation and Landscape Maintenance in Holland* (published posthumously in 1946). At Amstelveen, outside Amsterdam, only native plants are grown, yet the nature gardens comprising a mixture of habitats – bog, heath, meadow, woodland – reflect creative vision involving a total understanding of plants' needs with compositions of colour-rich borders of some sophistication.

Richard Hansen, originally a disciple of Karl Foerster, taught at Weihenstephan, the centre for perennial breeding, and in his book *Perennials and their Garden Habitats* (1981, English translation 1994) emphasized the importance of man-made plant communities in establishing long-lasting and self-sustaining perennial schemes – in fact naturalizing perennials, as Robinson advocated, but in a much more advanced and scientific way. In the garden at Weihenstephan, Hansen experimented with plant associations as much as with individual plants to create sustainable schemes of high aesthetic value. Working with nature involves choosing plants suitable for a site, rather than manipulating the aspect to suit certain plants. In stressing the importance of habitats Hansen's book permits gardeners to develop individual schemes based on long-term sustainability, but in any such scheme the importance of plant selection increases as the intensity of garden maintenance declines. Hansen's experimental work has led to exciting developments in perennial growing in German public parks. Today sweeping beds, developed as a hybrid between the wilder meadows and conventional borders, are planted with species and cultivars carefully selected for ecological reasons to suit the site, and chosen for their 'sociability' to co-exist in association with each other in man-made plant communities, an imitation of nature's ways (but not necessarily using native plants) that will need little maintenance or intervention.

Today in the United States Darrel Morrison, formerly Dean of Environmental Studies at the University of Georgia, Athens, and now at the University of Michigan, is influential in encouraging American gardeners to re-examine their attitudes to ornamental gardening. His message is for people to observe nature, to garden to conserve it and its natural resources, and even to re-educate their aesthetic responses, to see beauty in the more faded natural colours such as gold, tan and russet – the colours of seed-heads and dying grasses that conventional gardeners in the past dismissed as untidy, uninteresting or even a sign of bad housekeeping.

By the time of Robinson's death in 1935 (and ever since) the term 'Robinsonian' had come to be applied to any of the many forms of naturalistic gardening, in which hardy plants are combined together in natural ways. Robinson remains revered as the great prophet of planting naturalism, but, as we have seen, many other thinkers and designers have played major roles in encouraging gardeners to work 'with nature'. In fact practical gardeners have always being doing this, not only finding different microclimates in each garden, but also finding variations of soil, moisture, light, heat and cold in different parts of the garden, and choosing

Although native Californian plants are not always easy to transplant to gardens in other countries, the climate in Los Angeles allows for a very wide range of plants to be grown. Drought-tolerant plants from areas with similar environments such as Australia, South Africa and Chile are particularly adaptable and look natural together. In a garden designed by Chris Rosmini yellow kangaroo paw (*Anigozanthus pulcherrimus*) from south-west Australia, French or Spanish lavender (*Lavandula stoechas*) from dry Mediterranean hills and *Limonium perezzii* from the Canaries – the latter particularly well adapted to California – all thrive in the same conditions.

plants to suit these varying aspects, as is described in Chapter Two. Successful planting, in whatever style, depends on climate and other growing conditions – what we call the aspect. Lacking the extremes of hot and cold of continental Europe or of North America, the temperate climate of the British Isles provides almost unique opportunities to grow outdoor garden plants from a more diverse range of natural world habitats than in almost any other country or region of the world. Overall winters are seldom hard and summers are usually cool and damp. Inside this overall picture regional variations in climate and soil inspire different styles of gardening appropriate to each area. Each site is unique: even a next-door garden can give different planting opportunities. High-rainfall coastal areas on the west are washed with the warm waters of the Gulf Stream, providing microclimatic pockets and acid soil conditions for plants from similar habitats. Over the centuries, as plants have flowed in from other continents, this favourable climate has meant that the English have become passionate gardeners and plantsmen, experimenting with styles and testing – and succeeding with – new plants as they became available, in a way not possible elsewhere. The Dutch may have become the greater breeders and hybridizers, but all in all the gardens in the British Isles have become the envy of those who strive to garden in more climatic extremes and difficult conditions. Indeed, sometimes British gardens have been spoilt by the richness and variety of plants, grown at the expense of a coherent design. And because so many plants from foreign origins adapt so well to gardening in England, it has been less important to consider their ecological requirements.

In more extreme climates, such as those of North America, it is vital to take into account the precise requirements of the plants, as gardening 'against nature' becomes extremely time- and labour-intensive. The green 'English-style' lawn in the waterless south-west; rhododendrons and azaleas growing in sticky alkaline and caliche soils in Texas (caliche is hard when dry);

making a garden for Mediterranean-type plants in a wet clay, and trying to create an English-type perennial garden in the daytime heat (and hot nights) of the deep south – all are achievable (if not necessarily desirable), provided only that enough time, money, ingenuity and fertilizers are employed.

Today the application of Robinson's teachings has become much more urgent everywhere. As gardeners have taken fresh stock of what remains of wild landscape all over the world, ornamental gardening is increasingly committed to a more ecological approach to planting in differing climates. With wild flowers and countrysides disappearing, through exploitation and development, gardening (and, of course, forestry and National Park management) has become more closely linked with the natural environment and less concerned with experimental growing of a wide range of plants; it is certainly less concerned with earlier definitions of gardening as a fine art. In Europe native plant species are limited, and ornamental gardens depend for their greatest effects on foreign introductions; but even these gardens need to preserve a link with the landscape in which they are set, with native plants – essential for ancillary wildlife – and exotic plants that look like indigenous plants completing the picture.

Today every gardener is something of an ecologist. Instead of manipulating the garden soil or creating microclimates in order to grow plants with specific requirements, plants from similar habitats are matched to the specific given site. They are provided with conditions as close as possible to those of their natural environment. By selecting plants more precisely, there is less need to use nitrogenous fertilizers and pesticides against disease, thus avoiding damaging run-off to the water table. In natural gardening not only are acid-loving plants not planted in alkaline soils, but the erstwhile practice, commonly advocated even a decade ago by gardening magazines, of changing the soil to accommodate them (or even spraying with sequestrene, a remedial mix that releases minerals to acidify the soil)

'Old English' Transplanted to Ohio Landscape

Stan Hywet Hall in Akron, Ohio, was laid out for Frank and Gertrude Sieberling from 1911 by Warren H. Manning, a landscape architect from Boston. Akron is situated in the western foothills of the Appalachians, where soil is still predominantly acid, and with hot summers and cold winters. Set in a vast estate of 3,000 acres/1,200 hectares of gently sloping meadows combined with rugged areas of cliffs and ravines, Manning's design was primarily naturalistic in style and organization. It was laid out around a dramatic sandstone quarry on the north side of the house, in which lagoons were established. The materials chosen for the building were red brick, sandstone from the quarry, slates from Vermont and hand-carved oak. Basically the Sieberlings wanted farmland, woodland and the stone quarry turned into an environment conveying the ambience of an 'Old English' garden in the Robinson/Jekyll manner. The landscape was developed with an English-style lawn studded with naturalized bulbs in spring; behind, an essentially American landscape to the north and west stretched over the distant wooded hills. Formal borders, a spring-flowering peony garden and a cutting garden, the walled English Garden (most recently restored) and a Japanese Garden, with terraces falling to the north, were all features.

Warren Manning was the son of a prominent nurseryman in Reading, Massachusetts. Primarily a horticulturist, he had been trained in design in the offices of Frederick Law Olmsted and acted as horticultural adviser for Olmsted projects such as the development of the Biltmore Estate in North Carolina (1888–95) and the World's Columbian Exposition of 1893 in Chicago. As a passionate plantsman he was particularly interested in native flora, but in his designs for woodland and 'wild' places in the garden, he followed the Robinsonian tenet of encouraging planting of hardy exotics and natives in very natural ways. He was working on ecological studies long before 'ecology' became a household word, carrying on Olmsted's inspired legacy in his care for landscape conservation, and implementing in his own work a development of Jensen's concerns for vanishing countryside and native plants. At Stan Hywet, Manning even recommended filling in a ravine and constructing a retaining wall for the house rather than more conveniently siting the building in a flatter area, which he wished to retain as part of the landscape.

Manning worked on naturalistic lines, adapting his planting to suit

A detail of planting near the birch alley shows *Vinca minor* and lily-of-the-valley (*Convallaria majalis*) from temperate zones in the northern hemisphere growing together in harmony, expressive of William Robinson's recommendations to grow hardy plants from any part of the world adjacent to each other if they will thrive and spread in similar conditions. Although Robinson exaggerated the low-maintenance aspect of natural planting, nevertheless these sorts of plant combination demonstrate how the 'wild' garden works. In this case both plants can become invasive and, over a prolonged period, one will probably come to dominate and eliminate the other.

the topography of the site, although often incorporating into his designs (as at Stan Hywet) strong alignments and French-style vistas pushing through native forests. At Stan Hywet, besides the famous birch alley to the north, he planted an impressive avenue of London plane trees underplanted with native rhododendrons to the south, and, by cutting native trees, established an exciting viewpoint from the main hallway stretching some seven miles/twelve kilometres into the western landscape, thus uniting house, gardens, surrounding hills and the skyline in one continuous view.

He preferred to work on a site by instinct rather than drawing up elaborate blueprints. The walled English Garden was the most formal element at Stan Hywet, but even for its conventionally shaped beds and borders Manning made no detailed planting plans. In 1928 Ellen Biddle Shipman, the 'Miss Jekyll' of America – who also worked with Manning at nearby Cleveland on the Gwinn estate – revised the planting plans inside its walls.

This view from the terrace at Stan Hywet Hall in Akron, Ohio, in the American Midwest, allows a view far into the western countryside. Although preserving the native trees and under-storey in the vast estate, the designer Warren Manning liked to cut vistas through the forests and landscape very much like the French gardeners of the seventeenth century. Manning's approach to natural gardening and native plants in general showed the designer's skill in respecting nature, yet demonstrates the master hand of the gardener who controls the final picture.

At Stan Hywet Hall Warren Manning planted an alley of native birch (*Betula papyrifera*) underplanted with European periwinkle (*Vinca minor*), one of the more formal features in the garden, yet softened by the natural-looking planting style. Warren Manning, who did some of his early training in Olmsted's office in Boston, extended his interest in native flora throughout his designing career. However, like William Robinson in his garden at Gravetye, in his landscape work he always introduced some straight lines and firm structures around the house, extending the architecture of the house into the adjacent garden.

would be out of the question. Drought-loving plants and bog plants are planted where they will thrive naturally, so there is no need to provide extra drainage for the former or extra moisture for the latter.

Basically obvious, but not always considered, is the fact that plants requiring different sorts of planting situations also often have distinctively different appearances. They do not look natural grown together, however much horticultural effort has made it possible. Silver-leaved artemisia from stony Mediterranean soil simply looks ridiculous beside moisture-loving large-leaved rodgersias or gunneras. The nineteenth-century scientist and explorer Alexander von Humboldt attached special importance to the appearance of plants – their physiognomy – which relates to their own particular landscapes, and this can be translated into gardening. Aloes, agaves, cactus all look 'right' together; desert plants requiring similar conditions, their leaves and stems storing water. Today trends in natural gardening, in which growing conditions are taken into account, not only lead to lower-maintenance landscapes but also help to foster an appreciation of the redevelopment of long-term plant communities.

Many of the Robinsonian planting schemes that are feasible in England cannot be realized in more extreme climates, and the planting 'palette' necessary for creating any of his naturalistic schemes has to be adapted to suit other regions of the world. Of course it is the interpretation of Robinsonian principles rather than any form of 'Englishness' that is important. In fact *true* Robinsonian gardening is more exciting outside the British Isles, in continents such as North America and Australia where native plant schemes can draw on a much wider and more interesting range of 'local' species. 'Naturalism' is not necessarily a native-plant movement, although decisions to grow only native plants in various regions are a strong part of ecological thinking, sometimes assuming moralistic virtues, and undoubtedly useful in saving threatened plants and re-establishing lost plant communities.

Jensen, one of the first garden environmentalists in the United States, is most remembered for his emphasis on using native Midwestern plants rather than any exotics (although even he could modify his views to allow old and safe traditional garden favourites that did not endanger the ecological balance). In Britain, where native flora is limited in range – after the last Ice Age the English Channel prevented plants from re-establishing themselves as the ice-cap retreated north – it is hard to make decorative gardens using only natives, although an English wild-flower garden might sensibly include pre-Ice-Age plants, which grew in Britain when it was part of continental Europe. Native-plant gardening is much more viable in climatic regions of North America and in many other areas of the world where a far wider range of local species exists, although it is sometimes difficult to define its more exact interpretation in terms of native regions. In the United States the native-plant movement is mainly concerned with conservation of indigenous flora and with practical details such as saving water (and discouraging the use of nitrogenous fertilizer and pesticides and herbicides, which escape into the water system); at the same time it is also motivated by the rapid and dangerous colonization of many wild places and other open areas by alien plants, which do not support wildlife or permit regeneration of native species. Hall's Japanese honeysuckle (*Lonicera japonica* 'Halliana'), Californian privet (*Ligustrum sinense*), Russian olive (*Elaeagnus angustifolia*) and Norway maple (*Acer platanoides*) are all dangerous interlopers, one of the worst of all being Kudzu vine (*Pueraria lobata*), originally introduced for erosion control, which now blankets the southern landscapes. Even in Great Britain, where few foreign plants 'escape' from gardens, the spread of alien plants can potentially cause havoc to natural communities. Seedling sycamores contribute little to the foodchain, while *Rhododendron ponticum* spreading in peaty soils chemically suppresses all competitors in its path. Saving threatened plants, saving water – a vital necessity now in many gardening parts of

At Cruden Farm near Langwarren in Victoria, Dame Elizabeth Murdoch's avenue of native trees, the lemon-scented gums *Eucalyptus citriodora,* is magnificent. Planted close together in almost a continuous row like a hedge, these eucalypts display their wonderfully grey-pink shaft-like trunks. These trees shed their bark annually to reveal a creamy-white surface which colours with age. This avenue is an important and beautiful feature in the garden and the native trees, tender in maritime Britain, thrive here in the mild climate of their native land. Most gums acclimatize well in regions with similar environments, such as California, parts of Chile and in favoured Mediterranean gardens, where they are popular for their speed of growth. Unfortunately they also tend to colonize, preventing regeneration of regional natives.

the world but most vividly so in the American south-west – saving maintenance and saving the vanishing countryside and its wildlife are all part of a new awareness of threats to the living world.

In *Taming the Wildings* (1923) Herbert Durand listed various situations in which natives can, with advantage, be planted, and his advice is still timely at the end of the century. In the modest-sized garden (as Gertrude Jekyll and the Arts and Crafts designers also advised), natives can define and soften boundaries, linking the garden with the landscape in which it is set. In rural or suburban places the original charm of natural woodlands can be partly restored by planting natives, although a certain amount of manipulative 'gardening' will be necessary to sustain this as a natural ecosystem, especially when seeds of introduced plants blow in. In wilder country, such as seashore, woodland or a forest retreat, where exotics will look out of place, drawing attention to themselves just when nature should seem untouched, using native plants seems appropriate. Here, in the wild, nature needs conserving, although even this is not simple. In the great National Parks in western America, such as the Yellowstone or Yosemite, non-interference policies have had to be revised in favour of judicious clearing of undergrowth and more frequent burning, to prevent outbreaks of serious ecosystem-destroying forest fires – and to keep them accessible as amenity areas, also part of the management brief. In areas of waste land, recreational land, industrial sites and in large estates, native trees and shrubs blend in well with surrounding landscape and may be almost self-perpetuating, or at least will need minimum maintenance. In wildlife parks or sanctuaries native plants will provide essential wilderness habitats and be part of the natural food chain, and, once established, should be low-maintenance and require no fertilizing or pesticides, although any invasive exotics will need checking. Today sound ecological principles are applied to reclamation and replanting of despoiled and abused landscapes.

In eastern North America, where, after some initial

clearance by settlers, much of the land returned to hard-wood forest, natural, if not entirely native, plant gardening can consist of clearing the understorey and encouraging the existing wealth of wild flowers to prolif-erate, introducing other flowers and appropriate shrubs from similar world habitats to add interest. In the hot summers shade is a vital component of any outdoor life. Although Robinson never particularly advocated native-plant gardening, these labour-saving Robinsonian-type gardens might seem to reflect his influence, but are probably a pragmatic solution to regional conditions. In the open country of the Midwest, mostly today taken over by intensive agriculture or development, the native-plant gardener, whether in the backyard or in nature conservancy parks, tries to re-establish ecological prairie landscapes, originally the centuries-old products of extensive grazing patterns and periodic fires. This is an uphill task pitted against the invasion of germinating seeds of alien trees, perennials and grasses that contami-nate the natural balance; even when not combating exotics, in your gardening timescale you are fighting with change itself. The xeriscape or dry garden of the south-west is an eminently sensible response to a short-age of water, in which drought-loving natives can be combined with plants from similar habitats, and once established, need little if any supplementary water. In nature wonderfully floriferous shrubs and annuals clothe dry hillsides and even desert areas as soon as rain comes in spring, but most of the natives dry out and become dormant during the hottest season. Natural gardeners learn to appreciate the appearance of these seasonal changes. In the Pacific north-west, where the climate on the west and wet side of the Cascades approximates to that in Britain – though with hotter summers and colder winters – there is an all-too-familiar tendency to be greedy and grow *too many* varieties, from all over the world, in *too many* diverse ways, at the expense of coherent design. Huge trees, more often coniferous than hardwood, establish shade patterns to shelter native shrubs, perennials and ferns, many of which, introduced

to Britain by David Douglas in the 1820s, have become important elements of European garden design. Native-plant gardens containing salal (*Gaultheria shallon*), oceanspray (*Holodiscus discolor*) and madrone (*Arbutus menziesii*) in a setting with Douglas fir (*Pseudotsuga menziesii*) will establish a low-maintenance self-sustain-ing natural scene. Natural gardeners have adapted to the landscape around them by developing ecologically sensi-tive regional garden styles. Designers and garden-owners alike plant both natives and suitable exotics in their garden scenes, but there are sometimes compelling reasons for considering using natives only. Native plants are not only used to create low-maintenance gardens in natural-looking settings, but are studied for their role in re-establishing more complex natural plant communi-ties, while additional and suitable exotic plants added to a garden play their role in shaping man-made plant communities that are relatively self-sustaining.

Another consideration in natural gardening – apart from the ecological one – is the aesthetics. In conventional garden design plants are chosen for their form, shape, flower and leaf colour and texture and are arranged together to make a composition, almost exactly as a painter arranges his paints on his canvas. These schemes require intensive maintenance, with the gardener or designer often working against nature and the natural requirements of the plant. But in any natural gardening the plant's requirements become as important as the immediate visual aspect. The artistic ideal is reinter-preted with an emphasis on viable plant communities in gardens, rather than on individual plant associations, with plants chosen for their soil and climatic require-ments as much as for their beauty. Ecology and design may therefore seem to have opposing aims. But after choosing appropriate plants for any site they will still need to be arranged in aesthetic ways. In a native-plant garden, the gardener may become almost irrelevant – but because alien plants rapidly seed in and distort the natural balance, and because inevitably stronger plants push out weaker ones, a skilled ecologist-gardener with a deep knowledge of plant requirements must interfere, at least on a seasonal basis, or the 'garden' will cease to exist as a work of art.

In even more natural gardening, the choice of appropriate plants for a site becomes the most important factor for the practical and visual success of the scheme. Some natural gardeners develop a new sense of beauty, more related to how plants look in their natural habitat. To them planting in associations that are inappropriate for the plants is more aesthetically devastating than any garish flower or foliage clashing in a conventional garden bed or border. As Robinson did as a young man, natural gardeners study wild flowers in their natural groupings in their native habitats, enjoy their natural look, and learn a new sort of appreciation of beauty in buff and brown seed-heads and fading leaves, rather than looking for bright flower colours and emerald swards all through the year. Lawn areas can be valued for contrasts of grassy textures and a mix of flowers rather than velvet perfection – like wax-polished old wood rather than a synthetic varnish. But by studying plants' needs and by observing nature, the greatest designers and artists, such as Roberto Burle Marx in Brazil, have still managed to combine the principle of planting to please plants with aesthetically satisfying schemes. In his textured gardens he used sweeps of large masses of a given variety, painting broad brushstrokes on his landscapes.

In the wilder garden still, where labour is much less intensive, the aspect – soil, light and water conditions – of the site dictates which herbaceous ornamentals will thrive together. Plants are given suitable sites and then, in theory (or as Robinson advised), left to look after themselves. As Professor Hansen points out in *Perennials and their Garden Habitats*, although the labour required to look after an ecologically sound planting scheme is much less than that required for a conventional border, it has to be of a much more skilled and knowledgeable sort, as promoting self-regulation and removing unwanted disruptive species necessitates a degree of fine-tuning and decision making. An unskilled worker can tend the conventional planting scheme: weeding, cultivating the soil, fertilizing, watering, staking, cutting down, and transplanting and division are all routine tasks. Most gardeners realize now that wild gardens seldom live up to our horticultural or aesthetic expectations. Native or exotic hardy plants, arranged in Robinsonian drifts, are constantly invaded by alien weeds or disrupted by stronger plants overcoming weaker groups. It is impossible to isolate a wild garden or a truly native-plant garden from an existing environment, where there will be unwanted grasses, rooting brambles and other plants ready to invade, as well as a seed bank of 'undesirables' in the soil. Thus the wild garden, to achieve any sort of success, needs constant revisions, calling for a considerable depth of ecological and horticultural knowledge combined with aesthetic appreciation and skill in manipulating the overall picture.

In the following chapters the natural gardening approach is related to different garden habitats. Successful planting in the long term depends on choosing suitable plants for each area of the garden. These habitats can be defined as the deep shade of woodland, the 'brighter' woodland edge, the shrubbery in which woody and soft-stemmed plants mingle, planting in the open, in both dry and wet situations, and planting naturally in more conventional borders and in rock gardens, where plants have very specific requirements. In the first chapter that follows I have tried to define hardiness and adaptibility in relation to garden plants, and to show how an awareness of these factors can help us garden in a way that allows us to match plants to the conditions we can offer them. By increasing our detailed understanding of just where plants come from, how they 'work' and what they need, we become better able to garden with nature. Planting to please plants becomes the natural way to garden and at the same time – because the plants look 'right' together – satisfies our aesthetic intentions.

A Contemporary Plantsman's Natural Approach

The climate of Frank Cabot's garden, north-east of Quebec on the St Lawrence River, and lying between the granite mass of the Laurentian Mountains, clothed in the spruce, pine and fir of the boreal forest, and the river, is moderated by the fourteen mile/twenty-two kilometre wide expanse of water to produce a gardening climate of Zone 4. Deep winter snows cover and protect perennials and cool moist summers are reminiscent of more maritime situations. From the garden at Les Quatre Vents native deciduous shrubs, with a multitude of gold, red and orange hues in the fall, are framed by indigenous birch (*Betula papyrifera*), quaking aspen (*Populus tremuloides*), mountain maple (*Acer spicatum*) and majestic thuja (*Thuja occidentalis*). Shadbush (*Amelanchier canadensis*), stag's horn sumach (*Rhus typhina*) and suckering dogwood (*Cornus stolonifera*) grow among groups of local juniper (*Juniperus communis* var. *depressa*).

Les Quatre Vents lies 75 miles/100 kilometres north-east of Quebec city on the banks of the St Lawrence River, but with views westwards to the Laurentian Hills. It combines a natural approach to planting with some strong architectural rhythms and features. Since inheriting the property in 1965 Frank Cabot, a plantsman *par excellence* and a visionary designer, has expanded the formal elements in the flower garden, originally designed by two uncles, into informal naturalistic woodland and meadow scenes, by pushing the frontier of planting out into the woods and making skilful use of the native trees as background and 'borrowed scenery'. Soaring Italian Lombardy poplars (*Populus nigra* 'Italica') create contrasting drama.

Frank Cabot uses the undulations in the terrain for exploiting microclimatic planting pockets. The soil (as in most gardens in the American and Canadian north-east) is strongly acidic, and the ability of woody plants native to the north-east to thrive is limited only by the cold winters. The garden is a warm Zone 4, the worst cold mitigated by the broad expanse of the river estuary. Deep snow cover ensures that perennials from many different countries will survive the low winter temperatures. The growing season is short – frosts cease in early June but may be expected again in September – but long days and short nights at this latitude encourage perennials to give a fine performance. Grey-leaved American aspen (*Populus tremuloides*), paper birch (*Betula papyrifera*), spruce (mainly the white spruce, *Picea glauca*), eastern hemlock (*Tsuga canadensis*) and American arbor-vitae (*Thuja occidentalis*) – the climate at Les Quatre Vents limits the use of broad-leaved evergreens – link the garden with the natural landscape. Throughout the garden other regional natives unite more exotic planting to give a natural look. As a plant collector and explorer, Frank is fully aware of his plants' natural habitats and their requirements in a new environment. Without self-conscious emphasis on garden ecology, he is able through his own experience and knowledge of how nature 'works' to combine sweeps of hardy native woodland plants with Asiatic exotics – astilbes, primulas, miniature thalictrums, hostas, lilies and the like – some of which he and his wife Anne have themselves collected in

(Above) Paper birches, many with multiple stems, line a track on the fringes of the garden. Far and away the best of the north-east American birches for both garden and landscape, this tree makes a stately lawn specimen, combines in handsome groves or, as shown, forms spectacular alleys. The bark has an overall 'whiteness' not surpassed by the Asiatic birches.

(Above) A feature of Frank Cabot's garden is his use of native plants. The mountain ash, *Sorbus americana* (the North American counterpart of *S. aucuparia*, but less tolerant of hot summers), abounds in the wild around Les Quatre Vents. It has an open, upright habit, colourful fruit and vivid autumn tints. Planted in groups, it links the inner and outer landscapes.

the mountains of Korea and valleys of Nepal. All are planted in true Robinsonian style to thrive and spread in natural ways. 'It has taken years to get an understanding of how to fit plants into the larger landscape, in a way that demonstrates how the beauties of nature can be combined with classical structure to appeal to the senses, and show what a garden can do both to soothe and to stimulate the spirit.'

A natural stream, its banks planted with suitable moisture-loving plants – filipendulas and drifts of hardy iris – and backed by groves of shrubs, descends to a deep gorge crossed by rope bridges copied from those he saw in Nepal, where larger-leaved plants such as exotic rodgersias and rheums rub shoulders with petasites and arisaemas and native May-apples (*Podophyllum peltatum*) and *Tiarella cordifolia*, sheltered by tree canopies. Sunlit meadows, left unmown until the end of August to allow seeding, are planted with bulbs and 'wild' flowers from all corners of the world: species crocus, chionodoxa, puschkinia, muscari and scilla give way to the simple beauty of lupins, poppies, thermopsis and other perennials which thrive in the long grass.

(Left) In Frank Cabot's garden wild but coherent informality alternates with the tight structures of high hedges and long rectangular water canals. The trees framing the formal features are chosen for the conditions. The thuja hedges are a repetitive theme in the garden, and here they are reinforced with deciduous pleached lime, while tall Carolina poplars (*Populus canadensis*, a hybrid of the native *P. deltoides* and the Eurasian *P. nigra*) and paper birch, outlined against the sky, are reflected in the water. The main 'bones' of any garden should be of trees and shrubs that are native (or similar in habit to native plants) and suitable to the climatic conditions and the soil type.

PLANTING TO PLEASE PLANTS

*I*T IS INFINITELY complicated, but infinitely fascinating, to discover what plants need to grow – both in the wild and when moved into a garden. Plants respond to conditions offered locally by the changing seasons that enable them to make growth and to flower at the appropriate times. Given adequate supplies of light, moisture and nutrients, the main factors controlling the growth of a plant (and consequently its selection for the garden) are hardiness and appropriate soil. The gardener does not need to know the detailed physiological changes that take place in plants, but a basic idea of what is going on not only has thoroughly practical advantages (like preventing you from losing a moisture-lover by planting it in a dry spot, and from wasting effort on plants that cannot tolerate temperatures where you live), but also enriches gardeners' appreciation of the plants they grow and see in other people's gardens – especially those that come originally from halfway round the globe.

Knowing where a plant comes from is the first step in the natural gardening process. Not just the country, but the terrain that provides its local habitat. The natural approach simply means trying to provide the plant with a habitat as close as possible to its original home and surrounding it with plants with similar needs, probably coming from similar habitats in different regions of the world.

At the Huntington Botanical Gardens in California the frost-free desert garden, made on the site of a former reservoir, is overlooked by palm trees such as *Cocos plumosa* and fan palms. Large cactus plants, such as saguaros (*Carnegia gigantea*) were transported from the Arizona Desert, their roots protected by glass for the first few years after transplanting, to stimulate regrowth. Echinocactus, also from the south-western United States and from Mexico, are barrel-shaped with coloured spines and flowers emerging from the dense woolly crowns or areoles. These bizarre succulents are adapted to withstand water loss and strong sun. Water-storage tissues such as spherical stems (which also photosynthesize) provide maximum water retention, the body being as much as 90 per cent water with a waxy skin further reducing water loss and spines, hairs and ribs creating insulation. In deserts availability of water determines when plants grow, generally in spring and summer for most cactus habitats, but in coastal California rain usually comes during the winter months.

Gardeners are always working in this way – so frequently that we are unaware of doing so. When we act upon advice to 'plant in well-drained soil in sun' or position clematis 'with their roots in the shade' we are benefiting from the experience of generations of plant collectors, pioneering gardeners and nurserymen and from their accumulated knowledge in hundreds of books. Only professional botanists now collect plants (or their seed) from the wild, but when they do their expertise enables them to give a new species from, say, Nepal or Chile just the right combination of soil, moisture, light and temperature to allow it to germinate, grow on and flourish. At first the novelty is tested in the scholarly precincts of some botanic garden, but often it becomes more widely disseminated to gardeners. Also over generations well-known plants have physically become acclimatized, or breeders have made them so. What the experts cannot do for individual gardeners is know precisely what conditions we can offer plants in our own specifically situated plots.

Having suitable conditions is even more important in natural gardening, where – in allowing nature to take its course – the gardener interferes less than a more conventional neighbour who amends and improves the soil to be able to grow cherished plants, let alone one who draws on the whole artificial apparatus of hothouses and cold frames, sprinklers and sprays to coax a host of exotics to perform. The natural gardener may well help young plants to establish by such orthodox procedures as protecting, mulching, even staking, but on the whole will resort to these measures only rarely, instead matching plants to the site. Fortunately for gardeners, it appears that many species from the wild are, in fact, able to cope with a much wider range of environmental conditions than they experience in their original habitats. Introduced plants grown in alien garden conditions often show a surprising tolerance of the changed situation. However, natural gardeners need not only to be informed about the broad requirements of individual plants – their soil and moisture prefer-

ences, and the hardiness factor – but also to get to know all the potential microclimates of their own site (both favourable and unfavourable), within the broad climatic designation.

To a gardener a plant is hardy if it is programmed to grow successfully in the garden, surviving normal temperature fluctuations. To take the extremes of heat and cold of the prevailing climate into account is only the first step: the difference between maritime and continental influences is almost equally important (see page 43). We are also all aware that locally conditions such as altitude, exposure to wind and closeness to water make considerable differences to the gardening potential of any neighbourhood. Even more subtle are the localized microclimates dependent on the garden's aspect. The broad idea of microclimate is familiar to all gardeners, but not everyone realizes just how every decision in the garden has a specific effect of its own. You create a microclimate when you plant a single shrub (let alone a hedge, a tree or a wood) by introducing a degree of shadiness on the side away from the sun and by creating shelter for nearby plants by filtering winds. The plant will take moisture and nutrients from the soil, changing their availability for other plants. Even moving a stone can have an effect: the area on the sunnier, more exposed side becomes drier and brighter, while beneath the stone moisture is maintained and a mini-microclimate builds up. Observing such minor differences as well as being aware of the areas of sun and shade, soil dryness and moisture, exposure and shelter allow the gardener to build up a picture of the planting potential of a site.

How Plants Adapt to Climate

In order to survive in a particular habitat plants adopt various strategies that have evolved to cope with climatic extremes of heat and cold or more temperate situations. Access to moisture is a key factor, and where for periods of the year the climate precludes this, plants may cease active growth and become dormant; or they may die, having shed seed to ensure successors. In the tropics and in equatorial rain forests, plants have an endless supply of water and grow all through the year. They often have large, soft, smooth leaves, which shed rain, and there is no fear of frost damaging the lush foliage. In deserts and in very hot climates with only occasional rainstorms, plants compensate for the lack of a regular supply by storing water. Succulents use swollen stems and leaves and fleshy roots as water reservoirs. Mediterranean shrubs have leaves especially adapted for coping with hot sun (protective hairs give the appearance of silver or greyness; others have a waxy coating or contain aromatic oils); in really drought conditions, they shed them during the summer. At the opposite extreme conifers in Canadian forests have narrow evergreen leaves covered with hard cuticle to withstand cold, and to take maximum advantage of the short growing period in summer. Most garden plants come from climates that are less extreme – the cool temperate or maritime climates – but, adapted to deal with seasonal changes in their own regions, their success when introduced to a garden situation will depend on how close the characteristics of the site are to their requirements. Amazingly, they often succeed in conditions only approximating to their own.

Plants have developed a range of defence mechanisms against cold and heat. In winter deciduous trees and shrubs shed their leaves as a response to day length and cold; in hot countries they can shed their leaves as a response to summer droughts. In cold countries rising temperatures and lengthening days trigger renewed activity, sap rises and leaves unfurl from the dormant buds with photosynthesis resuming. In hot dry regions such as the Mediterranean and California, growth begins as the weather cools and rain falls. Even evergreens shed their leaves progressively. Broadleaved evergreens need moisture from their roots even in winter, when cold effectively prevents transpiration, and in severe conditions they will die of drought. Although conifers seldom shed most of their needles in response to cold or lack of water, they store water in sapwood, and thus have a

reserve if transpiration exceeds water supplied from the roots. Evergreens, from dry areas such as Mediterranean maquis, Californian and Chilean chaparral or the equivalent habitats in Australia store water in fleshy roots or reach underground moisture by having long tap-roots.

Most herbaceous plants with soft stems and leaves die down to ground level, their growing buds just below soil level and protected from frost by thick snow in continental climates, or by mulches in more temperate climates. Dead stems and leaves from the previous summer's growth also protect the crowns. In hot dry climates many perennials, evergreen in winter, go dormant like bulbs after flowering. Transferred to cooler and damper climate gardens they will lose their leaves in winter and produce flowers and foliage in the relatively cool summers. Acanthus go dormant in the summer in hot climates but are at their best through the summer in a maritime climate such as the British Isles. Bulbs, corms and tubers become dormant, storing nutrients accumulated while in leaf for the winter or summer; annuals die after seeding.

A tender plant, coming from a warmer climate into one with cooler summers and relatively cold winters, has an adverse reaction to cold, frost, wind-chill and dehydrating sun, which scorches evergreen leaves in winter (in cold climates decorative evergreens are planted under protective trees in woodland or against a north wall) and this is made worse if lack of hot sun in summer fails to ripen new growth. Large soft leaves, adapted to high atmospheric humidity and to permanently moist soils, have no method of avoiding transpiration and suffer in dry spells. Tender plants, if exposed to lower temperatures than they can tolerate, will have fatal tissue damage, split bark and drop their leaves and die or just fail to flower or flourish, typical reactions of plants growing in unsuitable situations. On the other hand some plants will die if given conditions that are *too* good – if 'grown too soft', as some gardeners will say – and allowed to produce lush juvenile growth vulnerable to cold. Every gardener knows that plants obtained from a

Shelter Belt Welcomes World's Flora to San Francisco

Established inside the already mature Golden Gate Park in the late 1930s, the Strybing Arboretum and Botanical Gardens have an exceptionally mild and regular climate. Temperatures through the year hardly vary more than 15 degrees above or below 60° Fahrenheit – a range of 24 down to 7° Celsius – with cool fogs rolling in from the Pacific in the hottest part of summer. This means that a wider range of different species can be grown here than in any other garden in North America. Today over six thousand species are found in the seventy acres/twenty-eight hectares, which includes geographically based gardens and some theme-based areas such as a biblical garden and a garden of fragrance. There are rhododendron gardens, separate New Zealand, Australian and Asian areas, a South American section, a garden of primitive cycads, a dry garden of aloes, agaves, yuccas and cactus, a tree-fern dell, a Cape Province garden, and a native Californian section, including a 'forest' of native redwoods. The New Zealand section was first established as long ago as 1915.

The Golden Gate Park, begun in the 1860s, was intended not only for beauty but to stabilize the sandy soil of the shifting dunes on the west of the city and to block the ocean winds. Thousands of Australian blue gum (*Eucalyptus globulus*) with its nitrogen-fixing qualities, Monterey cypress (*Cupressus macrocarpa*) and Monterey pine (*Pinus radiata*) were planted by William Hammond Hall in a pattern of alternating woodland and open meadow, to become successfully established in shelter belts. Space for the Strybing, based on plantings organized by geography and ecology rather than by botanical relationships, was left in the south-west corner, to be implemented after 1937. Helen Strybing's bequest, which made the arboretum possible, specified developing a botanical garden based on plants native to or characteristic of California. Eric Walther was appointed the first director, and his first action was to move a specimen *Magnolia campbellii* from another location into the park. Strybing provides almost perfect conditions for this early-flowering magnolia from the Himalayas. To accommodate the Californian native-plant collection a variety of habitats was created, including a rock garden, a meadow, an arroyo or dry stream-bed, a pond, chaparral and mixed woodland. Now named after Arthur L. Menzies (who worked in the Strybing from 1958 until 1973), this memorial garden of native plants was redesigned in 1986 by Ron Lutsko, a designer who specializes in Californian natives. Except for the adjacent woodland, planting of shrubs, perennials, herbs and groundcovers are in an open, sunlit space. Lutsko's design includes swathes of native bunch grasses (the predominant California grasses before the Spanish introduced cattle and European grasses for economic reasons). These combine with pale lavender iris, orange Californian poppies (*Eschscholzia californica*), baby blue eyes (*Nemophila menziesii*), manzanitas (*Arctostaphylos* spp.) and deep blue ceanothus to reflect an image of California before development. Lutsko chose these plants with special qualities of drought-resistance to harmonize with one another and to create an effect quite distinct from the often unimaginative plantings of exotics in many gardens on the west coast.

(Opposite) The temperature at the Strybing Arboretum on the west side of San Francisco shows little fluctuation throughout the year, with cooling fogs rolling in from the Pacific Ocean. This allows a wide range of plants to be grown from many parts of the world. Quaking or American aspen (*Populus tremuloides*) from North America is weak-wooded and short-lived but a grove makes an elegant canopy for a carpet of meadow foam, *Limnanthes douglasii*.

(Top right) In the Arthur L. Menzies Memorial Garden of Californian Native Plants at Strybing a dry stream-bed (known as an 'arroyo') has a cascade of delicate sun-loving native plants, many of which are much less decorative after the spring flush of flowering is over, when they dry up in the relative heat. In hot climates most indigenous plants flower in the spring (in deserts, of course, they flower after rain). Meadow foam (*Limnanthes douglasii*) gives a wash of background colour tying the planting together through the rock boulders, with the spiky grass-like *Juncus patens* used as a dot plant and Californian poppy (*Eschscholzia californica*) making spots of orange among the cream.

(Right) The beardless Pacific Coast iris (*Iris douglasiana*) is a rhizomatous iris with stiff, glossy evergreen grass-like leaves, flowering in April at Strybing with blooms covering a range of colours between red-purple, lavender-blue, blue, cream and white, produced on branched stems. In the cool fogs of San Francisco everything – including grass – grows well and one of the features of the whole 'garden' is the number of small plants that cover the ground either in open sunny situations or under the light canopies of trees and shrubs.

(Far right) In the Eric Walther Succulent Garden, part of the Strybing Arboretum and Botanical Garden, flower spikes of the Chilean bromeliad *Puya chilensis* are borne in early May. Storing water in the woody stem and with lance-shaped mid-green leaves, this puya can grow to fifteen feet/five metres. Because of the regular and mild climate it is possible to grow more different plants at Strybing than in any other garden in North America – six thousand species at the last count.

The maritime climate in Santa Barbara north of Los Angeles is mild and frost-free but can be too humid for many desert plants. Other succulents such as ice plants, valued for erosion control, enjoy the coastal climate. In a garden designed by Isobelle Greene in the Montecito area of Santa Barbara, ice plants (*Drosanthemum floribundum*) from southern Africa, prostrate-growing perennials, producing daisy-like flowers from summer to early autumn, colonize in sharply drained soil in full sun. Agaves, both *Agave americana* and *A. attenuata* in the foreground enjoy similar conditions. The dragon tree, *Dracaena drago* from the Canaries, is a slow-growing widely branched tree, resembling an inside-out umbrella when mature. The yellow daisy is *Arctotheca calendula*, a low-growing perennial composite from desert regions in South Africa, hardy to temperatures of 23°F/-5°C.

cold-climate nursery will establish better than those from a nursery where they have been protected. Some plants, however, must have harsh conditions to survive.

The final limiting factor may be a plant's tolerance of frost – not necessarily an *average* low temperature, as defined by zoning maps, but the rare occurrence of an extreme low. But plants' hardiness in a garden depends on other factors besides the extremes of cold or heat. Climatically their ability to survive depends on their being able to grow when it is warm and wet, and to survive the winters by various built-in mechanisms. A garden plant is hardy if it is able to adapt to its new situation without being killed by frost attacking unripe wood in autumn, by extreme cold in winter, by sharp frosts in spring after growth has begun, or by dehydrating winds. All these can be mitigated by natural factors, the whole aspect of the site: its elevation and latitude which affect temperature, shelter from wind, the heat and amount of sun in summer, a shady situation with frost and sun protection given by overhead canopies, cloud cover and rainfall, heavy snow and good drainage. Although for every 100-metre elevation above sea level the temperature drops by 0.6° Celsius (330 feet and 1° Fahrenheit), even this is modified favourably or unfavourably by the slope and aspect of a garden, the extent and density of cloud cover, and the rainfall. In high latitudes a shorter growing season reduces the ability of woody plants to withstand less severe low temperatures than they experience in their own habitats. A woody plant from a region of long hot summers may be unable to ripen wood sufficiently to withstand even mild winters if the intensity and/or the duration of sunlight are less. With lower light levels and shorter summers – especially in coastal regions with a lot of cloud cover – plants from regions with hotter summers may well survive, but fail to fruit and flower in the cooler, greyer climate. Other soft-stemmed plants, which need a longer growing season to reach flowering maturity, may be cut off by autumn frosts and thus fail to flower altogether.

Wind exacerbates both cold and drought, so natural or man-made windbreaks provide modified shelter. Frost-hardy plants from regions where severe cold occurs only in still conditions cannot withstand wind. Other plants, adapted to icy overland winds in their own regions, cannot survive warmer (but salt-laden) sea gales.

Plant growth and gardening are affected by the difference between a maritime or temperate climate, with even rainfall throughout the year, cool summers and relatively mild winters (the British Isles, maritime areas of north-west Europe, parts of the mid-Atlantic coast of North America and the Pacific north-west coast), and a continental climate with extremes of winter cold and summer heat, where it is generally drier in winter but with heavy spasmodic rainfalls in the summer (central Europe and much of the Midwest of America, and part of the east coast). Although higher latitudes bring colder winters, these are less severe in an oceanic climate, where with water heating and cooling much more slowly than landmasses, there is much less variation in maximum and minimum temperatures. In the northern hemisphere with vast landmasses inland, continental climates endure very cold winters; in the southern hemisphere with huge oceans and less land, summers are cooler and winters milder. In maritime climates, frequent warming-up periods, followed by the return of sharp frosts, especially damaging in early spring, can kill plants that come from much colder areas, where low temperatures are sustained all winter, with a late spring moving rapidly into the heat of summer and short autumns before the winter cold. Thus many plants from harsh climates are tender in milder ones with 'stop-go' winter climates, such as that of the British Isles washed by the Gulf Stream. Young plants with fewer reserves are more likely to suffer from the stop-go syndrome. On the whole, as plants mature they become hardier, although certain short-lived hot-climate species (including lavenders, cistus and ceanothus) become more vulnerable to temperature swings in winter as they get older and more woody. The alternating heat and cold also affects the flowering of shrubs. Flowerbuds of tree magnolias from Asia may well be prompted to swell too early in a mild spell in Britain, only to be blackened by an untimely frost, and every gardener knows how important it is to not to place camellias and tree peonies where early-morning sun will thaw their buds too quickly.

Zoning maps, based on winter isotherms connecting areas of consistent annual average minimum temperatures, give the lowest temperature a plant can endure (see page 192). Although useful inside a general landmass such as the United States, where most of the country has severe winters, these can be misleading in regions affected by oceans, especially in north-west Europe, with plant survival often depending more on the difference between maritime and continental climatic conditions rather than on absolute cold. In maritime high-latitude countries where temperatures are alternately cold and mild, a mean temperature chart reveals nothing of the false starts and subsequent checks. The presence of broad masses of water also reduces the risk of hard frosts, and shelter from cold winds protects plants from the dreaded wind-chill. The complex realities of plant hardiness and climatic variability do not always fit in with the meteorological patterns produced by joining the isotherms. In California, where the variable topography combines with maritime exposures to produce an assortment of growing situations, twenty-four separate growing zones have been identified by *Sunset Magazine* to help the gardener, these being more concerned with sea-fogs, heat and drought than with cold.

Zones give temperatures below which a plant will probably not survive, although it is recognized that in many gardens there are naturally favourable (and unfavourable) microclimates, which extend or limit the range. In natural gardening these are created by neighbouring plants; in more artificial circumstances they can be man-made. Writing about America in 1940 Alfred Rehder in his *Manual for Cultivated Trees and Shrubs* reminds the gardener to be wary of absolute reliance on zoning attempts: 'There are ... many other factors beside temperatures in winter which will influence the hardiness and growth of certain plants, [such] as soil, its physical as well as chemical composition, exposure, rainfall, humidity of the air, exposure to cold winds. As a rule one may say that plants stand cold better in a drier situation than in a wet one and that deciduous trees and shrubs prove hardier in an exposed situation and in climates with higher summer temperatures, while evergreen plants prefer a sheltered situation, and like a more humid climate and less extreme summer and winter temperatures; for this reason many deciduous species grow best in the East while evergreen plants, and particularly broad-leaved evergreens, will do best on the Pacific coast.'

Success in gardening also depends on the number of growing days in each season, between the last frosts in spring and the first frost in the autumn; this is further dependent on soil types and moisture, with some soils warming up much more quickly than others. In general plants start to grow at temperatures over 43° Fahrenheit/6° Celsius and cease with the first frost. Plants in gardens are also affected by heat and although it is known at what point plants will cease growing in a hot climate (all growth stops when temperatures reach 108° Fahrenheit/45° Celsius), it is much more difficult to assess general heat tolerance, especially when heat is combined with humidity and hot nights.

In general frosts occur in depth during the northern-hemisphere winter from December to March; in Europe this is the result of high pressure over Scandinavia drawing down very cold Siberian air from the east to affect Europe and Britain. The greatest sufferers in a prolonged spell of deep frost are evergreen trees and shrubs that cannot continue transpiration. Radiational frosts occur mainly in spring and early summer but, because unpredictable, cause more damage to marginally hardy plants. During the day the sun warms the atmosphere and is absorbed by the earth; as the sun goes down the earth gives off heat, and temperatures fall. Heat-loss is greatest

In the temperate climate of the British Isles it is possible to grow a wide range of plants from different habitats. At Inverewe on the west coast of Scotland, washed by the Gulf Stream, conditions are even more favoured with few late frosts or stop-and-go winter conditions. Celmisias, rosette-forming perennials or alpines, with silvery-white leaves and daisy flowers, from high-altitude screes in New Zealand and Tasmania, thrive in cool moist climates in sun or half-shade if given humus-rich peaty soil and good drainage.

where there is no overhead shelter such as natural tree or shrub canopies (horticultural fleece can be used in more artificial situations – and is well worthwhile until immature plants have become established). In the 1840s John Claudius Loudon experimented with a simple but flimsy protection against frost. He suspended a cambric handkerchief six inches/fifteen centimetres above a patch of grass when frost was predicted. The temperature beneath the handkerchief remained between 7 and 11° Fahrenheit/4 and 6° Celsius higher than the surrounding area. These frosts often occur after a mild spell has stimulated new growth or development of early flowerbuds. Cold air is denser and heavier than warm air, and flows down slopes and hillsides, collecting in a frost pocket. These frosts, especially at the bottom of a slope, wither the new growth and may kill a young plant. For a gardener simple measures such as creating openings in walls and fences to drain off night frost can make a difference, but for commercial fruit growers and nurserymen choosing a site can be all-important. Young woody plants, without reserves to draw on, are particularly susceptible to unexpected frost or wind chill.

In continental climates as winter ends, plant growth is prompted by a continued increase in day length and temperatures, encouraging rapid growth with hot sun ripening and hardening the wood. In more temperate conditions with cooler summers and mild autumns, lax growth continues to be made for a prolonged period of mild autumnal weather without hot sun to ripen and harden wood, and this is cut back by the first hard frost, weakening the plant's metabolism. A tree such as *Paulownia tomentosa* from China or trumpet vines from the United States will thrive in Zone 6 in the eastern states of North America but will hardly thrive in a much higher Zone 9 in Britain, and rarely flower. Conversely, the performance of humidity-loving plants such as heathers will deteriorate as you travel further into the drier conditions of the continental landmass (eastwards in Europe, westwards in America). Many plants native to cool mountainous areas of the world thrive only in the

Microclimates Maximize Potential in Zone Four

Whatever the climate, soil and situation, the passionate gardener is always pressing to extend the frontiers of planting possibilities. Frank Cabot does this by making the most of all the different aspects of his site, Les Quatre Vents. In broad terms the garden is relatively favourably situated. The garden benefits from the proximity of the St Lawrence River – fourteen miles/twenty-two kilometres wide at La Malbaie – and enjoys a microclimate of Zone 4 (with temperatures expected to fall to some −20° to −30° Fahrenheit/ −29° to −34° Celsius, and a growing period of approximately 100 days) in an area some twenty-five miles/forty kilometres square. This is surrounded by a relatively narrow band of Zone 3 that soon becomes Zone 2. The river not only keeps temperatures up in winter but keeps them down in summer – summers are usually warm and moist, with cool nights and the fogs and mists of a maritime climate.

Despite these mitigating factors, at Les Quatre Vents the cold winters typical of the clear-cut seasons of continental climates give many plants from the Himalayas and the plateaux and valleys of south-west China an advantage denied in more maritime climates with fluctuating winter temperatures. The ground normally has an insulating blanket of snow through the worst winter months, allowing successful experiments with perennials and bulbs from much warmer climates by keeping them thoroughly dormant all winter. (Lack of the typical snow cover during winter a few years ago led to a considerable number of losses at Les Quatre Vents.) The cold winters do severely restrict the range of woody plants that can be grown – the trees and shrubs that not only provide visual structure to the garden, but also offer protection to smaller plants below. On the other hand the hot summers help to ripen wood, increasing winter hardiness and encouraging flowering the following summer; this advantage is, however, tempered by several factors – cool summer nights, low light levels and a short growing season.

As Frank Cabot has said, 'The principal drawback to gardening in northern zones is the limited choice one has of trees and shrubs, yet this limitation does simplify the landscaper's task.' In the garden he uses many native or naturalized species for the backbone of his plans, with conifers represented by spruces (*Picea abies*, *P. glauca* and *P. nigra*), balsam fir (*Abies balsamea*), American larch (*Larix laricina*) and pines, including *P. strobus*,

In his garden near La Malbaie Frank Cabot takes advantage of all environmental opportunities. Just as the expanse of water moderates the winter and summer temperatures to create a microclimatic situation for the whole garden, turning a potential Zone 3 situation into a Zone 4, so within the garden trees and valleys, streams and meadows provide shelter and varied habitats for plants from many different lands, by creating further small pockets of favourable microclimate. In the wood with hemlock and some remaining spruce, looking down over the gorge and at the rope bridge, native species meadow lilies (*Lilium canadense*) spread into comfortable groups.

P. resinosa and *P. banksiana*. *Thuja occidentalis*, which grows to majestic proportions along the St Lawrence, is used in formal sequences throughout the garden – as gardeners in the British Isles might use English yew. The mountain ash (*Sorbus americana*) is everywhere, as are the quaking aspen (*Populus tremuloides*) and

several kinds of grey-stemmed amelanchier. Both yellow birch (*Betula alleghaniensis*) and paper birch (*B. papyrifera*) are found in the forest, the latter by far the better tree for landscape purposes.

A knowledgeable plantsman and skilled horticulturist, Frank Cabot enjoys creating small favourable microclimatic situations for favourite plants of his, which 'officially' lie outside the broad range of plants that he should grow; in the main, however, he plants in broad Robinsonian sweeps, carefully selecting plants appropriate to the situation rather than risking more tender specimens which he might lose in a bad winter. Although woody plants have to be carefully chosen, hardy perennials grow quickly in the long summer days at this latitude. Moreover, the cool nights extend their performance at flowering time: further south, intense heat may reduce the length of flowering to a few days rather than weeks.

Much depends, of course, on many other factors besides temperature extremes. Fortunately for gardeners, plants are able to tolerate a much wider range of environmental conditions than they experience in their own natural habitats. Gardeners can optimize their chances by selecting plants that have partly acclimatized themselves in the wild. For instance, the Lombardy poplar (*Populus nigra* 'Italica') and the Carolina poplar (*P. canadensis*) are used extensively in the garden, with the Amur maple (*Acer ginnala*), a graceful medium-sized tree hardy to Zone 2. Plant species grown from seed from the highest mountains of their native regions will adapt most easily to a colder climate. As a plant collector and explorer Frank Cabot has often seen exotics in their own habitats and understands the subtler nuances of plants' requirements. Because most of us do not wish to grow only our own native plants, we can usefully study the native environment of desirable exotics in order to understand how our own climate and aspect differ, and then encourage the introduced plants to adapt to conditions as close as possible to what they require.

(Left) A view from the garden looking over one of the ponds to the Laurentian Hills to the west from which aggressive winds can sweep down into the garden. The gardens lie on the left bank of the St Lawrence River, where it widens to extend eastward fourteen miles/twenty-two kilometres, providing an expanse of water to modify the effects of winter cold and summer heat. The invasive hardy *Petasites japonicus*, from China, Korea and Japan, has sweetly scented flowers in early spring before the spreading leaves emerge. A plant of moist ground and damp woodland, it enjoys the climatic situation at Les Quatre Vents.

(Above left) In the white garden at Les Quatre Vents, philadelphus, delphiniums and campanulas flower as well as (if not better than) they do in the temperate maritime climates of the British Isles. Cool nights – the air temperature is kept down by the adjacent river – ensure a long period of flowering in spite of the very short growing season between the last frost in early June and the first frost in September. Although the choice of trees and shrubs (especially evergreen) is severely limited by the climate, fortunately deep snow almost invariably covers and protects perennial plants through the long winter months. A year with little snow can bring many casualties.

microclimatic conditions of the extreme south-west of Britain or of Scotland's west coast, influenced by the Gulf Stream, where there is little frost but high humidity. Even in a country as small as Britain incidence of rainfall affects what plants can be grown with ease, with high precipitation of some sixty to seventy inches/1,500 to 1,750 millimetres on the western hills in the route of the prevailing winds, and a very low rainfall of some twenty inches/500 millimetres on the east. Similar gradations are very marked in the United States, with predominantly north–south mountain ranges.

The actual plant metabolism needs time to adjust to seasonal changes. In all except tropical climates plants are subject to freezing from time to time. If dormant, plant cells contain little water and damage from frost is limited. If full of sap, ice crystals form in the cells and rupture the membranes. In autumn warm days followed by cold nights, with high daytime transpiration and respiration at night curtailed by low temperatures, combined with the plant's adaptation to day length and temperature, lead to an optimum rate of slowing down in a plant's metabolism. The plant accumulates a store of carbohydrates, and less water, in its tissue, which will protect the cells from frost damage. Some plants protect themselves from frost by having a concentration of cellular compounds that act as an 'anti-freeze'. Severe daily fluctuations in temperature are common throughout North America in oscillating patterns that repeat through the winter months. In northern Texas, where freezing winds from the Canadian plains can lower Gulf temperatures of 90 or 100° to 32° Fahrenheit/from 32–8° to 0° Celsius in a few hours, plants from other habitats, without regional adaptability, having little time to adjust, are often damaged. Hardy plants can also be harmed when frozen, if thaws set in too quickly. Any plant even slightly inclined to doubtful hardiness in the garden should be placed where it will be protected from early-morning sun by an overhead canopy. It should never be given an eastern exposure.

Of course, favourable microclimates in a garden make

In Quillota in Chile, the gardens of Pedro Thomas Allende, designed by Juan Grimm, have groves of jacaranda (*Jacaranda mimosifolia*) as a backdrop in front of the mountains. Most frequently seen as street trees in warm climates, such as southern California, south-west Asia and sufficiently humid coastal areas of the Mediterranean such as Portugal and southern Spain, the elegant deciduous trees have white-throated pyramidal panicles of purple-blue flowers. From Bolivia and the Argentine, these trees will withstand minimum temperatures of 41–5°F/ 5–7°C.

At Mount Cuba in Delaware native pink shell azaleas (*Rhododendron vaseyi*) and *Phlox divaricata* grow under the tall tulip poplars (*Liriodendron tulipifera*). At the Mount Cuba Center the mission is to conserve the local Piedmont flora and encourage its appreciation by the public. The centre is propagating cultivars of interest to gardeners (such as *Aster laevis* 'Bluebird', *Heuchera micrantha* 'Palace Purple' and new forms of *Solidago rugosa*) and releasing them to the nursery trade.

it possible to grow plants beyond their usual cold or heat tolerance. But in general what a gardener in any region calls a hardy plant is biologically programmed to survive in that particular garden. Trees, shrubs and perennials collected as seed from the high altitudes in their own regions are most likely to thrive in a garden in a colder area. Many plants also become more hardy as they grow more mature, so if they can be got through the first winter, especially if they come from a nursery in which they have had protection, they will continue to thrive.

Unless in very extreme climates, perennials, unlike trees and shrubs (which must have conditions approximating to those in their countries of origin), can be made to perform more or less successfully in almost any conditions – given a large degree of intensive management. If tender, they can be protected by mulches in winter, they can have their water requirements monitored and attended to, and the soil enriched and amended to suit them, and be divided and replanted to ensure optimum performance. But perennials can also be grown with much less effort and very little maintenance if given conditions as near as possible to their regions of origin, as in more naturalistic gardening. Of course, in certain climatic conditions traditional English-type perennial borders are not possible. In the south-eastern states of North America days and nights in summer are too hot. Other areas of the world such as deserts are also too hot and dry or too cold. Most perennials recommended for growing in natural-style gardens in western Europe and in North America come from temperate regions of the world, generally with cold or dry winters and wet summers. Many will survive low temperatures at least to about 23° Fahrenheit/–5° Celsius, but most survive much colder situations with temperatures dropping to –4° Fahrenheit/–20° Celsius. More specialist rock-garden plants, originating from mountain snow-lines, may require special methods of growing, ensuring good drainage, dry winters and coolness in summer. Perennials from warm countries, their dormant buds protected at ground level, can survive to very low temperatures in a much colder garden if there is a natural covering of snow (or if they are given a thick layer of mulch). Perennials of doubtful hardiness like the alpines mentioned above, and tender shrubs from the Mediterranean areas, will do best if given good drainage and kept dry in winter. In cold continental-type climates where frost can lift plants out of the ground, a wigwam of conifer branches applied after the first hard frost will be most effective, preventing plants from thawing out in a mild spell by keeping the frost in the ground as well as protecting them. In British gardens, with less severe frosts, thick mulches can be added while the ground is still warm to give roots a longer growing period. Mulches influence soil temperature, making the soil cooler in summer and warmer in winter, and slowing the rate of seasonal temperature change. A mulch will help to make it possible to grow warm-climate plants in areas with cold winters, and cold-climate plants in areas with hot summers.

In general the plant's origin will be the best guide to tolerance of heat in summer, with a difference between dry heat and heat with humidity. Perennials from the Himalayas and west China, where there are cool summers and a lot of summer moisture, will not thrive in extremes of summer heat or drought. American woodlanders from mountain ranges on the east coast need moisture and an acid soil, often going dormant after flowering is over through the hot summers. Perennials and bulbs from Mediterranean countries or regions of the world with similar climates generally flower early in spring or in the autumn as the cool weather returns, but are dormant through the summer. Some perennials – irises from exposed rocky slopes in eastern Europe or western Asia, peonies from dry woodlands and exposed sunny sites from Europe and from richer soils in Asia, and dahlias and salvias from Mexican mountains – have swollen roots or rhizomes, which will store and retain moisture through periods of drought.

Growing perennials successfully is easiest when winters are mild and summers are relatively cool. Most perennials from other parts of the world, from often rather different climatic conditions, seem to adapt well to the English climate (where the native flora is very restricted) and regions such as the Pacific north-west in America. English perennial borders are almost entirely composed of exotic plants. The extremes of cold, heat and humidity of much of North America make growing perennials from other parts of the world, unless with similar climates, difficult. Fortunately for American gardeners many of the best perennials actually come from North America, natives of woodland or more open prairie, while others originate in similar habitats in parts of eastern Asia, Siberia and eastern Europe. There are also very definite regional climates throughout the United States all rich in native flora, many of the plants of which have travelled to enrich European perennial gardens: prairie flowers and grasses from the rich soil of the Midwest, Mediterranean-type perennials, bulbs and annuals from California, woodland asters from New England woods, and the more difficult mountain plants from the southern Appalachians (Georgia, South Carolina, Tennessee, North Carolina, West Virginia and Virginia).

Hardy perennials, covered with a thick mulch or a protective blanket of snow in winter, can grow very successfully in northern New England and Canada, where many familiar shrubs cannot be attempted. The growing season is short, with perhaps only 120 days without frost compared to 330 in England, but with hot sun during the day and cool nights, plants grow tall in the long days of the higher latitudes.

Perennials from other climates often behave quite differently in a new environment. Perennials from cool mountain areas may well need shade when grown in gardens at lower altitudes. Plants familiar in open sunny gardens in England, when translated to North American gardens with much hotter summers, will require shade. As said above, Mediterranean plants such as acanthus, dormant in summer in their native environment and in similar climates such as California, are important foliage plants and summer-flowerers in cooler climates, with stems dying down after frost, and crowns given protection through the winter with a thick mulch.

In the wild many perennials and bulbs flower in woodland in spring, before deciduous trees and shrubs get their leaves. They survive the summer with very little light, many retreating underground to dormancy through the hot dry months. Plants from exposed steppes where there are no shade-bearing trees or shrubs are accustomed to sun and require open situations, although alpines from almost similar habitats (but requiring moisture for their deep roots) can be burned off in a dry sunny situation. Many of the best bog plants from the Far East and from North America come from damp or marshy woods, and in cooler summer climates such as that of the British Isles survive full sun as long as they have enough moisture. Primulas, astilbes and hostas, although their origins are damp woods, will all thrive in open situations in western British gardens if given appropriate soil and sufficient moisture. Blue poppies from the Yunnan and north-east Burma, growing in scrub and wood, need acid soil, humidity and cool shade.

The natural gardener can help plants on the margin of hardiness survive by placing them under the natural overhead canopies of other plants and by protecting their roots and crowns with a deep mulch. Shallow-rooted shrubs such as Japanese maples and rhododendrons can be mulched in winter to keep the roots from repeatedly freezing and thawing, and mulched in summer to keep in the moisture. Gardeners can go to great lengths to protect shrubs with shelter belts and screens, or by wrapping them individually with woven straw mats, or hessian or burlap.

Working with the Soil

The raw material of soil comes from weathering of rocks into mixtures of different particle sizes. The soil itself is a complex mixture of inert minerals, chemicals and organic materials, the nutrients. It is also colonized by millions of microscopic organisms which by their actions make the vital nutrients available to the plants. To perform their function, roots need water and air as well as nutrients. Earthworms are the most important soil organisms; they are literally fertilizer factories, digesting the soil, aerating it and thus making channels for plant roots and for moisture.

The pH of soil measures its acidity or alkalinity, which affects the availability of plant nutrients. These are nitrogen (for rate and vigour of growth), phosphorus (for root growth and ripening of seed and fruit) and potassium (as potash, speeding the production of sugars in the leaves and the ripening process, and having close links with nitrogen), but also calcium (necessary for young plant growth, and for making heavy clay soils workable), magnesium (for the manufacture of chlorophyll) and other trace elements such as iron, manganese, boron, copper, zinc and molybdenum, essential for growth of some plants. But it is the three main nutrient elements that are responsible for the growth of most plants.

Soil pH is largely controlled by the parent rock from which the soil is formed. The pH range for good plant growth lies between 5.5 pH and 7.5 pH, with 6.5 as an optimum. Most plants are reasonably tolerant of this range but gardeners quickly learn which plants, mainly ericaceous, will not thrive in a soil with high pH (calcifuges) and others, although more rare, that need strongly alkaline conditions (calcicoles or calciphiles). When planted in soil of the wrong pH plants suffer from mineral deficiences and become much more susceptible to pests and diseases. In alkaline soils with a high pH there may well be shortages of manganese, boron, phophorus and, in some soils, calcium. In low-pH soils plants will be short of phosphorus and there may be a toxicity of manganese and aluminium. Even if the pH of the soil is not measured, the basic soil type and likely pH can be guessed by observing plants in the district, both native trees and shrubs and garden plants that flourish in neighbouring gardens.

In nature, in forests and when natural ways of gardening are pursued, falling leaves decompose and nutrients are re-absorbed by the roots of the plants, or leaves are composted to be reapplied to the soil, a natural recycling equivalent to the farmer putting back manure on his land. In practice if soils are too wet and lack oxygen or too cold or too acid, decay is very slow. On the floor of rain forests nitrogen in the acidic soil is constantly being leached away. In gardens soils are often contaminated and depleted by outside influences. In very intensive gardening (such as vegetable growing) force-fed plants benefit from extra fertilizers. When growing plants from other environments it may be worth knowing what particular type of soil and which nutrients are most important to their survival. In natural gardening using artificial means to lower a pH in order to be able to grow acid-loving plants such as rhododendrons in an alkaline wood is hardly appropriate.

Clay soil has the smallest particles of all soil types; it is self-binding, water-logged and easily compacted in winter and bakes as hard as cement in summer. Squeezed between finger and thumb, it will form a sticky ball. In compacted clay there are few earthworms. The addition of organic compost and gravel helps particles to aggregate into larger workable 'crumbs'. At the opposite extreme to clay is a light sandy soil with large soil particles. Although nearly always easy to work, sandy soils are fast-draining and drought-prone, needing irrigation. Unable to store nutrients, they need frequent addition of bulky organic matter. Silts have particles intermediate between clay and sand. They tend to compact easily but are, in general, water-retentive and fertile. Loams, described scientifically, have a combination of large and small particles. To the gardener 'loam' denotes the very best possible soil type with an optimum combination of good drainage, moisture retention and good nutrient-holding capacity. This ideal soil is the sort of tilth found in an old well-worked kitchen garden: Americans describe it as having the consistency of a good moist chocolate cake.

Whatever the soil, digging in organic matter will improve texture and workability and help the essential micro-organisms to thrive. In a new garden, topsoil may be found to have been compacted by heavy machinery and, sometimes, is so poor that new topsoil has to be imported. Obtaining new topsoil is not easy. Old definitions of topsoil as the original surface layer of grass or cultivated land (the coveted loam) are no longer realistic and soils available may well be composed of subsoils with a mineral base, enhanced by organic matter and nutrients. A healthy soil structure of beneficial soil life, with a steady release of nutrients, adequate moisture retention and drainage ensures healthy plants, which in turn will be more pest- and disease-resistant.

Plant Adaptability, Past and Present
Ever since people have travelled they have brought plants with them to their new homes, and have sent back novelties found in the new regions. Some cultivated plants (and attendant 'weeds') have thus been growing and adapting in different environments for hundreds and even thousands of years, gradually acclimatizing. The process of plant exchange speeded up first with plant collecting expeditions and then with the expansion of ornamental gardening into a leisure industry. Over the years new garden varieties arose by chance, and breeders increased both the range of cultivars and their ability to tolerate various kinds of stress.

THE ART OF PLANTING A NATURAL PICTURE

In 1970 the painter Ton ter Linden bought a small run-down farm where he could start his garden on what was neglected meadowland in the Drenthe region of north-eastern Holland. The sparsely populated rural area, a pattern of small fields and hedgerows with thatched farmhouses, provided the peaceful atmosphere he required. Nothing remained on his almost four acres/1.6 hectares at Ruinen except a few ancient apple trees, providing him with an empty canvas for his pioneering gardening, which was to become an important ancillary to his watercolours.

Naturalism in planting is not the main aim of the garden in a strictly ecological sense; nevertheless the flowing borders in which plants suitable for the environment are grown together as neighbours have a spontaneously 'natural' look. At Ruinen the gardening compositions change every year as self-seeding plants (combined with creative weeding) – all controlled by the artist's eye – are encouraged to establish new patterns as they demonstrate their adaptability to the site. Interweaving colours give way to the fading tones of stems and flowerheads, creating beautiful and ever-changing pictures very different from conventional herbaceous borders, in which plants are allotted confined spaces and deployed in preconceived relationships.

As a young man ter Linden regularly visited the nature gardens in Amstelveen, going there to paint. Influenced by the writings of Dr Jacques P. Thijsse on nature conservation and landscape maintenance, the municipality there had, since 1939, developed a series of gardens in which only native flora was grown. In contrast to more pedestrian native-plant parks and landscapes, at Amstelveen the grouping of the wild flowers in consciously composed aesthetically pleasing ways was advocated. Achieving this required extensive knowledge and practical experience of ecological factors so that the maintenance was appropriate, but also called for creative vision – a 'mix' of naturalness and artistic quality control. Ton ter Linden saw that the first essential in his flat landscape at Ruinen was to plant a wind-break inside which, using specimen trees and subdividing hedges (of yew, hornbeam and less formal plant materials), he could create an inner microclimate for plants as well as the bones of his design. Today there are twenty-two different spaces: gardens for the seasons include a spring and an autumn garden; there is a woodland garden, a fern garden, and colour borders of different combinations, mainly based on red, white and

yellow, with silvery elements – usually artemisias – weaving other colours together and forming a link between them.

Gardening methods emphasize naturalism. No cutting down is done in autumn; instead ter Linden enjoys the fading buffs and browns of stems and seed-heads through the winter months. In spring herbaceous stems are cut into eight-inch/twenty-centimetre lengths and dropped on the ground to decompose into a nutrient-rich mulch. The beds are weeded and all staking is done with natural brushwood: 'Birch is ideal because it is so pliable, but I also use a lot of oak twigs. I start staking plants like delphiniums and thalictrums when they are about two feet tall, but I also stake surrounding plants. In this way I create a network of brushwood which I hope will survive the inevitable gales. After staking I cut away all the superfluous wood, so nothing remains in sight.'

(Right) The painter Ton ter Linden combines naturalism with artistic effects in his garden at Ruinen, making use of the nuances of his environment, and planting very much to please plants as well as to satisfy his own aesthetic concepts. Flowing borders, interweaving colours and permanent planting, which means choosing plants carefully for the environment, combine to show how 'naturalism' can be manipulated inside quite old-fashioned views of conventional garden beauty. In the picture spikes of self-seeding atriplex, veronicastrum, *Cephalaria gigantea* and penstemons are enriched by the late-flowering eupatorium on the right.

(Left) Ton ter Linden uses plants with different shapes and colours, such as short-lived verbascums (in this case, perennial *Verbascum chaixii* 'Album'), to create effects that may last for just a few years or only one season. Many verbascums are biennials, found on dry stony hillsides; in gardens they will often seed to flower *in situ* in the second year following. Ton ter Linden's borders are constantly changing, creating their own dynamic, as some plants disappear and others, such as spreading silver-leaved anaphalis and artemisia (which are invasive in well-drained soil in full sun), gradually establish new relationships with adjacent plants, creating artificial plant communities based on habitat. In the background are pink phlox and the hardy upright purple-flowered *Verbena hastata* from North America.

(Right) The queen of the prairie (*Filipendula rubra*) from north-east America is a grand plant for large boggy gardens, flourishing in sun or half-shade. The cultivar 'Venusta' has deep rose-pink flowers, paling as they age. Ton ter Linden uses the filipendula in damp areas of his garden. Here with sanguisorba, they flank a stretch of water, framing a seat. To create naturalistic garden pictures plants need at least to appear to have been given situations they will enjoy; in actual fact the gardener can often 'cheat' to get the best aesthetic effects. If water features are artificial with adjacent dry soil, moisture-loving plants appropriate to the ambience can still be introduced with the aid of an irrigation system.

Today trees and shrubs in particular are being especially bred to increase their hardiness and/or heat tolerance, and for tolerance of different soil conditions, providing greater choices for gardeners wanting to grow familiar genera in more extreme climates. Hardier strains of philadelphus and azaleas will make it possible to grow these plants, with improved cold-resistance, in more northern climates with low winter temperatures. Other breeders struggle to find cultivars able to withstand the hot nights and days of the southern states and to adapt to different day-lengths in widely separated altitudes. In the world of perennials others have worked on Japanese iris (*Iris ensata*) to produce cultivars viable in alkaline soil. Hemerocallis and many other perennials are bred with shorter stems to avoid the necessity of staking, and with a longer flowering period and longer-lasting individual flowers. To many this sort of breeding seems self-defeating, the quality of a plant being lost as other characteristics are emphasized. On the whole soft-stemmed herbaceous plants, perennials, biennials and annuals can, with intensive preparation and maintenance, have soil and moisture requirements manipulated to allow almost any artificial but decorative combination.

At first, however, it must have been a matter of trial and error when plants were taken to different countries and climates. Most of the foreign plants grown in early times in the temperate gardens of northern Europe were fruits and aromatic plants used for medicine, coming from the Mediterranean region or from western Asia. While more northern deciduous shrubs experience wet and cold in winter and need moisture during the summer, Mediterranean shrubs are adapted to summer heat. Their grey or silvery leaves enable them to survive almost drought conditions in summer, but they tolerate little frost. Gardeners nevertheless learned to plant these valuable additions in favoured spots, to offer them protection and nurture them as far as possible, until many of them have become familiar garden plants in cooler latitudes on both sides of the Atlantic.

Other plants came from central Asia: it was found that

fruit trees, almonds, cherries and plums from central Asia did well in northern Europe, especially if they came from wet regions around the Caspian and Black Seas. Those from the colder steppe areas also do well in Midwest America, where climatic extremes of heat and cold are similar. A plant is on the tender side if it is liable to be killed or damaged by cold. Evergreen shrubs with leaves that transpire all winter need moisture, which they cannot get if the air is too cold and dry and roots are in frozen ground. In Britain native European evergreens such as holly, ivies and conifers are adapted to these conditions, but most Mediterranean shrubs such as rosemary, bay and myrtle, and evergreens from Chile, New Zealand and California, are under stress, as likely to die from poor drainage allowing water to freeze around the roots as from low temperatures. The Mediterranean climate, influenced by the warm air mass of the Sahara Desert (which in southern Spain and southern Portugal meets the Gulf Stream to give a climate similar to Florida ten degrees of latitude further south), produces hot summers and cool winters, during which most of the plants do their growing. In the Mediterranean climate, growth begins as summers cool off and rain encourages growth. Bulbs and most perennials flower in winter or early spring and go dormant during the hot summer. Evergreen shrubs from the warm climates of the southern hemisphere such as Chile and New Zealand wait for the more settled spring before starting to grow.

In Britain and north-west Europe and other cool-temperate maritime climates, such as the Pacific west coast of North America, south-west Chile and parts of New Zealand, the cool summers and relatively mild winters provide plants from a very wide range of habitats with a possible garden home. Plants from these regions do well in Britain, where the favourable growing conditions are enhanced by warm westerly winds and by the Gulf Stream that travels from the Gulf of Mexico to the west coasts of the British Isles, making the climate warmer than in regions of the same latitude on the American east coast.

The North American climate is influenced by cold radiating from the land- and ice-masses in Canada, only tempered by the eastern and western mountain ranges, running north and south, and by the warm waters of the Gulf of Mexico. On the north-east coast the ocean is less of a moderating force because the prevailing winds do not blow west off the Atlantic, although the effects of the Gulf Stream influence climate as far north as Cape Cod; on the west coast, beyond the Rockies and more coastal ranges, the winter climate is much less harsh. Deciduous trees and shrubs from eastern and central North America, where the winters are cold and summers hot and often wet, do better in a continental climate – if soil conditions are suitable – than in more maritime regions. Trees such as American walnut (*Juglans nigra*) and osage orange (*Maclura pomifera*) from further west in Kansas thrive and fruit in central Europe (but rarely in England); shrubs such as kalmias and liquidambars, many of which also prefer acid soil, do better in the extremes of the continental climate of Europe. In the eighteenth century collectors realized that new American exotics, introduced in many cases through Mark Catesby and through John Bartram, American botanist and plant-explorer, needed special acid soil conditions, so the plants were collected together in 'American Gardens'. In these, recently introduced trees such as red oaks (*Quercus rubra*), American walnuts and tulip trees (*Liriodendron tulipifera*) might be planned for eventual forest cover, while groves of trees and shrubs such as magnolias and liquidambars and rhododendrons from the south-east states (Pacific north-west rhododendrons did not come to Europe until the nineteenth century), and kalmias and vacciniums, were planted in specially provided or prepared peat-based soil. Many of the smaller eastern North American woodland flowers also need acid conditions and would only grow satisfactorily in similar beds.

Dr John Fothergill (1712–80), the botanist with the celebrated garden at Upton, West Ham, described his planting conditions for American woodland plants in

In the Santa Barbara Botanic Garden, an exceptional site up Mission Canyon, under the Santa Ynez mountain range, native Californian plants are encouraged to spread in natural plant communities, with the Cathedral and La Cumbre sandstone peaks making a backdrop. Plants are arranged by plant type or natural habitat. The central meadow is a field of wild flowers, in which coral bells (*Heuchera*), native to New Mexico, grow with Californian poppies (*Eschscholzia californica*) from similar habitats. The native flora of California is extremely varied, with plants coming from a wide range of settings – desert, alpine, coastal and interior valley – with about one-third of the total five-thousand-odd species being endemic. Many are not suited to the maritime Santa Barbara climate, which is too humid for desert species and some alpines.

William Robinson is best remembered in *The Wild Garden* for his advocacy of growing plants in natural ways, and his dislike of artificial bedding-out schemes. Nevertheless recognizing the need for linking house and garden, he terraced the area around Gravetye Manor and used traditional paving and flat lawns backed by flowerbeds. Growing roses in geometrically shaped beds seemed a contradiction of all he had preached but he believed that 'the only true test of all such things is the artistic one – do they make for ugliness or for beauty?' In Peter Herbert's restoration of the gardens at Gravetye he has followed Robinson's ideas in using plants appropriate to the situation, not replacing Robinson's rose garden.

1772: 'Under a north wall I have a good border made up of that kind of rich black turf-like soil, mixed with some sand, in which I find most of the American plants thrive best. It has a few hours of the morning and evening sun, and is quite sheltered from the mid-day heats. It is well supplied with water during the summer, and the little shrubs and herbaceous plants have a good warm covering of dried fern thrown over them when the frosts set in. This is gradually removed when the spring advances, so that, as the plants are never frozen in the ground while they are young and tender, I do not lose any that come to me with any life in them.' Elsewhere in his wilderness Fothergill, having first cleared out laurels and weeds, grew, in the shelter of the remaining trees, shrubs from north-east America: 'Kalmias, Azaleas, all the Magnolias and most other hardy American shrubs. It is not quite eight years since I made a beginning so that my plants must be considered young ones. They are, however, extremely flourishing. I have an Umbrella tree (*Magnolia tripetala*) about twenty feet high, that flowers with me abundantly every spring; but the great Magnolia (*M. grandiflora*) has not yet flowered; it grows extremely fast. I shelter its top in the winter; he gains from half a yard to two feet in height every summer, and will ere long, I doubt not, repay my care with his fragrance and beauty.'

Plants from cold areas such as Russia and Siberia, north-eastern Asia and high mountains of the Far East, unharmed by extreme cold in their own countries, may succumb to the fluctuation of an English winter. They are also accustomed to hotter summers, and shrubs such as koelreuteria may seldom flower without the extra heat to ripen the wood. The cold tolerance of trees and shrubs from the Himalayas, the mountains stretching from Pakistan to western China, with cold dry winters and warm, very wet summers, is closely related to the altitude from which they come. Some of the best plants for woodland gardens in Britain come from the mountains and valleys. Spring and autumn are warm, dry and sunny, with monsoons between June and October. Success with plants from the Himalayas depends on

The climate in the North Island of New Zealand ranges between the warm temperate or subtropical climate of coastal regions and the mainly temperate maritime climate found inland. In Gordon Collier's gardens at Titoki Point (named for titoki, *Alectryon excelsus*) in the south-east of the North Island of New Zealand, tree ferns (*Dicksonia squarrosa* and *D. fibrosa*) and the taller silver tree fern (*Cyathea dealbata*), which need humidity and an almost frost-free environment, grow in the Damp Garden with some specimens of the native rimu (*Dacrydium cupressinum*) planted in the 1930s by Mr Collier's parents, together with phormiums (*Phormium tenax* and *P. cookianum*). Plants from other parts of the world also thrive in the moist conditions where heavy clay makes drainage for some plants difficult: hostas and ferns such as the shuttlecock fern (*Matteuccia struthiopteris*) and the sensitive fern (*Onoclea sensibilis*) flourish with skunk cabbages, primulas, astilbes and ligularias. An interesting native is the strange drooping *Pseudopanax crassifolius*. Originally a bare hillside, the garden lies 450 metres/ 1,500 feet above sea level, with summer temperatures up to 84°F/28°C. Rainfall is 38in/960mm, there is little snow and 15°F/10°C of frost is rare.

giving them forest shelter as well as providing enough moisture. Western China has a very similar climate, with most shrubs flowering in May before the rains start. Soils vary widely from acid to alkaline, with many rhododendrons, calcifuge in gardening situations, found growing in thin, acid soil on limestone in the wild. Many moisture-loving perennials also come from this area, introduced to western gardens towards the end of the nineteenth century.

In the Pacific north-west of America, north of California, the climate resembles more closely that of much of Britain, characterized in coastal regions by cool to hot summers and mild wet winters, although it can vary a great deal depending on aspect – with temperate coastal forests with high rainfall alternating with dry east-facing slopes and dry valleys. Many of the large conifers from the west coast adapt to the wetter regions of Britain and some of the understorey shrubs, ferns and perennials thrive in British gardens. Oregon grape (*Mahonia aquifolium*), first taken east by Lewis and Clark in 1805, adapts well to northern Europe, and many of David Douglas's shrubs, such as *Garrya elliptica* and salal (*Gaultheria shallon*), together with deciduous species such as *Ribes sanguineum* and *Holodiscus discolor*, collected in the 1820s, thrive in England.

Many of the evergreen shrubs from New Zealand and Tasmania acclimatized to a maritime climate with salt-laden winds are especially suitable for coastal areas and milder districts in temperate climates. Before attempting to grow them, it is worth considering the exact location of their habitat. In New Zealand, divided by mountains up to 6,000 feet/1,800 metres, north-westerly winds bring high rainfall to the west coast, while on the eastern lee-side dry winds bring drought conditions and possible frosts during the 'winter' from May until August, with occasional frosts in any month of the year. The climate varies between oceanic and insular in the south-west to warm-temperate in the north. In general the

vegetation is more sensitive to wind and to 'wet' and 'dry' than to any other climatic aspect, although the altitude from which a plant comes affects its hardiness in gardens. New Zealand plants seem to tolerate most soil types. Although coming from such extremes as high-rainfall bog in the south-west of the South Island (with almost 200 inches/5,000 millimetres of rain) to almost drought conditions in a sandy soil on the east coast near Christchurch (which receives only 26 inches/650 millimetres), many New Zealand shrubs seem able to adapt to differing wet or dry garden situations: brachyglottis, corokia, griselinias, hebes, hoherias, leptospermum, daisy bushes (*Olearia* species), pittosporums and ozothamnus are all good seaside shrubs for the British Isles, with *Brachyglottis* 'Sunshine' (syn. *Senecio* 'Sunshine') most commonly seen even in colder gardens. Many of these shrubs from the high-rainfall forests dominated by southern beech, which contain four distinct *Nothofagus* species in different regions at different altitudes, in the western portion of the South Island, enjoy the wet or humid conditions found in Cornwall and on the west coast of Scotland. Tree ferns (*Cyathea dealbata* and dicksonias) thrive as understorey in the damp humid valleys. New Zealand flax (*Phormium tenax*) grows in swamps and damp areas, while mountain flax (*Phormium cookianum*) grows on mountain slopes as a neighbour to cabbage trees (*Cordyline australis* and *C. indivisa*). Hoherias, an endemic genus, have distinct habitats, with *Hoheria glabrata* growing on the wet west-facing mountain slopes, and the similar *H. lyallii* on the drier eastern flanks. Olearias are the most neglected of evergreen garden shrubs; given a site that pleases them, they are much less tender than often supposed, with excellent foliage and very floriferous. The hardiest come from high altitudes in the South Island or from the mountains of Tasmania, while *Olearia* 'Henry Travers' (syn. *O. semidentata*) and *O. chathamica* need the humidity of an island climate to survive.

COSMOPOLITAN NATURALISM IN NINFA'S CLEMENT CLIMATE

Ninfa is an oasis of beauty in the plain south of Rome. The village was deserted at the end of the fourteenth century and remained in ruins until the early years of the 1900s, when the Caetani family drained the malarial marshes surrounding it and started planting among the medieval ruins a garden full of flowering roses, irises, arum lilies and exotic trees. Rushing streams provide abundant water, now canalized for maximum utility; they combine with hot summers and relatively mild winters to make possible acclimatization of a wider range of plants than in the normal Mediterranean-type climate. In general the lands surrounding the Mediterranean are warm and dry in summer; plants grow during the mild wet winters, but stop all growth during the hottest periods of summer. Tropical and subtropical plants expect higher humidity and rainfall. At Ninfa abundant water, mainly supplied from a reservoir above the house, cools the air as well as providing moisture, and allows plants that grow all the year in their native habitat to survive. Although the collection is eclectic, with plants coming from many countries, the natural scenery and the relative ease with which plants grow give this strange garden a very naturalistic (as well as romantic) ambience. The main 'bones' of the garden come from the village streets, their formality now reinforced with lines of Italian cypresses; old ruined houses and church façades provide the high walls over which wisteria and banksian roses cascade and twine, with climbing hydrangeas and ivies in the shade. Sunlight and shadow alternate through the garden thanks to the tall pines, plane trees, cedars and evergreen oaks planted by the Caetani family in the 1920s.

The place has always been renowned for its wild flowers: in the eighteenth century the German historian Gregorovius described how 'over Ninfa waves a balmy sea of flowers', and Augustus Hare saw flowers which 'grow so abundantly in the deserted streets, where honeysuckle and jessamine fling their garlands through the windows of every house, and where the altars of the churches are

thrones for flame-coloured valerian'. Ninfa provides a favoured site for growing plants in very natural ways. The sculptural leaves of gunnera (*G. manicata*) from the Brazilian cloud forests give a tropical feel to the river; arums and irises line the water channels; roses twine up cypresses and grow so luxuriantly over walls as to look completely spontaneous. Rare pines from Mexico, magnolias from Asia and North America, ceanothus from California, buddlejas, viburnums, dogwoods and maples all grow in seemingly careless abandon, thriving in the favoured climate and fertile soil, sheltered from winds by high hills.

Ninfa is now a charitable foundation. Lelia and Hubert Howard, the last private owners, created a nature reserve in the area.

(Far left) A domed umbrella or stone pine (*Pinus pinea*) stands out by one of the old walls of the village, revealing the much more arid Mediterranean-like terrain on the hill outside the garden. Calla or arum lilies (*Zantedeschia aethiopica*) enjoy the available moisture by the river with their roots in the water, continuing to flower for much of the year. These plants, with arrow-shaped leaves, come from swamps or lake margins in east Africa. In colder climates the callas will only survive low temperatures below 50°F/10°C if in a greenhouse and planted out in summer or if, planted in pots, their crowns are submerged under water, safe from frost.

(Left) The mild winter climate at Ninfa, with hot summers but plenty of water, provides planting conditions for a diverse range of trees, shrubs and perennials. The giant-leaved *Gunnera manicata* from Brazil grows along the riverside in reach of scrambling roses and citrus fruit, with tall rustling bamboos and acanthus in the background. The dominating umbrella pines (*Pinus pinea*) and Italian cypresses (*Cupressus sempervirens* 'Fastigiata') confirm the overall Mediterranean atmosphere. The abundant water keeps the atmosphere humid, even in the hottest time of summer, to which tropical and semi-tropical plants with lush vegetative growth contribute.

(Right) A close-up of the clump-forming giant timber bamboo *Phyllostachys bambusoides* from China shows the beauty of the thick, shining deep green canes. Like the native *Acanthus mollis* growing among their rhizomes, these bamboos need a fertile, humus-rich, moist (but well-drained) soil and thrive in sun or half-shade. In full sun in a hot climate the acanthus loses its leaves in summer, retreating to dormancy until rain and cool weather encourage growth in autumn. In a climate with more severe winters, acanthus leaves are killed off by frost and the plant behaves like any deciduous perennial, performing and flowering in spring and summer.

CHAPTER THREE

WOODLAND AND WOODLAND EDGE

*T*HIS CHAPTER is about woodland, but it is also more generally about planting in shade. A Robinsonian woodland garden conjures up a scene adapted from an existing wood of fine deciduous trees, with the gardener merely taking advantage of the shade and humus-rich soil to 'embellish' natural effects by appropriate planting. This ideal is beyond the reach of many gardeners today, but is a useful model even on a far smaller scale. Observing how plants cope in the vicinity of woodland provides inspiration for integrating small groups of trees – or even single specimens – into the domestic garden picture. The key here is largely understanding how plants respond to degrees of shade. In nature shade is generally cast by tree cover (occasionally, however, it is a feature of sunless slopes); in *gardens*, however, areas of shade are the inevitable adjunct of the very buildings and boundaries that define the site. Every gardener has to cope with shade – not necessarily 'woodland shade'; but some appreciation of how woodlands 'work' can help the gardener choose plants for shady areas, and see that they thrive.

A woodland is composed not of trees alone but of structured layers in which tree canopies shade, and shield from wind, the understorey of shrubs and forest-floor plants, including lower-growing woody plants, flowers, bulbs, ferns and mosses, kept cool and moist by thick mulches of decomposing leaves. Shade, shelter and a cool, humus-rich root run are thus the chief characteristics of a natural woodland habitat. Most woods (other than coniferous forests) are not

In one of the gardens designed by the Oehme and van Sweden partnership in America, *Ligularia dentata* 'Desdemona', with vivid yellow-orange flowers and brownish leaves, purple on the undersides, grows in a swathe under the tree, behind a drift of liriope (*Liriope muscari*) with miscanthus grass and calamagrostis to the left, as woodland edge fades into brighter sunshine. All ligularias – mostly from central and east Asia – are found in moist or wet grassland and in damp woodlands. Wolfgang Oehme and James van Sweden are known for their planting in massed abstract patterns, not naturalistic in style, but with much attention paid to the conditions that plants enjoy – matching plants carefully to the site.

uniformly dense, and tree planting will open out at intervals into glades of filtered light – a space open to the sky can be created overnight when a tree falls, and larger glades may be cleared by fire (part of a natural cycle in Californian and Australian woods). Such openings will be quickly colonized by germinating seedlings taking advantage of the light, woody plants eventually shading out perennials as the forest is re-created. At the woodland edge, too, plants from the understorey will drift forward from light shade towards sunlight. Shade-tolerant native shrubs and perennials will often find their way unaided into an established wood, while others, perhaps seeking a bit more light, will spread into groups at the edge of wood or shrubbery. True woodland plants are those that will thrive in low light density, the sort of light filtered by leaf canopies, with their roots in a deep layer of composted leaf litter or duff, built up over years by accumulations of fallen leaves. It is by trying to imitate these effects and conditions that you create a woodland garden, as opposed to a mere wood.

For a gardener, the deciduous or mixed woodland habitat provides exciting opportunities for introducing an understorey of a variety of plants of suitable hardiness, all of which require similar soil conditions and climate. The natural woodland garden, as opposed to a natural forest, can have an assembly of plants from many parts of the world. They will look right together because they have the same basic requirements for growing. In a woodland garden, as opposed to ordinary woodland composed only of natives, it is possible to introduce exotic plants, as long as they enjoy similar conditions. Gardening is an artistic and artificial process rather than simply an ecological conception, and can draw on any

Just north of Boston and close to the Atlantic Ocean, Catherine Hull has a woodland and rock garden. Its structure was designed by Fletcher Steele, but Mrs Hull is the plantswoman who has made the garden not only a collection of rarities – and many ordinary natives and exotics suitable for woodland – but also beautiful. I know of no other garden where small woodland plants are grown more successfully. *Glaucidium palmatum* from mountainous woodland in northern Japan thrives in a rich moist acid soil in deep shade, sheltered from drying winds. With fresh green palmate leaves, it bears its type flower of soft pinkish mauve in early spring. The white form shown far left, *G.p.* 'Leucanthum', is less often seen.

(Left) *Arisaema sikkokianum*, a jack-in-the-pulpit from Japan, grows with white trillium (*Trillium grandiflorum*) in a shady moist corner of Catherine Hull's garden.

suitable plants from wherever they originate, to extend the beauty and interest of the horticultural range. The key to garden success in woodland, as in more open situations, is the compatibility of the plant to its place. And the key planting tactic is to imitate nature's broad sweeps. As William Robinson said in *The Wild Garden*, rather than dotting plants about, 'we must group and mass as Nature does. Though we may enjoy a single flower or tuft here and there, the true way is to make pretty colonies of plants, one or two kinds prevailing in a spot; in that way we may secure distinct effects in each place...' Shrubs, perennials and bulbs can be happily naturalized to spread, either by suckering or seed, in simple drifts beside the original natives, or adjacent to each other, in the filtered light under the tree canopies. The style of planting in the understorey of a wood should imitate nature, with spreading overlapping drifts of shrubs or perennials, with planting patterns established by shapes of the overhead canopies – like the patterns made by the trees' shadows – making gentle blending outlines, layers of woody shrubs fading into clumps of ground-hugging perennials and bulbs.

This embellishment of woods – and of course of other 'wild' areas – in a way that seems almost completely 'natural' is typical of how twentieth-century gardening has developed. And once established it should be almost self-supporting, the gardener's task being to remove unwanted intruders and to edit the rest, adjusting areas where stronger plants edge out the weaker. In more domestic garden styles plants, even trees, are manipulated and contained, but the essence of woodland planting is its apparent freedom, a very Robinsonian conception. Its practice and adaptation all over the world, in many diverse climatic regions, has established a relaxed gardening tradition where maintenance can be almost minimal (although it has to be quite skilled, as it depends on a knowledge of plant needs and behaviour) in the outer areas of a garden, with the style becoming increasingly intensive and manicured the nearer the woodland area is to the house.

Plants that are naturally shade-tolerant are able to utilize what light there is in a deciduous wood better than others, either through having thin evergreen leaves which photosynthesize all year, taking advantage of extra light in winter when trees are leafless, or by growing and flowering early in spring before the canopies give deeper shade and the soil dries out. Plants for the natural woodland have to be suitable to the aspect of a site. They are either native from the region or come from similar habitats in another part of the world. Shrubs, perennials and bulbs that do demand shade originally come from forests in their own countries or from shady slopes of north-facing hills. They and their root-systems are used to a relatively cool situation out of the sun's glare. They will do best in deep natural humus, made from an acidic accumulation of fallen leaves, which helps retains adequate moisture. Many plants are not all that particular about soil, but some, the real calcifuges, must have acidic conditions in order to grow at all. They may also be fussy about the amount and quality of what light is available. Shade-lovers will probably do quite well on the edge of woodland or under the canopy of a deciduous tree, but plants that are most suitable for the woodland edge may well reject the deeper shade of the forest, or the sunless border.

It is important to appreciate the different kinds of microclimate that can prevail in shade. Shade conditions vary greatly, from areas receiving no sun to those receiving a few hours of filtered sunlight each day, the depth of shade varying with the seasons and depending on the latitude of the garden. In winter the low sun may penetrate into areas below trees, which it would not reach when high in the sky during summer. The quality of the shade in a wood depends a good deal on the nature of the main tree canopy. Mixed broadleaved woodland – perhaps with a sprinkling of evergreens and conifers – is generally the most hospitable. Shady habitats vary greatly from the dense, dry shade in a conifer wood to the more hospitable shade under deciduous trees, where a rich layer of decomposed leaves retains moisture, to conditions of flickering sunlight on the woodland edge, where the range of plants that will flourish is greatly extended. The lack of moisture and nutrients under trees is as important to plants as the lack of light. Tree roots absorb much of the moisture and goodness in the soil, although, because competitive grasses and other weeds are not present in shady conditions, the shade-tolerant plants can survive the lack of light, moisture and nutrients more easily. Also on the plus side is the higher humidity caused by vegetation and the relative coolness of the forest, controlling transpiration and reducing evaporation from the soil. The roots are kept cool by natural mulches, which retain the moisture. As William Robinson wrote, 'A great many beautiful plants haunt the woods, we cannot change their nature easily: and even if we grow them well in open places, their bloom will not be so enduring as in the wood.'

Sometimes the only shade in a garden is found under a specimen tree or provided by high walls. Gardeners also have to cope with the special conditions that occur on the sunless side of a wall, which may also be in a rain shadow, creating shade and drought. The soil in the shade cast by trees may be not only dry, but also full of surface roots, making it almost impossible to cultivate successfully. Alders, poplars, robinias, wild cherry, Norway maples and, of course, beech, have very dense root systems, which make it difficult for plants to establish themselves. In the dense beech woods of oceanic Britain only the native wood anemones (*Anemone nemorosa*) and bluebells (*Hyacinthoides non-scripta*) are normally found, with perhaps a few brambles; even these disappear when the leaf-canopy closes.

In the most trying dry conditions with shade and tree roots, creeping evergreens such as *Lamium galeobdolon*, ivy, cyclamen and periwinkle are possibilities in the British climate. Spring sun penetrates through branches of overhead deciduous trees before the trees leaf out and the ground is still moist enough for spring-flowerers to flourish. Sweet woodruff (*Galium odoratum*), Solomon's seal (*Polygonatum*), pulmonarias and various wood anemones (*Anemone nemorosa* and *A. blanda*) will all flower and die down. In North America, in the mainly deciduous woods of the east and Midwest, *Pachysandra terminalis* from Japan and Baltic ivy (*Hedera helix* 'Baltica'), the most cold-tolerant of the ivies, are efficient groundcovers for deep garden shade, although the former needs irrigation to flourish, but are also used extensively in situations where there is a much larger choice of both native and introduced, almost self-sustaining understorey plants, where a mixed planting scheme would really look much more natural. Bloodroot (*Sanguinaria canadensis*), bunchberry (*Cornus canadensis*), dicentra, false Solomon's seal or false spikenard (*Smilacina racemosa*) and native ferns tend to associate well with 'foreign' woodlanders, plants such as annual honesty, European ginger (*Asarum europaeum*) and spring-flowering snowdrops.

The summer shade cast by a horse chestnut (*Aesculus hippocastanum*) is so dense that only early-flowering winter aconites (*Eranthis hyemalis*), content to have their dormant period in dense, dry shady conditions, will grow successfully. On the other hand deciduous oak trees were generally considered in William Robinson's day to make the best high canopies for gardeners with the soil beneath them leafy, humus-rich and moisture-retentive, in natural conditions sheltering an assortment of hollies (forms of *Ilex aquifolium*) and hazel in their light shade. Evergreen oaks are not so hospitable. European holm oak, the evergreen *Quercus ilex*, although excellent for wind protection and a magnificent forest tree, has a dense canopy, impenetrable to rain, its roots extracting moisture and nutrients from the soil. American live oaks have different problems. Their root systems, prone to disease if damaged, dislike interference or the additional watering necessary to get other plants established under them. In nature in various parts of the south and southwest certain native plants are adapted to growing with and under the oaks, but in a garden situation drought- and heat-tolerant ophiopogons and liriopes work better than grass or other low-growing plants.

moisture, and with overhead canopies screening rain showers. A few woodland plants such as *Arum italicum* ssp. *italicum* 'Marmoratum', autumn-flowering cyclamen (*Cyclamen hederifolium*) and some of the evergreen ferns, such as *Asplenium scolopendrium* and *Polystichum acrostichoides* (from north-east America) have beautiful leaves during the winter months to enrich the scene, thriving even in dry soils.

Hellebores, epimediums, *Tiarella cordifolia*, *Tellima grandiflora*, tolmieas, Solomon's seal and woodrush (*Luzula sylvatica*) all grow naturally in dry shade. Many more plants will succeed in shade in wetter conditions. Most ferns love damp shade. Some are evergreen: tender holly fern, *Cyrtomium falcatum*, from the Far East, and various native polystichums, as well as *Polystichum munitum* from the wet woods of the Pacific west coast of North America. On woodland pond-edge candelabra primula and other moisture-lovers thrive, their roots in the deep silt. At the edge of the wood where there is more light, possibilities increase: many of the best perennials originate from woodland habitats with hotter summer climates than those experienced in the British Isles and, when translated into cooler garden conditions (with more sunlight, but not too much heat), will become more vigorous. Equally, plants from high altitudes, growing in sun in their own habitats, may need shade in lower altitudes where summers are hotter. Plants for woodland edge and almost sunless borders include taller varieties, European foxgloves, aquilegias and aconitums, American actaeas, cimicifugas and golden rods and toad lilies from the Far East.

An overhead canopy of trees helps protect all plants from damaging spring frosts and frost-laden winds, particularly dangerous for exotic shrubs from more continental climates growing in the temperate British climate, in which warm periods through the winter encourage premature growth. In areas with continental climates such as the north-east part of North America, spring is much shorter, but once it comes no more frosts occur. It is followed immediately by summer, hardly

A great sweep of ostrich ferns (*Matteuccia struthiopteris*) grow in the woods at Bois des Moutiers near Dieppe in France. Ferns are found in a very wide range of habitats from rocky crevices to true swamps, but overall ferns will do well in garden conditions in moderate moisture if given some shade – bright shade rather than deep shade – as all ferns need some light. Most gardeners can find a suitable spot, if not in woodland – ferns do not like the competition of tree roots – at woodland edge or under a hedgerow or beneath a north-facing wall, where soil can be amended to suit the ferns chosen. There are ferns for dry and damp shade and for acid and alkaline soil and, of course, they vary in stature from the dramatic tree ferns of New Zealand and south-east Australia to small elegant adiantums and blechnums.

Most plants that thrive under trees are low-growing and give their best performance in spring. Many bulbs, corms and tubers, which store nutrients, grow rapidly as the weather warms in spring, flower, ripen seed and then go dormant. Snowdrops, scillas, *Cyclamen repandum*, delicate wood anemones as well as *Anemone apennina* and *A. ranunculoides* and the small yellow *Tulipa sylvestris*, all naturalize in deciduous woodland, enjoying the humus-rich moisture-retentive medium made by fallen leaves, and joined by common European primroses (*Primula vulgaris*) and violets. The soil dries out in summer, with tree roots absorbing most of the available

RARE WOODLANDERS SAVED BY SANCTUARY AND SCIENCE

Planting started at The Garden in the Woods at Framingham, near Boston, Massachusetts in 1934. The founders were Will Curtis (previously a student of Warren Manning), and Howard 'Dick' Stiles. The two men collected wild flowers from all over America into a flower sanctuary 'where plants will be grown, their likes and dislikes discovered, and the knowledge gained passed on in an effort to curb the wholesale destruction of our most beautiful natives'. In 1965 they entrusted the garden's future to the New England Wild Flower Society, whose charter's purpose is to promote the horticulture and conservation of American plants. The garden is now the Society's headquarters.

For more than forty years Curtis and Stiles collected wild flowers, ferns, shrubs and trees and established them in both natural and modified settings, developing woodland groves, rockeries, swamps and lily-ponds, pine barrens, meadows and screes, in the original thirty acres/twelve hectares of glacial ridge, ravines and bogs, to provide the varied habitats necessary and to establish desirable microclimates. The site, with mainly acid soil, had existing trees and shrubs typical of New England woodland. Hemlocks, sugar maples and birches predominated, with an understorey of viburnums, huckleberries, blueberries and dogwood. Curtis used his designer skills to integrate the diverse habitats, with winding paths connecting the various 'cultures'. The aim was to grow and propagate as many American plants as possible at latitude 42° north of the equator, with hot summers and cold winters typical of Zone 5, but also to demonstrate that ecological priorities did not exclude making an aesthetically pleasing garden. In the end, having created suitable sites for American natives, they also planted exotics that originated in similar environments, thus broadening the depth of interest of the garden.

Today visitors in April see trailing arbutus (*Epigaea repens*) and hepaticas; in May they see yellow lady's slippers (*Cypripedium calceolus*) and trilliums; in June there are prickly pear cactus (*Opuntia*) and pitcher plants (*Sarracenia*); Turk's cap lilies and blazing stars (*Liatris*) appear in July, cardinal flowers (*Lobelia cardinalis*) and turtle-head (*Chelone*) in August, followed by autumn colours. Seeds and plants are offered for sale to interested enthusiasts. Once-rare natives include *Epigaea repens*, the Massachusetts state flower, which had been picked in the nearby woods nearly to extinction, but is now micropropagated and available for sale from the nursery. Also growing is Oconee bells (*Shortia galacifolia*) from the mountains of North Carolina, a plant first discovered by André Michaux near the headwaters of the Savannah River and held as a dried specimen in his Paris Herbarium until noticed by Asa Gray in 1839. It was finally rediscovered in the wild in 1877. Still rare in its habitat region, it is now propagated and available in many nurseries. Turkeybeard (*Xerophyllum asphodeloides*), pixie moss (*Pyxidanthera barbulata*), swamp pink (*Helonia bullata*) and *Cypripedium reginae*, one of the rarer lady's slippers, are all propagated by microculture. Today when commercial (if illegal) collecting in the wild threatens plant communities, pioneer work such as the propagating at The Garden in the Woods is both making these rarer plants available to gardeners and helping to raise public awareness of threats to wild flora.

(Opposite) In May lady's slipper orchid (*Cypripedium calceolus*), still found in drifts in New England woods, flowers in front of maidenhair fern (*Adiantum pedatum*), and behind the European *Galium odoratum*, sweet woodruff. The lady's slipper is also found in northern Europe and in Britain but is now nearly extinct in the wild in Europe. William Robinson was sent the moccasin flower (*C. acaule*) with pink flowers from Philadelphia for his garden at Gravetye but although planted in 'boggy moss' it vanished without trace. After establishing The Garden in the Woods, both Curtis and Styles added exotic plants if they seemed to suit the mood of the site. Rare and scarce plants are now propagated at the garden, and made available to gardeners.

(Above) Emerging fiddleheads of the hardy ostrich fern (*Matteuccia struthiopteris*), from European, east Asian and North American woods, in The Garden in the Woods. Beautiful early in the year, this adaptable fern prefers a damp, but well-drained, deep acid soil, but will also adapt to harsher drier conditions, growing happily with suckering rhizomatous roots contained in ornamental pots.

(Above) Native plants are grown in The Garden in the Woods. *Amsonia tabernaemontana* is a clump-forming many-stemmed perennial with dense rounded cyme-like panicles of pale blue flowers, very similar to the oriental *Rhaza orientalis*. Both need an open situation, the leaves colouring vividly in autumn, and here grow in a sunny glade in the garden. Woodland planting is at its most attractive if dark shade is succeeded by sunlit open-meadow effects, where woodland-edge plants that require more overhead light will thrive. The Garden in the Woods has varied habitats and microclimatic sites. Winding paths connect the various and varied planting schemes, the whole demonstrating that ecological needs do not rule out aesthetically pleasing effects.

leaving time to plant as the frozen earth thaws. Autumn is a period of six to eight weeks with hot days and cold nights, quickly building up the sugars that contribute to the bright reds, crimsons and oranges seen in an American fall, but hardly experienced in an island or temperate region where long slow autumns of continuous growth can be dangerous for shrubs, which make lax new growth, unripened by sun.

Each woodland site is a unique planting area, but a great deal can be learned by studying good examples of old-established woodland gardens and seeing how their designers have worked with the terrain. Some have been made from existing woods, others from deliberately created plantations, which eventually mature into woodland. Some gardens, especially among deciduous trees in eastern North America, are carved out of woodland. In these, trees may be pruned or taken out to increase light, and soil can be amended to increase its nutrients and moisture-retention characteristics. Fortunately there is nearly always a plant that will grow, even in the most difficult or odd situation. In Britain most woodland gardens have been made in the last few hundred years, often beginning as arboreta with collections of exotic specimen trees newly arrived from America or later from eastern Asia. Often these, once the high canopies and humus-rich soil had been established, developed as rhododendron gardens, with attendant Ericaceae and other suitably compatible calcifuge shrubs, as well as the smaller woodland plants – although rhododendrons do not tolerate any competitive and close plant association or groundcovers growing under their canopies to compete with their roots. Herbaceous plants from similar habitats revelling in the same sort of conditions, such as primulas, meconopsis, giant lilies from Asia and many of the small woodlanders from the Alleghanies mentioned below, should be planted clear of the rhododendron bushes.

The range of rhododendrons possible is greatest in a sheltered light woodland with a maritime influence but those that come from colder climates – such as the Russian far east (surviving to –50° Fahrenheit/–46° Celsius) or New England – may suffer in typical British winter vacillations, with warm spells encouraging premature growth being followed by harsh spring frosts. The cooler the climate, the less summer shade is needed, but in a true continental climate the leaves of evergreen rhododendrons can be severely scorched by both summer and winter sun. Many originate in monsoon regions in country bordering the Himalayas, on the mountain slopes above the plains, where heat is tempered by altitude to produce a climate of cool winters – colder as you go higher. In their native habitats, rhododendrons never lack for moisture. There is rain all year, peaking in the monsoons between July and October. It is wetter in the eastern regions than in the west, because rain-laden monsoons blow from the east. These are the rhododendron heartlands, where there is always sufficient rain during the growing season to provide essential moisture for the shallow roots.

In many garden situations, summer rains are not the norm, and as woodland gets drier during the summer months, irrigation is often necessary – at least while plants are being established. Rhododendrons need an uncompacted moisture-retentive yet well-drained organic soil (a pH of between 4.5 and 5.5 is ideal) in which they develop their root system very close to the surface. Forking around rhododendrons is never advisable. They benefit from applications of loose acid-based mulches of decayed leaves (oak and beech leafmould is ideal), bracken or pulverized bark.

At Westonbirt Arboretum, Holford's first tree planting in 1827 was done in quite formal style with forest blocks divided by rides. Gradually shapes and habits of individual trees have taken over some of the geometry to make the planting more naturalistic, allowing canopies and underplanting to provide undulating rhythms to reveal tree and shrub association, dark wooded areas succeeded by open glades – many with planting of acers – and overhanging branches give natural protection to an understorey of shrubs. In the 1840s Sir Joseph Hooker took part in major plant-hunting expeditions, in particular in Sikkim, from where he brought back *Rhododendron arboreum* and many other plants requiring similar conditions of climate and soil. Working at first in Glasgow, before succeeding his father as Director at Kew, he realized how suitable high-rainfall west-coast gardens, warmed by the Gulf Stream (in the south-west tip of Scotland, the Gulf Stream from Mexico locally raises the climate almost to subtropical standards), were for growing choicest acid-loving tender plants, especially if some sort of shelter belt was established for protection against the prevailing south-west salt-laden winds. His influence on garden development with a strong emphasis on habitat planting in woodland predated William Robinson's influential writings. Many of the great woodland gardens in the wet, mild, almost frost-free regions of Cornwall, such as Trewithen, Trengwainton and Trelissick, are in the same genre, with trees, rhododendrons and other shrubs from the Himalayas, from E. H. Wilson's expeditions to China, and from Japan, from where plants tend to be highly calcifuge, demanding a high rainfall.

At Trewithen, Major George Johnstone established a new woodland garden in an existing beech wood in the early years of the twentieth century. Today sweeping wings of mature trees and shrubs frame the attractive eighteenth-century house. Tall *Rhododendron arboreum* and giant deciduous magnolias from Asia, specimen eucryphias, *Nothofagus procera* and *Laurelia serrata* from Chile, with smaller shrubs such as the red-berried *Viburnum betulifolium* (a 'Chinese' Wilson plant), *Fothergilla major* from the Appalachian mountains in eastern North America with its brilliant autumn foliage, and tender Chilean myrtles (*Myrtus lechleriana*, now *Amomyrtus luma*), enjoy the same sort of climatic conditions and soil, but also appreciate the protective overhead canopies.

Some seventy miles/113 kilometres to the east the Garden in the Wood at Knightshayes in Devon was created in the last fifty years by judiciously felling trees to create glades of light between areas of shade, allowing a wide range of new plantings. Although on a frost-draining slope, Knightshayes does not have the favourable Cornish climate, but raised beds, edged with peat blocks, along the contours of the hill have made it possible to grow many small acid-loving American woodlanders in the dappled shade (see pages 100–101).

In The Garden in the Woods at Framingham in Massachusetts only native shrubs and perennials grow in the marshy woodland and are allowed and encouraged to spread in Robinsonian drifts. The garden was begun in a spirit of plant conservation and now collections of thousands of shrubs, wild flowers and ferns have been established in natural and modified settings, with woodland groves providing appropriate canopies for shade-lovers, but also extended to include typical swamp, meadow and scree environments for more open planting. Now owned by the New England Wild Flower Society, the site today has on its forty-five acres/eighteen hectares the largest landscaped collection of wild flowers in north-east America.

Many other gardens in North America are made in natural woodland, where there is already a build-up of leaf litter. In the eastern states of America most of the dense forests are of hardwood deciduous trees and shrubs, even though rarely virgin woodland but secondary growth; these can be opened out for shade gardens. Before adding suitable plants it may well be necessary to get rid of 'unwanted' aliens, which seeded in during regeneration. Japanese bittersweet (*Celastrus*), Japanese honeysuckle, multiflora roses, *Ampelopsis glandulosa brevipedunculata*, tree of heaven (*Ailanthus altissima*), poison ivy (*Rhus radicans*), catbrier (*Smilax*) and in the south-east Kudzu vine (*Pueraria lobata*) are all dangerous invaders. Norway maple (*Acer platanoides*) is another alien carrying a toxin in its roots poisonous to other plants.

The wooded mountains of North Carolina with their deep acid soil have the richest native shade-tolerant flora, some of which have very specific natural environments – magnolias, rhododendrons (rosebay, *Rhododendron maximum*, will grow as far north as Maine), *R. catawbiense* and deciduous azaleas (including the pink-shell azalea, *R. vaseyi*), *Hydrangea arborescens* and *H. quercifolia*, *Itea virginica*, pieris, mountain laurel (*Kalmia latifolia*), *Leucothoe axillaris*, yellowroot (*Xanthorhiza simplicissima*), hay-scented ferns (*Dennstaedtia punctiloba*), cinnamon fern (*Osmunda cinnamomea*) and many interesting smaller flowers, including *Galax aphylla* and Oconee bells (*Shortia galacifolia*) – once rare, but easily increased, and now popular in suitable woodland gardens. All these plants, except perhaps the hydrangeas, need very similar growing conditions in a garden. The native flora in any region, produced by the particular climate, topography and shade, will tell the local gardener what exotics from similar habitats will flourish.

In the darker coniferous forests of sitka spruce, Douglas fir and hemlock in the Pacific north-west, gardeners have almost too much shade, although natives such as madrone (*Arbutus menziesii*), salal (*Gaultheria shallon*), oceanspray (*Holodiscus discolor*), huckleberries (forms of *Vaccinium*) and kinnikinnick (*Arctostaphylos uva-ursi*) spread wherever there is some light. All of these, except the more tender madrone (its seed sent to England by David Douglas in 1827), translate well into woodland gardens in Great Britain, requiring a deep acid soil. *Gaultheria shallon* is very invasive, revelling in lime-free soil under a dense canopy, and rivalling the smothering effect of Ponticum rhododendron in situations it enjoys. Other deciduous shrubs from western North America such as snowberry (*Symphoricarpos*) grow in all types of soil and are excellent cover among the roots of trees and under dripping branches; 'their chief value is for undergrowth in woods or for ornamental covert (as birds eat the berries) and will flourish everywhere'. They are well established in European woodland, as companions to other shade-loving shrubs such as the evergreen *Lonicera pileata* from China.

But woodland gardens are not always, or indeed often, carved out of an existing wood. Some plants suitable for planting in naturalistic woodland in the outer regions of the garden, where tidiness is less important, may also be used under specimen trees in the main garden area, where they will be more carefully tended. Woodland gradually fades to woodland edge and shrubbery, the more formal flowery garden near the house drifts gently into less manicured shrubbery and copse. In temperate England most gardeners welcome an open, sunlit south-facing terrace without shade trees to steal the light, but in climates with hotter summers, such as North America, trees near the house become essential for comfort. Thomas Jefferson, writing at the end of the eighteenth century after his grand tour of gardens in England, recognized the need for shade before all else in the making of new American gardens. Often only one specimen tree and its combination with house walls will provide shade-loving plants with a suitable garden site. A border under a north-facing wall without competitive tree roots offers a healthy site for plants that require moist rich soil, such as mahonias, hellebores, woodland asters, actaeas and toad lilies, provided the ground is prepared beforehand with a good quantity of moisture-retaining humus.

Other shade gardens have to be created in open situations and sometimes in a field or building site with no original trees or shelter. The first essential for any sort of woodland gardening is to provide shade and coolness out of the sun's fiercest rays. Although it will take many years to develop into a true woodland, a few trees planted as specimens or in groves and backed with some large shrubs will almost at once, by providing cover, make it possible to grow drifts of smaller shade-demanding plants, at least on the shady side of the tree and, as the canopy widens, under its spread. In the hot Californian climate when trying to establish companion-planting with a range of native oaks, different sorts of plants will thrive under the oaks on different orientations. Some need shade almost all day, others need early morning sun, others do best with a western exposure. Evergreen trees provide shade but also take moisture from the soil and little rain penetrates their canopies even during the winter months. At Tintinhull in Somerset the thick evergreen canopies of two tall oaks (*Quercus ilex*) at the bottom of the garden give wind protection from the south-west but create a pocket of very dry shade, ensuring a very definite change of pace in planting design from the rest of the flower garden. The roots of the trees take all the available moisture. Only shrubby evergreen *Arbutus unedo*, cyclamen, hellebores and massed *Vinca difformis*, all companion plants in their native Mediterranean habitat, will thrive under the branches. I have seen exactly the same combination growing in the holm oak woods near Siena in Tuscany.

In natural gardening, although microclimates exist, it is preferable not to influence soil pH or radically alter its type, so that properly selected plants will continue to thrive. In all more artificial gardening, different habitats are created by artifice, soil can be amended, and microclimates created to stretch out the range of plants that can be grown. But in a woodland garden nature must appear to reign, even though, in a new garden, as areas of shade increase – often accompanied by a drier soil as roots grow and spread outwards taking up most of the available moisture – planting can be adapted. Once the desired soil and light conditions have been created, the right plants will spread and multiply in natural ways. Even the deep shadow of a house wall can provide cool and moist conditions in which many woodlanders will thrive, essential little microclimatic pockets, in which shrubs, perennials and bulbs can be planted from the outset as long as the soil suits their needs.

As a style, woodland gardening and planting lie closer to natural laws than any other and each shrub or flower needs to be planted in naturalistic drifts or, if on a large scale, in great sweeps. Gardening with nature, by choosing plants that like the environment offered, does not mean ignoring the aesthetic side of gardening. An awareness of suitability can combine with pleasing

Heale House on the River Avon north of Salisbury in Wiltshire is renowned for its bulbs naturalized under trees and on banks falling away to the water meadows and river in the valley. Thousands of bulbs of one sort or another thrive in great drifts, reminiscent of Robinson's own massive planting in his fields above the lake at Gravetye. As he says, 'the beauty of the Wild Garden is that we get away from the need of ceaseless care of ordinary gardening'. Here ivy-leaved *Cyclamen hederifolium* grows in woodland, flowering in early autumn and showing its marbled leaves from October to May, needing little attention even if ground-elder roots creep in among its corms.

associations. The more suitable the actual plants are for the site, the less maintenance will be required; if only one type of plant was used (like the Baltic ivy suggested earlier – efficient but unimaginative), it might need virtually no maintenance at all, but inevitably, however carefully adjacent plant groups are chosen, some plants will be more or less vigorous than others. The tougher plants, shrubs or perennials, will gradually push under the weaker ones. In general many hardy plants will thrive better in rough places than they ever will in a flower border. Under the protecting canopy of trees and among trailing shrubs and ferns, shade-lovers will flourish and naturalize, and other plants will take over from them as they fade and decay in natural progression.

CREATING WOODLAND SHADE FROM SCRATCH

Woodlands are often in three layers, the tree canopy overhead, shrubs with spreading branches and shade-tolerant carpeters on the forest floor. Here the planting in broad sweeps with virburnums hanging over ferns, hardy geraniums and foam flowers divided by bark-covered paths, has a very natural look, although few plants are British natives. The trees have been 'limbed up' to give a more open aspect – a pattern of sunlight and shadow – and to allow contrasting forms and textures of foliage to have as much importance as seasonal flower colours. Regular mulching to conserve moisture and prevent weed-seed germination makes the shade garden relatively labour-free.

Beth Chatto's garden near Colchester in Essex was started in 1960 on waste land considered too poor for farming. Arid, gravelly soil with a south-western exposure and water-retaining silt in the north-east hollow – one area too dry and starved, the other perpetually waterlogged – presented her with plenty of challenges. Rainfall in East Anglia is very low, and Beth's first ambition was to create a water-garden oasis out of the sodden ground by damming the spring-fed stream.

A few ancient oaks and hollies rising above a tangle of blackthorn and brambles provided the canopy for her future woodland garden, and other areas, planted with small trees and shrubs, have become natural shade gardens. Beth always gives credit to her husband Andrew for introducing her to the importance of studying the natural environment of garden plants; the care given to soil preparation and plant selection throughout the garden is evidence of the emphasis she places on this aspect of natural gardening. Today Beth Chatto is internationally acclaimed for the 'suitability' of her planting, and for making a garden based on ecological ideas. What is interesting about her approach is that she did not work 'ecologically' with her given site, but has gone to great lengths to modify it, and *then* planted 'ecologically', with great success.

The starving gravel soil is regularly improved with garden compost and spent soil from the nursery, while heavier clay and silt-textured soils are mulched with layers of gravel and coarse grit, as well as organic manures. Regular mulching between newly planted specimens prevents evaporation. Although it is not possible to reproduce exactly the conditions of soil and climate of the region from which a foreign plant originated, nevertheless microclimates can be created – an empty windswept site can be turned into a sheltered plant haven – or, as in Beth's case, a dry wood can provide sites for shade-lovers, provided they are not ones that require constant humidity and a high rainfall. By reducing the deepest shade, by planting the right plants – many of them perennials and bulbs that flower early and set seed before the full overhead canopies of deciduous trees leaf out – and by choosing shade-tolerant plants that do not require summer moisture, a wide variety of plants can be grown, including many with delicate foliage which cannot thrive in more open situations. Plants from cool mountain-tops can need shade even in the moderate heat of an English summer, just as other plants found growing in shade in their naturally warmer climates need sun in England's temperate climate. Similiarly, plants such as many rhododendrons, found at high altitudes in mountainous areas of North America and Asia, need humidity and high rainfall to survive in the British Isles (appropriate acidic soil and woodland conditions are found in the south-west and on the west coast of Scotland, but not here in East Anglia). Azaleas grow naturally as understorey plants where they are found in Japan and America. Success in a shade garden depends on many factors: the degree of light and shade (whether deep shade or dappled, allowing some light to filter through for periods of the day), on the rainfall and degree of moisture plants will obtain, and, of course, on other climatic considerations.

(Right) The stems of the bamboo (*Fargesia nitida*) rise out of a carpet of Irish ivy (*Hedera helix* ssp. *hibernica*). The clump-forming fountain bamboo, from damp woodland in central China and the north-eastern Himalayas, needs fertile, moisture-retentive soil and humid sheltered conditions, disliking cold, dry winds. It has dark purple-green erect canes. Although most effective beside water, few bamboos enjoy permanently wet soil. Irish ivy is a vigorous carpeter or climber, a fairly shallow-rooter and not needing a lot of moisture, it may well control the spread of the bamboo. Both plants prefer to grow in half-shade.

(Far right) *Trillium cuneatum* (syn. *T. sessile* of gardens) has nodding, dark red flowers smelling slightly of rotting meat, in its native habitat of the mid- and eastern states of North America attracting pollinating flies. The leaves are marbled chocolate and green, with a central flower, the dark petals of which are held stiffly upright. Most trillium species are from North America, with a few from the western Himalayas and north-east Asia. They thrive in a moist shady bed of acid or neutral soil or on a peat bank where they cannot be overwhelmed by neighbouring plants. In their native habitats they grow among humus-rich decomposing leaves.

(Right) In the dappled half-light of Beth Chatto's shade garden, vigorous cranesbill geraniums and foam flower (*Tiarella cordifolia*) make a background matrix for *Pulmonaria saccharata* 'Reginald Kay' and a splash of vivid colour is provided by *Silene dioica* 'Richmond'. Beth Chatto studies the natural requirements of her plants and then provides environments as close as possible to those of their origins, thus planting to please plants by amending soil and creating microclimates, rather than selecting only plants suitable for the natural conditions of the site. In gardening there is a fine balance between manipulating nature's conditions to extend the range of plants possible to use successfully and choosing plants that will succeed over a long period. Soil types and textures can be changed most easily for shallow-rooted perennials but woody plants, with deeper and wider root systems, soon grow beyond amended soil areas.

In woodland the understorey should not be planted in geometrical patterns but in naturalistic sweeps. Woodland gardening is painting pictures rather than working to a rule book, although the trees and larger shrubs providing the top layer of canopy may well establish some sort of rhythmic pattern. The arboretum at Westonbirt owes some of its attraction to the original nineteenth-century layout with trees in definite alleys and glades, thus providing a framework for lower-growing plants. Although William Robinson's ideal woodland garden, needing no alteration for fifteen years or so, hardly exists, nevertheless if plants are chosen which associate together so well that they become a self-perpetuating man-made plant community, they should need little attention. Areas of natural woodland need no amendments; as the gardener makes them more sophisticated, they benefit from annual top-dressing to prevent shade beds filled with tree roots from drying out in a dry summer.

Understorey plants which, in the wild, grow in woods and on the cooler northern slopes of hills are the most suitable for woodland gardens. They need either dense shade or the dappled shade found on the woodland edge, that transition zone between wood and more open grass or lawn, those originating in woodland needing shelter from drying winds. Among shrubs most tolerant of deep shade is the North American snowberry (*Symphoricarpos albus*), which 'acclimatizes' in Britain and Europe to make dense thickets under deciduous trees, making a cover for wildlife. It tolerates poor soil and dark shaded corners in the garden, although fruiting more positively if given a more open place. It seems indifferent to soil type, growing happily on chalk and limestone soil in woods and hedges, where native English box, spurge laurel, *Daphne laureola*, and drifts of woodland spurge (both *Euphorbia amygdaloides* and *E.a. robbiae*) are found. Oregon grape (*Mahonia aquifolium*) is found in Douglas fir forests in the Pacific north-west, with an almost comparable climate to the British Isles; it prefers more moist conditions but is surprisingly unfussy about soil. European butcher's broom (*Ruscus aculeatus*), as William Robinson says, 'may be planted under the drip and shade of trees where few other evergreens could exist' and is one of the few that will spread under a beech canopy. Its relation from the eastern Mediterranean, the more tender Alexandrian laurel (*Danae racemosa*), with more glossy decorative leaves, will also tolerate shade.

Many of the best hardy shade-tolerant evergreen shrubs come from the same cool, wet mountain slopes in western China where rhododendrons are found, and prove surprisingly tolerant of soil type. Their chief requirement is shelter from drying winds. *Lonicera pileata* and *Viburnum davidii* with turquoise berries, another 'Chinese' Wilson plant, both from west Sichuan, are excellent groundcover under trees. Japanese plants are often calcifuge, and many of those bearing the specific epithet '*japonicus/-a/-um*' originated in China and are much more tolerant of alkaline soil. Forms of *Euonymus japonicus*, the taller *Aucuba japonica* and *Osmanthus heterophyllus* thrive in light woodland shade, the latter most attractive in the less common green-leaved type. *Ilex aquifolium* is native in Britain and Europe, an evergreen stand-by in English woods, with many different leaf forms and varieties. Many evergreen hollies from Europe do well in alkaline shade in a temperate climate, cultivars of *Ilex aquifolium* and the more tender hybrid *I.* x *altaclerensis*, but Japanese hollies and many of the American species need a lower pH and hotter summers. *Ilex glabra* thrives in northern New England in very wet acid soil, needing moisture around its roots in winter. Cherry laurel (*Prunus laurocerasus*), grown in Europe since the sixteenth century, survives in limy soil but is invasive in more acid conditions. Slightly more tender but suitable for dry shade are laurustinus, *Viburnum tinus*, Portugal laurel (*Prunus lusitanica*), *Arbutus unedo* and *Phillyrea latifolia* from the Mediterranean garigue, all surviving in shallow soils over chalk. Although from damper montane forests in China and the Himalayas, species of small Christmas

At Bois des Moutiers, Varengeville, near Dieppe, hydrangeas are a speciality in the woodland. This part of France has a maritime climate similar to the British Isles – although without the extra benefit of the Gulf Stream on the west and south-west of Britain. Laid out originally by Edwin Lutyens – who also remodelled the house for the Malet family in 1898 – and Gertrude Jekyll, trees, rhododendrons, hydrangeas and ferns grow in the sheltered valleys, with a formal garden around the main buildings. The 'blue' hydrangea is *Hydrangea* 'Blaumeise' (syn. 'Teller Blue'), a lace-cap with flat inflorescences which are deep blue, becoming more indigo in acid soil. The leaves are mid-green, shining wide and rounded. Most of the Teller series have a reputation for tenderness and will not thrive in inland gardens.

box, *Sarcococca*, flourish even on dry chalk soils and scent the edge of woodland in January and February with small tassel-like white flowers, followed by red or black berries. Shrubs that will thrive in woodland or garden shade but are totally calcifuge include many of the Ericaceae – rhododendrons, kalmias, ericas, camellias, gaulnettyas, gaylussacia, leucothoes, pachysandras, vacciniums and some viburnums, plants from North American mountain ranges and from Asia and Japan. Manzanitas (*Arctostaphyllos*) are also ericaceous but not all will enjoy shade, many originating from Californian chaparral. *A. patula*, the greenleaf manzanita, from open glades in coniferous forests in Oregon and other neighbouring states, has pink flowers and enjoys summer drought. Hardy bearberry or kinnikinnick (*A. uva-ursi*), from northern Europe and North America, is a low groundcovering creeper, sun-loving but tolerant of some shade, very useful for making rippling green carpets drifting in and out at wood edge.

Perennials hardy in the British Isles come from all corners of the world. Those tolerant of the shade of a mature woodland throughout the year generally come from mountain forests, the north side of mountain slopes or from such high cold that they require shade even in the cool English summers. Many will grow equally happily in half-shade where they get some hours of sunshine each day. Many flower early in the season before the canopies leaf out and then fade away, disappearing as shade gets denser and the soil dries out in summer. The smaller plants have been mentioned earlier. Shade can be dry or moist, dense or dappled, and most plants have distinct preferences. Some of the perennials are quite fussy about soil acidity and alkalinity. In British woodland gardens many perennials will adapt to the changeable climate, the overhead canopies of trees and shrub layers giving that extra protection in periods of what we call stop-go, when warm periods are followed by sharp drops in temperature and late spring frost and freezing winds tend to damage plants grown in the open.

Although many woodland perennials, especially those from the mountains of north-east America, need deep acid moist soil, many others are tolerant of both alkalinity and acidity, but show preferences for dry or damp situations. Among perennials most tolerant of dry shade are some of the early flowerers, bulbs, corms, tubers and plants with a rhizomatous root system storing moisture and nutrients to help survival through the dry season – wood anemones (forms of *Anemone nemorosa*), *Anemone blanda*, so-called Japanese anemones (many forms all originating on the Chinese mainland but cultivated in Japan for many years and first introduced from there), *Arum italicum* varieties with handsome leaves in winter going dormant through the summer, lily-of-the-valley (*Convallaria majalis*), a rhizomatous creeping perennial producing its fragrant flowers in early spring before the leaves appear and disappearing through the summer, the Gladwin iris (*Iris foetidissima*) and its pretty variegated leaf form.

Dry shade exists under heavy evergreen canopies, occurs among greedy tree roots and beside spreading hedge roots, and on the shady side of high walls where rain seldom penetrates. Perennials that can cope with this include blue-flowered *Brunnera macrophylla*, which may die back in drought but recovers with autumn rains, and creeping yellow-flowered *Waldsteinia ternata*. Other plants need a damper but well-drained situation: Solomon's seal (forms of *Polygonatum*), epimediums, red and white-berried actaeas, the much smaller yellow windflower (*Anemone ranunculoides*), European gingers (*Asarum europaeum*) with dense glossy leaves and tiny hidden flowers, sweet woodruff (*Galium odoratum*), nettle-leaved campanula (*Campanula trachelium*), various European fumitories (corydalis – but not the bright blue *C. flexuosa* from Asia), most foxgloves (species of *Digitalis*), stinking hellebore (*Helleborus foetidus*) and many other hellebores in dappled shade or under the shadow of a wall, lime-tolerant hepaticas, martagon lilies, the spring pea (*Lathyrus vernus*), dog's mercury (*Mercurialis perennis*), usually thought of as a weed but a

In shade by the stream at Newby Hall in Yorkshire, hostas and drifts of yellow *Primula florindae* flower among foliage of skunk cabbage and spiky iris. Most woodland gardens have areas of dry shade which, although suitable for small spring flowerers, can seldom put up a performance during the later seasons as the canopy thickens and trees take moisture from the ground. If the area is naturally boggy or there is a natural stream bank on which plants grow, their roots reaching the water, many summer-flowering plants, equally happy in shade or sun as long as the soil is moist, dramatically extend the range of plant possibilities.

useful spreader with greenish flowers), blue-eyed Mary (*Omphalodes verna*), and forms of *Vinca minor*. The Mediterranean *Vinca difformis* is slightly tender but thrives in dry shade, as will biennial *Smyrnium perfoliatum*, and the prolific seeding Welsh poppy (*Meconopsis cambrica*). Some of the hardy cranesbill geraniums will thrive in quite dense shade, especially *Geranium nodosum*, a good seeder, and *G. sylvaticum*. Shade-tolerant plants requiring humus-rich lime-free soils include those from Japan, many of which have a natural affinity with plants in North America, needing shade and moisture. Early-flowering plants with underground storage organs include arisaemas, delicate mauve-flowered *Glaucidium palmatum* and *Hylomecon japonica*. The miniature *Hacquetia epipactis* comes from the Pyrenees and American natives include May-lily (*Maianthemum bifolium*), *Vancouveria hexandra* from the Pacific northwest and the tiny *Iris cristata*, which will make a ribbon or drift of blue, with leaves golden in autumn.

For less dense shade or areas on the edge of woodland, where there are more hours of sunlight all through the year, and for the more garden-like settings where planting is under the edge of specimen trees or in the shade of a wall, the list of suitably shade-tolerant perennials expands: masterworts (forms of *Astrantia*), Apennine anemone and *Anemone blanda*, dicentra, barrenworts (evergreen and deciduous epimediums), hellebores, perennial honesty (*Lunaria rediviva*), the greater woodrush (*Luzula sylvatica*) which, in dry acid soil, will spread to cover large areas, omphalodes, primroses, lungwort (pulmonarias with spotted, blotched or plain leaves, and flowers in shades of red, pink and bright blue), comfrey (the best groundcover is *Symphytum grandiflorum*, but the taller blue-flowered *S. caucasicum* tolerates shade and seeds prolifically), *Tellima grandiflora* and foamflower (*Tiarella cordifolia*). All these plants will need some regular garden maintenance, even if it is only dead-heading for appearance's sake and to prevent spreading further than required.

In lighter shade of wood-edge or in more open glades

The Arboretum as a Work of Art

In the deeper shade of Pierce's Woods strong dark verticals of tree trunks contrast with horizontal-growing swathes of American foamflower, *Tiarella cordifolia*, and *Heuchera* 'Montrose Ruby'. W. Gary Smith has used existing taxodiums (*Taxodium ascendens*) and other native trees such as amelanchiers and *Nyssa sylvatica* to define his spaces with banks of evergreen mountain laurel (*Kalmia latifolia*) and deciduous shrubs (fothergilla, *Rhododendrum atlanticum*, *R. serrulatum*, *R. viscosum* and *Viburnum nudum* 'Winterthur') filled in with drifts of native perennials, all designed for artistic effects rather than planned as assemblies of native-plant communities.

Pierce's Woods at Longwood Gardens in Pennsylvania have recently been redesigned with the aim not of faithfully copying nature, but of abstracting the essence of nature's 'intentions', while planting in artistically pleasing broad sweeps of native groundcovers under the overhead tree canopies. W. Gary Smith, the designer of the modern layout, uses plants indigenous to the local woods, but has also drawn upon his aesthetic sense to create a garden as a work of art, improving and embellishing nature rather than faithfully reproducing it, interpreting rather than simply making a copy. 'Unlike many gardens which emphasize natives, this one makes no effort to re-create natural ecosystems,' he says. 'Rather, it borrows visual ideas from nature, abstracting them and exaggerating them to make a bold statement.' His major goal at Pierce's Woods was to attract attention to the beauty of native plants rather than to promote natives as part of an ecological and moral crusade.

The original owners were the Pierce brothers, Quakers from Bristol, who believed in the study of nature as a way of understanding the Almighty. Quakers, including John Bartram, the first American botanist, had always been in the forefront of natural

history and botanical study. The Pierces' first plantings in 1798 included feathery bald cypress or swamp cypress from Louisiana (*Taxodium distichum*), exotic ginkgos from China – a 'fossil tree' only rediscovered and brought into the nursery trade in the eighteenth century, and cucumber magnolias (*Magnolia acuminata*) from Georgia, all mainly assembled in broad avenue planting. In a natural woodland nearby native tulip poplars sheltered spicebushes, arisaemas, May-apples and spring beauties, as they still do in natural woodland in the area. Almost certainly many other trees and shrubs were dug from neighbouring woodland, and others obtained from John Bartram's sons' nursery outside Philadelphia or from the Prince Nursery in Long Island, one of the earliest to offer a list of native and exotic trees and shrubs. By 1853 plants in the arboretum included a collection of indigenous east-coast magnolias and American chestnut (*Castanea dentata*), as well as tree of heaven (*Ailanthus altissima*), paulownias and Japanese pagoda trees (*Sophora japonica*), all from Asia. The arboretum flourished until 1880, when upkeep of the park deteriorated.

Pierre Du Pont purchased the site, then consisting of about 206

Native perennials associate under the canopies of tall trees. May-apples (*Podophyllum peltatum*) spread in front of phlox (*Phlox divaricata*) and foamflower (*Tiarella cordifolia*). May-apple leaves emerge from the ground like closed umbrellas, gradually unfurling as they reach 2ft/60cm. The flowers are single white, nodding under the leaves, producing a greenish round fruit in May, hence their name. It is a genus of one rhizomatous species, spreading rapidly to colonize with its underground stems, and preferring rich soil, moist in spring. Even in this natural habitat one or more of these plants will overwhelm the others and plant 'spreads' need editing every year after flowering is over.

acres/83 hectares, in 1906 – the first part of what was to become the Longwood Gardens. His first objective was to save some magnificent old trees from destruction. By 1992 the decision was taken to remove plantings of Asian hybrid azaleas, planted during the 1960s, and replace these with native azaleas such as *Rhododendron arborescens*, *R. austrinum*, *R. atlanticum*, *R. candelulaceum* and *R. vaseyi*, and other eastern North American shrubs such as *Hydrangea quercifolia*, *Fothergilla gardenii*, *Viburnum acerifolium* and *Leucothoe fontanesiana*, allowing them to define spaces or 'rooms' in the forest as part of the design process. In the same year thousands of herbaceous plants, including the native *Pachysandra procumbens* and white foamflower (*Tiarella cordifolia*), blue *Phlox stolonifera* and heucheras (*H. villosa* and *H. americana*), were being propagated to cover the ground under the shrubs. Gary Smith's aim has been to plant in large sweeps, evoking the spirit of the eastern deciduous forest, limiting his palette for the sake of establishing an appropriate scale, rather than going for maximum variety.

Although native plants are often promoted as low-maintenance alternatives to 'horticultural' plants, in reality they often require as much attention as non-natives. Pierce's Woods are primarily a 'garden' and much attention is paid to keeping groundcover masses in their groups rather than allowing the natural 'mingling' that would occur in a natural forest system. Tree canopies have to be thinned periodically to allow the native azaleas to receive sufficient light to flower, and even natural leaf litter needs sweeping and raking to ensure that paths are kept clear and that woodland flowers are not smothered. Even when the replanting in Pierce's Woods is completed, adjustments to keep the desired design effects will continue over the years.

Today Pierce's Woods form a small part of a vast horticultural display garden covering 300 developed acres/120 hectares, with another 700 acres/280-odd hectares of meadow and woodland. Some extremely large trees remain from the original Pierce plantings. They include a cucumber tree and a giant ginkgo.

Cyclamen coum, snowdrops and winter aconites growing under the bole of a beech tree at the Dower House, Barnsley, Gloucestershire and in full flower in early spring. These sorts of effect can be achieved in any garden with a good-sized specimen tree. The little bulbs and corms benefit from the light and moisture received during the winter months, and accept the dry shade under the summer canopy when they have all retreated to dormancy. In his description of making his garden at Gravetye, Robinson states that the 'The Winter Aconite ... is very free and welcome, but does best in limestone drying out in cold soils.' He refers to the common *Eranthis hyemalis*, but today a few other species broaden the range: *E. cilicica* from Turkey to Afghanistan, its hybrid with *E. hyemalis*, *E. x tubergenii*, and *E. pinnatifida* from Japan.

hostas and astilbes perform best grown in great drifts, perhaps separated from each other by epimediums such as the evergreen *Epimedium perralderianum*. As well as these there are some evergreen shade-tolerant ground-covers, which will withstand mowing and reduce tiresome edging, and can be planted where woodland fades into lawn. These include purple bugle (*Ajuga reptans*), creeping Jenny (*Lysimachia nummularia* and its golden form), comfrey (various forms of *Symphytum*) and periwinkles (forms of *Vinca minor*). Taller later-flowering species, which do best on the edge of woodland rather than in deep shade, include many North American plants: asters from the New England woods, especially the woodland aster (*Aster divaricatus*) and the large-leaved aster (*A. macrophyllus*), bugbanes (*Cimicifuga*), the 'distinct and graceful' *Gillenia trifoliata*, false spikenard (*Smilacina racemosa*), hostas (originally from Japan), and arching willow gentian (*Gentiana asclepiadea*) and foxgloves from Europe, and, if the site is sufficently moist, hardy astilbes originating from Asia and *Kirengeshoma palmata* from Japan.

There is a whole group of American shrubs and small woodland plants that revel in deep shade and a damp acid peaty soil. Many come from the Appalachian Mountains, most prolifically from the Alleghanies and Blue Ridge but also from further north in the Catskills and Adirondacks. These, given the right conditions of soil, moisture and light, can be used to carpet the forest floor, making gently spreading drifts as they would grow in nature. Too few of us in Britain are fortunate enough to have the requisite environment. In many parts of the United States, where gardens are carved out of natural forest, the layers of humus-rich peaty soil are already there for planting in. In these conditions woodland plants, shrubs and perennials, especially natives, may well form a natural close groundcover, spreading and multiplying with a minimum of maintenance. Among the most beautiful and successful are those lime-free woods in the eastern states where tall trees shelter native dogwoods (*Cornus florida*). These in their turn stretch their light flowering canopies above low-growing spring performers. Native spring flowers that accompany the dogwood are baneberries (*Actaea*), *Aquilegia canadensis*, American ginger (*Asarum canadense*), yellow lady's slipper (*Cypripedium calceolus*), Virginia bluebells (*Mertensia virginica*), blue-flowered sweet William (*Phlox divaricata*), creeping phlox with blue and white flowers (*P. stolonifera*), May-apple (*Podophyllum peltatum*), foamflower (*Tiarella cordifolia*, with attractive autumnal leaf colour), trilliums and *Uvularia grandiflora*.

Lower-growing plants requiring damp, lime-free soil include bunchberry (*Cornus canadensis*) and Allegheny spurge (*Pachysandra procumbens*), a much better plant than the frequently planted Japanese pachysandra, and bloodroot, both single and double flower forms (*Sanguinaria canadensis* and *S.c.* 'Flore Pleno'). The very low-growing checkerberry (*Gaultheria procumbens*) and partridgeberry (*Mitchella repens*) need sites with almost pure humus-rich acid soil and thrive in pockets between natural rock outcrops. Further south in damp, humid almost subtropical conditions exotic *Aspidistra elatior* and caladiums flourish in shade under evergreen oaks.

Not all the accompanying flowers in an American woodland scene need to be native, but they must come from a similar environment. Fortunately many plants that are found in alkaline areas will grow quite well in more acid-type soils if other environmental aspects are satisfied, although acid-lovers cannot thrive in lime soil. Hostas in general, although amazingly adaptable to dry conditions, flourish when given a moist and fertile soil. They are best in drifts at the edge of woodland or in a north-facing bed, or the edge of a bog garden.

Shade-tolerant grasses and sedges include Japanese sedge (*Carex morrowii*), *Carex pendula* (which will also tolerate drier conditions), the tufted grass (*Deschampsia cespitosa*), the greater woodrush (*Luzula sylvatica*) and the Japanese spreading grass *Hakeonechloa macra*, which is mainly represented in gardens with the form *H.m.* 'Aureola'. None of these is particular about soil.

In very sticky alkaline soils where I have worked in Texas, the palette changes. Plants elsewhere grown normally in sun require shade in the greater heat and glare. Woodland plants suitable for growing in shade under the spreading evergreen oaks and yaupons (*Ilex vomitoria*) include *Acanthus mollis*, *Aspidistra elatior*, holly ferns (*Cyrtomium falcatum*), the Turk's cap (*Malvaviscus arboreus* 'Drummondii'), *Salvia regla* and river ferns (*Thelypteris kunthii*). Grassy *Liriope spicata* and mondo grass (*Ophiopogon japonicus*) grow under the live oaks (*Quercus virginiana*) planted as lawn specimens, as grass cannot be irrigated above their vulnerable roots. In California Nancy Hardesty introduced me to oakwood culture. In the Portola Valley project, near Palo Alto where I was working with her, she has developed a nature preserve dominated by five different oaks with native shrubs in a progressive residential community: evergreen coastal live oak (*Quercus agrifolia*), canyon oak (*Q. chrysolepis*), blue oak (*Q. douglasii*), black oak (*Q. kelloggii*) and valley oak (*Q. lobata*) sheltered a natural understorey of coffee berry (*Rhamnus californica*), lemonade berry (*Rhus integrifolia*), cream bush, also known as ocean spray (*Holodiscus discolor*), toyon (*Heteromeles arbutifolia*), bay laurel (*Umbellularia californica*), shade-tolerant manzanitas and fuchsia-flowered gooseberry (*Ribes speciosum*) and in more open areas various sages. This is a native-plant situation, but Mediterranean-type shade-tolerant shrubs would succeed equally well in similar conditions: *Arbutus unedo*, phillyreas and laurustinus.

Most ferns do well in the cool dappled shade of high trees or on wood edge where they are found in the wild, and will flourish on the dark side of a wall as long as they have some light from overhead. They all thrive with a layer of thick humus-making mulch, but need adequate drainage. Most prefer a moist soil through the year, but a few grow in very dry conditions. Although a few ferns thrive in alkaline soil, most prefer soil slightly on the acid side. Of course, some of the most spectacular of the exotic ferns are distinctly tender, such as *Woodwardia radicans* or Australian tree ferns (*Cyathea*

At Heronswood, the nurseryman Dan Hinkley's garden west of Seattle, the woodland is full of excitement. With an equable maritime temperate climate, benefiting from the proximity of the Pacific Ocean and the protection of overhead canopies of Douglas firs (*Pseudotsuga menziesii*) many unusual plants – trees, shrubs and perennials – are grown and are available in the nursery. Winter temperatures fall only to 25°F/–5°C with summer heat rising to 80°F/27°C. The sandy loam has a pH of 6.5– 6.8. In the relatively bright shade of the overstorey specimen *Lindera obtusiloba*, *Hydrangea macrophylla* 'Kluis Superba', a rare *Dasyphyllum diacanthoides*, *Hemerocallis* 'Stafford' and *Drimys lanceolata* are set against the vivid golden foliage of *Robinia pseudoacacia* 'Frisia' and *Rubus cockburnianus* 'Golden Veil'.

and *Dicksonia*), and in Britain need the warm humid climate found in Cornwall or similar environments. Robinson understood the value of graceful fern fronds in woodland glades and for 'sheltered half-shady nooks' or awkward corners in the garden. Lacking the bright appeal of flowers, and being more difficult for the amateur to identify, ferns are generally undervalued and underused in all parts of the garden, but they are particularly appropriate planted at a wood edge or in hedgerows. Growing under high tree canopies, ferns make perfect companions for wood and Apennine anemones, for wood sorrel (*Oxalis acetosela*) and for woodrushes such as the airy *Luzula sylvatica* – in fact for all the little woodlanders already mentioned. Many retain their fronds, giving a welcome greenness through the winter, and only cast the old as new 'fiddleheads' unroll in the spring. Among the 'evergreens' are the ordinary British native hart's tongue fern (*Phyllitis scolopendrium*) and its many mutations, which thrive in dry shade and only need cutting tidily to the ground in the spring if in a garden situation – not if in the wilder wood. Soft shield fern (*Polystichum setiferum*) and its many cultivars also keep their evergreen look and enjoy dry shade, while hardy evergreen blechnums, cyrtomiums and polypodiums need cool shade and a slightly moister soil. *Polystichum munitum* from western North America, known as sword or Christmas fern, is much larger and spreads through the woods of gardens near the Pacific Ocean. The ostrich plume fern (*Matteuccia struthiopteris*), the invasive sensitive fern (*Onoclea sensibilis*), cinnamon fern (*Osmunda cinnamomea*) and the royal fern (*O. regalis*) are all deciduous. They will thrive under tall trees or shrubs if the soil is sufficiently moist, and the royal fern is lime-tolerant.

Many spring-flowering bulbs need light woodland conditions; they grow best in areas shaded or partially shaded for much of the year, but more or less open to the sky during winter and early spring. They usually flower before the overhead canopies leaf out. Even a few flowering or fruiting trees, the equivalent of a grove or

shrubbery, scattered through the garden, will provide the light shade under which bluebells, snowdrops and anemones will spread and multiply, all bulbs which, when dormant, welcome shade in summer rather than baking sun. Deciduous trees, which allow rainfall to penetrate during the growing season, make the best hosts to the smaller spring bulbs, and many, such as cyclamen and muscari and *Tulipa sylvestris* will naturalize on the shady side at the base of a hedge. The bulbs best adapted to growing under large trees are aconites, chionodoxa, crocus, scilla and muscari, while erythroniums, narcissi and snowdrops prefer a lighter shade canopy with more moisture. On the whole the pH of the soil – the measure of its acidity and alkalinity – is less important for bulbs than its texture and structure. Peat (or a peat substitute), mushroom compost and leafmould will lighten heavy soils and improve water retention in sandy ones. Drainage can be improved with sharp sand and grit.

Among the autumn-flowering woodland bulbs the Mediterranean *Cyclamen hederifolium*, opening pink or white flowers in September, must be one of the easiest to naturalize in dry shade, in an appropriate climate. Later its attractive marbled leaves cover wide expanses of earth during the winter. There are woodland cyclamen for almost every month of the year.

Robinson established clumps of bulbs under the spreading branches of his deciduous English oaks (*Quercus robur*) at Gravetye Manor, but in fact snowdrops (and bulbs such as erythroniums) 'do' best in cooler and moister situations, benefiting from a covering of organic mulch during the dormant season. At Tintinhull carpets of blue chionodoxa and scillas have naturalized under the canopies of deciduous shrubs flowering before the 'woodies' come into leaf. In other gardens a deciduous tree, a lime or horse chestnut, allows winter rain and spring sunshine to encourage winter aconites, wood and Apennine anemones, scillas, arums, European and American gingers, small spring-flowering corydalis, sweet woodruff and many other

bulbs that require light to flower in winter and spring but tolerate the shade of the dense foliage through the summer months. Spring and summer snowflake (*Leucojum vernum* and *L. aestivum*) flourish in the same conditions, while martagon lilies will survive denser shade and drier soil. The giant lily (*Cardiocrinum giganteum*) succeeds in semi-woodland shade in humidity and deep rich acid soil – similar conditions to those needed by the velvet-leaved Himalayan poppy, blue-flowered *Meconopsis betonicifolia*, its various cultivars and yellow-flowered relatives from Asia.

True woodland conditions with understoreys of shrubs provide better, cooler summer conditions for many bulbs than an isolated tree specimen. Leaves from the woody plants provide essential humus, making layers of moisture-retentive compost in which native wood anemones and all forms of dog-tooth violets will thrive, never drying out in summer. In the natural woodland Robinson recommended wood anemones (*Anemone nemorosa*), lily-of-the-valley (*Convallaria majalis*), Lent lily (*Narcissus pseudonarcissus*) and snowdrops (*Galanthus nivalis*).

Henry Du Pont's garden at Winterthur in Delaware was laid out in a natural forest of tall tulip trees (*Liriodendron tulipifera*), tall straight trunks and canopies providing the cover for swathes of pink and white Indian azaleas and for banks of smaller native American and exotic flowers. The tree cover has been manipulated to provide just the right degree of shade for the bulbs in the March Walk and elsewhere in the garden, giving light at flowering time and shade when they are dormant. In some places Du Pont has mixed his colour drifts; aconites (*Eranthis hyemalis*) from Europe, but hardy in the United States, except in the colder north, flower almost simultaneously with and are interplanted with crocuses, scillas, spring snowflakes (*Leucojum vernum*) and snowdrops to make an oriental carpet pattern. In other places, and perhaps more effectively, the secret has lain in planting with great masses of one sort rather than mixed-up varieties, as would be

At Forde Abbey in Dorset snowdrops and crocus have naturalized under the trees in much of the garden. This is the sort of 'wild' gardening, with early spring flowers in turf, that William Robinson loved and advocated. A great advantage of this sort of gardening is that it does not interfere with the flowerbeds at all and, if the situation is right, the plants look after themselves. Winter aconites, crocus and snowdrops are followed by narcissus suitable for naturalizing, all grown under deciduous trees and flowering before the leaves of the trees unfurl. Snowdrops do best if obtained in the 'green' just after flowering and before the leaves die down, disliking drying out after being dug for planting in autumn.

likely to occur in natural conditions. In early spring as the snow melts at Winterthur a great drift of Amur adonis (*Adonis amurensis*), natives of Siberia with brilliant yellow petals, make a golden carpet, near to an even larger and ever-spreading sweep of misty species *Crocus tommasinianus*, which flowers earlier than the larger-flowered Dutch hybrids and whose graceful shape looks much more natural.

THE WILD GARDEN REINTERPRETED AT WINTERTHUR

The gardens at Winterthur, north-west of Wilmington, Delaware, are the most beautiful naturalistic gardens in North America. Their special quality comes from the design and colour sense of Henry Francis Du Pont, a member of the horticulturally famous Du Pont family, who have been responsible for many of the great Delaware and Pennsylvanian gardens, gardens of the Brandywine valley, made since their arrival from France in 1800. Hagley or Eleutherian Mills, where the first powder mills that established their fortunes were started, formal French-style gardens at Nemours, the display garden of Longwood and Winterthur Gardens are the best known. Many other members of this gardening and botanical family created private gardens of distinction during the last two centuries. In 1990 the American Horticultural Society honoured the entire Du Pont family with its special National Achievement Award in recognition of their services.

Henry Francis Du Pont was born in 1880 and inherited Winterthur in 1926. Already trained in horticulture, he had worked closely with his father in developing the estate, but he brought to the gardens a new artistic viewpoint. Familiar with William Robinson's writings on the wild garden and with Gertrude Jekyll's colour theories for the garden, he adapted their English teaching to his own woodland, planting both native and exotic woodland plants in drifts under the tall trees. Du Pont's sense of colour and meticulous planning for seasonal effects remain his own, but the concept of Robinson's 'wild' garden has seldom been better interpreted. In the eastern deciduous forest, tall trees – including second-growth American chestnuts (until these were destroyed by blight in the early years of the century), red, white and black oaks, the fast-growing tulip poplar (*Liriodendron tulipifera*), white ash, red maples, hickories and occasional groups of American beech – provide the highest canopies. Beneath these a layer of smaller trees survive with less light, then shrubs and forest-floor wild flowers, ferns and mosses. The particular mix of plants depends on many factors, including climate, soil structure and

neighbouring plant species. Native shrubs include early-flowering *Lindera benzoin*, the black-twigged spicebush, scattered through the wood, with the early pink azalea and white- and pink-flowered dogwood at the wood's edge. Mertensias, trilliums, May-apples, celandine poppies, ferns and *Phlox divaricata* thrive and spread naturally, their spring season augmented by exotics: aconites, adonis, Spanish bluebells, chionodoxa, narcissus, corydalis, Apennine anemone and snowdrops all thrive and blend with the natives in ever-widening sweeps.

In 1859 the botanist Asa Gray published his thesis based on the common origin of the flora of north-eastern America and of eastern Asia and Japan. Before the glacial epoch all northern-hemisphere plant species would have been homogenous; after the ice retreated, mountain ranges – sometimes new creations – controlled re-establishment and movement of plants northwards. In both North America and eastern Asia, flora either escaped the worst ravages or were able to move north without making genetic adaptations, leading to a close relationship between floras from each area. In practical terms this meant that American gardeners could grow successfully the Asian counterparts of North American dogwoods, witch-hazels, cherries and rhododendrons. At Winterthur full advantage has been taken by the extended range of suitable plants.

(Above) Blue and white European bluebells (*Hyacinthoides hispanica*) flower beneath azaleas in the contoured woodland. Henry Du Pont extended the Robinsonian theme by using shrubs such as azaleas to broaden his colour palette and to give layered structure under the tall trees and above the small bulbs. Du Pont used different combinations of Dexter hybrid Asian rhododendrons, bred for hardiness, as well as experimenting with the possibilities of growing kurume azaleas (which first flowered at Winterthur in 1918 – coming into bloom at the same time as the native dogwood, *Cornus florida*) two years before they were officially introduced to North America by E. H. Wilson. Du Pont loved the azaleas 'grouped in harmonious colours and pleasing contrast. They naturalize in every imaginable terrain and contour ... and are perfect with countless varieties of bulbs and wild bloom.'

(Right) In the wood at the back of the main house at Winterthur, sweeps of native *Phlox divaricata* flower and spread under deciduous trees, American beech (*Fagus grandifolia*) and tall tulip trees (*Liriodendron tulipifera*), in exactly the sort of situation they enjoy. Wild gardening, or gardening with nature, means selecting plants suitable for the site. In woodland many of the small groundcover plants flower early before the leaves of overhead canopies have unfurled, and later they retreat to summer dormancy as the soil dries out – with trees taking all available moisture – and the canopy thickens to exclude light. In the distance Japanese torch azaleas (*Rhododendron kaempferi*) at the edge of the Azalea Woods draw the eye. Henry Du Pont naturalized woodland plants from many different areas of the world to create what we still call a Robinsonian style of gardening, adding his own dimension of colour aesthetics.

(Above) In very early spring the March Bank at Winterthur is carpeted with golden-yellow winter aconites (*Eranthis hyemalis*) and with the Amur adonis (*Adonis amurensis*), native to Siberia and related to buttercups and peonies. The flowers of both unfold as soon as the plants push through the ground. The latter, although not grown as frequently as the aconite, enjoys similar conditions. At Winterthur these plants require little attention except for scraping away fallen leaves in winter. These plants under the tall tulip trees and beech date to Henry Du Pont's time.

CHAPTER FOUR

SHRUB BORDER AND SHRUBBERY

SHRUBS, AS OPPOSED to trees, are woody plants that tend to branch from the base. We grow them for their beauty in the landscape, for their shapes, foliage, bark, flowers and fruit and for their use in appropriate associations with either trees or smaller plants. The range available to gardeners today is wider than ever, yet as topics the shrubbery and the shrub border seem neglected. In a modern garden the term 'shrub border' has an uninspiring, functional sound; it tends to be planned for low maintenance, shrubs growing close together after a few years and leaving no space for other flowers. The shrubbery, too, got itself a bad name, partly because of the dreary connotations of the almost flowerless Victorian shrubbery, but also because shrub shapes and leaf forms, however beautiful each individual shrub, often fail in visual impact – except for the actual seasonal moment of flowering – and do not make a natural-looking composition; associated shrubs lack the glamour of forest trees and the summer impact of flowery borders.

In nature shrubs do not grow by themselves but are part of complex plant communities, where overhead tree canopies provide changing patterns of light with protection from sun, wind and frost for the shrubs below. The shrubs themselves, even those that form thickets, associate with native, semi-wild or exotic perennials and bulbs that come from similar environments, need the same sort of climatic conditions of soil, moisture, sun or shade and look 'right' together. In gardening jargon the 'mixed' border is a traditional herbaceous

Along the wall in John Brookes's walled garden at Denmans some bulky shrubs such as variegated holly and purple-leaved smoke bush (a form of *Cotinus coggygria*) and roses are planted above feathery fennel and oriental poppies. In natural planting shrubs and perennials growing together in a scheme should all have the same sort of climatic and soil requirements but soil and drainage can be adapted for shallow-rooting perennials more easily than for woody plants, whose roots will ultimately depend on the natural soil conditions of the area for their success. None of the plants shown are at all fussy about soil, but rhododendrons and other members of the Ericacae would require a more acid soil.

border with a few shrubs to give structure and winter shapes, but the 'shrubbery' in our preferred Robinsonian sense features woody plants accompanied by an appropriately chosen understorey, establishing a natural pattern of growth, and mutual dependency.

From a horticultural point of view there is very little difference between wood-edge and shrubbery – indeed, often shrubs grow at the edge of woodland, and the perennials and bulbs associated between the shrub groups are much the same. But for many gardeners who have no space for groves of trees, a shrubbery environment will provide the nearest they can get to woodland atmosphere, with small trees and larger shrubs sheltering the lower-growing plants and providing them with a cool root-run in Robinsonian style. For other gardeners, anxious and willing to avoid more conventional high-maintenance herbaceous borders or 'mixed' borders (with just a few shrubs to give perennials strength), the shrubbery is also the flower garden, in which evergreen or deciduous shrubs create dappled shade to alternate with wide open spaces in which a whole assembly of semi-wild perennials – as opposed to highly bred border perennials, which need the well-cultivated soil of a flowerbed and full sun – can be grown, to give colour when most of the spring shrubs are quiet during high summer. The traditional herbaceous border has a two- to three-months' display when perennials perform in summer, but the well-planned naturalistic shrub border or bed has interest all year. The best perennials and bulbs for the shrubbery are those that will grow and flower both in open situations and in semi-shade, so that the earth is covered and planting groups overlap and intermingle at the edge.

William Robinson had plenty to say on the topic. He inveighed against the contemporary late Victorian shrubbery, calling it, in typically didactic Robinsonian terms, an assemblage of 'costly rubbish', but he himself emphasized the aesthetic and horticultural merits of the 'mixed' border, partly his own invention, or the invention for which he is given the credit. In *The English Flower Garden* he hints at how this can be arranged so that appropriately chosen perennials, which need less maintenance, can weave beautiful patterns to run in and out between the shrubs: 'A frequent way in which people attempt to cultivate hardy flowers is in what is called the "mixed border", often made on the edge of a shrubbery the roots of which leave little food or even light for the flowers.' Instead he recommends that 'The face of the shrubbery should be broken and varied: the shrubs should not form a hard line, but here and there they should come full to the edge ... it is generally best to use plants which do not depend for their beauty on high culture ... and there are a great many of them such as the evergreen Candytufts (*Iberis sempervirens*), large-leaved rockfoils (*Saxifraga*), Acanthus, Day Lilies (*Hemerocallis*), Solomon's Seal, Starworts (*Aster*), Leopard's Bane (*Doronicum*), Moon Daisies (*Chrysanthemum leucanthemum* [now *Leucanthemum vulgare*]), and hardy native ferns. A scattered dotty mixed border along the face of a shrubbery gives a poor effect, but a good one may be secured by grouping the plants in the open spaces between the shrubs, making a careful selection of plants, each occupying a bold space.'

If well planned and suitably planted in naturalistic style, the shrub border should be beautiful through the seasons and need little maintenance. The shrubs provide protective canopies almost exactly as the trees do in woodland, although in the shrubbery many of the woody plants will have an upright, broad or fan shape from the base rather than a spreading head on one tall trunk. (For this reason shrub specimens in lawns are seldom satisfactory, as they do not make a dense enough broad canopy to prevent grasses and weeds coming up next to their bases.) A shrub bed represents a distinctive habitat, where – depending on aspect and soil – suitable woody plants of different shapes and sizes can be arranged in apparently natural layers and groupings by deploying smaller shrubs or soft-stemmed plants around their bases to cover the soil and keep it cool and weed-free. These smaller plants, supported by the framework

In an open sunny border in an English garden designed by Helen Yemm, *Buddleja alternifolia* from China, with slender arching branches weeping over neighbouring lower-growing plants, and with fragrant lilac flower wreaths, is a perfect companion in a border, casting little shade on its neighbours. This buddleja can be grown shrub-like with multiple stems or trained as a standard. Good border shrubs create a distinctive habitat with smaller shrubs and soft-stemmed plants around their bases, keeping the soil cool over their roots. In the picture euphorbias grow in full sun and hostas take advantage of the light shade under the buddleja.

At Long Hall, at Stockton in Wiltshire, a billowing cloud of scented philadelphus towers behind a purple-leaved smoke bush and provides the focal point of double borders. In the bed opposite upright magenta *Geranium psilostemon* gives a splash of colour along the front, backed by the glaucous-leaved *Rosa glauca* with pale pink flowers. Philadelphus species and cultivars are very useful summer shrubs, with fragrant white flowers, their range covering a long flowering period through June and most of July. Insignificant and slightly scruffy when not in flower, they attract attention only during their blooming period. With small leaves and often with an upright habit, they make natural companions for perennials that do not relish shade.

of shrubs, should have year-round qualities rather than just short-term flowering beauty and, however carefully chosen for the site, will need some annual adjustments and weeding, protecting more invasive species from those of slower growth. But shrub beds, while keeping a natural look, also need to be planned to look attractive, with contrasts of flower and foliage and form between both the shrubs themselves and the more seasonal soft-stemmed flowerers, which run in and out making natural but abstract patterns between them.

The shrubbery is much more part of the designed garden picture than is 'natural' woodland, and there is no question of leaving it to look after itself – as Robinson might have recommended for the wilder

garden. However, by choosing appropriate plants to associate with each other, either individually or in groups, the planting will look and behave as naturally as possible. In British gardens – depending on their exact location – the temperate climate makes it possible to create beds combining shrubs and flowers from many different but similar habitats. This so-called shrubbery is peculiarly – but not exclusively – English in its planting style and Robinson cannot be given all the credit. Nevertheless in his own garden at Gravetye Manor he covered the ground between trees and shrubs with a selection of plants that would look after themselves. It is a style with very natural overtones, so that the smaller plants associated with the shrubs are allowed to seed and spread (as long as they do not disrupt the planting as a whole). It can be adopted in any suitable location. Patterns of growth are determined by the combined effects of climate (and microclimate), light and shade, soil and nutrient supply, moisture and drainage.

In the milder parts of Britain drought-loving Mediterranean-type shrubs (often from California, Australia or South Africa – or from other similar world habitats) with specially adapted grey, silver or aromatic leaves to withstand hot sun, will thrive in well-drained or dry (and often alkaline) soil. They can be accompanied by 'natural' colonies of other sun-lovers: evergreen self-seeding rock roses, asphodeline, grey-leaved euphorbias, spreading silver-leaved anaphalis and perennial artemisias, all of which grow between the shrubs and – once established – need little attention or renewal. Some of the Mediterranean-type shrubs which, in their own countries of origin, stop growing during the hottest part of the season will remain in leaf in a cooler British summer climate, retreating underground to escape the colder winters. In shrubberies with a neutral or alkaline soil the British climate allows for a vast range of shrubs and perennials from all parts of the world. Some of the best effects may come from combining shrubs and perennials that would grow together in their native regions. Viburnums and species roses, buddlejas and caryopteris from Asia can be interspersed with tall groups of *Thalictrum delavayi*, day lilies and Japanese anemones (originally from China). Quieter effects are achieved by planting drifts of European ginger (*Asarum europaeum*) with glossy leaves in summer and/or scented sweet woodruff (*Galium odoratum*) to carpet the bare earth between the shrubs.

For north-facing mixed borders in Britain some of the woodland plants mentioned in Chapter Three are self-proliferating seeders: foxgloves, hellebores, wood spurges (forms of *Euphorbia amygdaloides*), Solomon's seal – all with handsome leaves as well as flowers. In colder climates the very hardy evergreen *Viburnum* x *pragense*, a hybrid between the lime-tolerant *V. rhytido-*phyllum* and *V. utile*, both E. H. Wilson introductions from China, will thrive with tough perennials from steppe lands of northern Europe or western Asia, such as *Achillea millefolium*, *Campanula glomerata*, *Veronica spicata* and burning bush or gas plant (*Dictamnus albus*) from dry gravelly calcareous soils. *Iris sibirica*, filipendula and goat's rue (*Galega officinalis*) prefer damper soil, as does large-leaved *Inula magnifica* from the Caucasus mountains. At the opposite extreme are shady borders in which lime-haters cling together. The damp, rich peaty loam with high rainfall and humidity typical of British coastal areas washed by the Gulf Stream is a 'natural' home for the best of the rhododendrons and Ericaceae in general as well as for companion plants such as desirable Himalayan poppies and primulas from Asia, and small American woodlanders from the Alleghanies and the Pacific west coast.

In colder regions with continental climates the hardier rhododendrons (many from North America), Japanese and American hollies (the latter both evergreen and deciduous) and deciduous viburnums and the fringe tree (*Chionanthus virginicus*) make the woody framework. Interplanting can be spring-flowering trilliums (there are trilliums for different soil types and for different altitudes, growing on higher mountains in lower latitudes); mertensias, *Veratrum viride* and the cinnamon fern (*Osmunda cinnamomea*) and creeping phlox, which can grow around the base of the deciduous shrubs, dying back as the shrubs leaf out and the soil dries; also interspersed are wedge-shaped sweeps of taller summer-flowering and berried baneberries (actaeas), asters from the New England woods, and bugbanes (cimicifugas) from North American and Asiatic woods and Asian astilbes and toad lilies (*Tricyrtis*). Among the best garden shrubs are those from Asia, many of which are acid-lovers, which have an affinity with north-east American trees and shrubs, many of the same genera such as *Chionanthus*, *Hamamelis*, *Hydrangea*, *Styrax* and viburnums occurring in both continents. Asiatic shrubs suitable for gardens in north-east America, with cold winters and hot summers, include *Styrax* species, Japanese *Viburnum dilatatum* for its bright red berries in fall, and *V. sieboldii* and *V. sargentii* (and its bronze-leaved form *V.s.* 'Onondaga'), with spring-flowering companion perennials such as *Dicentra spectabilis* and poppy-like *Glaucidium palmatum*, all giving a better performance in the continental extreme than they do in the British Isles. One of the finest monkshoods, *Aconitum carmichaelii*, comes from Kamchatka. Japanese *Kirengeshoma palmata*, hostas and tricyrtis will grow in a neutral or faintly alkaline soil but prefer moist acid conditions. Many shrubs from north-east America, thriving in climatic extremes and low-pH soils, are good border plants: amelanchiers with striking grey bark, sweet gale (*Myrica pensylvanica*), *Clethra alnifolia*, scented sweet fern (*Comptonia peregrina*), sumachs (forms of *Rhus*), deciduous viburnums and hydrangeas (*Hydrangea arborescens*). Unlike many perennials, which are found in greatest variety in alkaline soils, the greatest abundance of flowering shrubs comes from regions with infertile, acid conditions. Introduced to garden situations with richer nutrients, shrubs such as *Cornus florida*, rhododendrons, kalmias, roses and hollies will give a better 'garden' performance.

Obviously, between the extremes of sun-drenched or deep-shade beds are other distinctive categories dominated not so much by soil acidity or alkalinity but by soil type and texture; in these different sorts of plants will thrive. Clay, which can be alkaline or acid, sticky to work in winter and baking hard in summer (but usually rich in nutrients) suits hollies, aucubas, osmanthus and most viburnums (though the latter prefer free drainage); perennials such as aconitums, hellebores, eupatoriums and daisy-flowered heleniums with strong root systems will thrive even before the texture of the soil is much improved. The opposite extreme is poor, fast-draining sandy soil needing constant mulching to improve moisture content, in which shrubs such as amelanchiers, elaeagnus, sea buckthorn, perovskia, phlomis and sages will develop well, while most perennials, while enjoying

the free drainage, will need plenty of additional nutrients. All soils can be manipulated by the gardener in the short term, but for best long-term effects should be stocked with groups of woody and soft-stemmed plants with requirements appropriate to the natural soil conditions.

The shrubbery is a project in which plants may reach suitable maturity after about ten to fifteen years. Other shrubs and perennials can be removed and replaced as they outgrow their positions; in general, shrubbery plants can expect more day-to-day care and manipulation than those in a wood. The original planting, with adequate space left between the 'woodies' for future growth and development of their distinctive habits, should also ensure plenty of scope for soft-stemmed plants, which give additional foliage shape, texture and colour as well as flowers, in wide pockets between the shrubs to make the planting scheme seem much more natural from the very beginning. There are plenty of potential pitfalls in this sort of 'infilling'. As the shrubs grow the spaces between will become smaller and, even, at some point, may disappear altogether. And from the beginning there must be vigilance to prevent vigorous herbaceous perennials, planted to cover the bare ground to give an impression of luxuriance, from crushing and eliminating the burgeoning shrubs, which, like all plants, need air and light to grow. Many perennials for these semi-wild conditions (but not the fussier border plants) are able to adapt to the constantly changing conditions as shrubs grow closer together, and are suitable for growing in moderate sun and shade, weed-suppressive but not too invasive.

From the point of view of shrubbery planting, small trees, with the largest shrubs, such as abutilons, amelanchiers, tree ceanothus, drimys, escallonias, eucryphias, magnolias, etc., chosen judiciously to become dominant features, give an architectural quality to the planting. Ultimately to get the best out of plants it is not only necessary to know what sort of aspect or soil they need to thrive, flower and fruit, it is also important

Hydrangea aspera villosa, an erect deciduous shrub, covered in lace-cap flowers in summer, is one of the few hydrangeas that will grow as well in alkaline soil as in acid. In alkaline soil the flowers are pinkish mauve, in acid loam distinctly bluer. Often damaged by late frosts when grown in a maritime climate such as the British Isles, where warm periods in late winter encourage premature growth, this plant is best grown where its buds are protected from early morning sun. The bulbous late-flowering summer hyacinth, *Galtonia candicans*, from southern Africa, needs a hot well-drained site but moist soil throughout the summer growing months. In areas of severe winters galtonias can be lifted and potted up to be overwintered in a cool green-house. This planting is unusual as although the hydrangea and galtonias are growing together, the bulbs should be in an open sunny border in which they will not be overwhelmed by shrub growth in future years.

to think in terms of their ultimate height and width. Some shrubs achieve their best only when mature and may be considered for their appearance fifteen or twenty years ahead. Among their number are tree magnolias, fringe trees (*Chionanthus virginicus* and *C. retusus*, from North America and Asia respectively) and the larger viburnums, which must be planted sufficiently far apart to allow for final maturity with space for the colourful soft-stemmed (or smaller woody) infillers. Other shrubs perform well from the beginning; they can be pruned judiciously through the years but retain their essential qualities, always leaving room for the accompanying smaller plants, which add to the richness of the whole

scheme. Plants from drier and more temperate regions flower when young, responding to pruning out of old wood: beauty bush (*Kolkwitzia amabilis*) from the higher gorges of the Yangtze River in Hupeh, species shrub roses, smoke bush (*Cotinus coggygria*) can all be pruned back to allow the smaller plants to thrive.

Large shrubs in shrubberies or shrub borders rapidly create their own dappled shade. If chosen apppropri-ately they will protect and encourage each other and provide suitable growing conditions below their branches for small bulbs and creeping perennials. For the more flowery shrub border, wide spaces drifting back into the rear of the border are also kept for smaller shrubs or soft-stemmed summer performers. How the scheme works will depend on the aspect. The back of a shrub bed or a freestanding shrubbery away from the sun will inevitably be in semi-shade almost from the start and all planting will be of a woodland type. The front of a sunny-facing bed will receive a lot of light and warmth, making it possible to grow sun-loving shrubs and both small 'woodies' and meadow plants, strong clump-forming perennials, along its front edge and in back-drifting groups, with shade lovers towards the rear. Other compass orientations, depending on latitude, will receive more or fewer hours of morning or evening sunlight, and of summer and winter sun. The flower-buds of some early-flowering shrubs are threatened by a quick thaw after frost, so camellias and tree peonies need a west-facing aspect. Even in a natural garden with appropriately chosen plants, the gardener can encourage favourable microclimatic situations, just as happens in nature. These provide extra protection from prevailing winds or the dangerous, rarer and often colder abnormal gales. Soil, too, can be improved, especially at planting time, to suit plants' needs (giving a plant a good start differs from changing soil acidity and alkalinity, which will have only temporary effects). Protection can be 'natural', with appropriate shrubs sheltering each other, or temporary and artificial; many shrub borders are backed by protective high walls or dense hedges. In

Shades and Glades in a Devon Wood

At Knightshayes, on the edge of the woodland garden, a purple-leaved beech dominates the view at the end of the mown ride, with long grass edging the 'flowerbeds' of shrubs and rhododendrons. The latter are shallow-rooted, and woodland-edge or shrubbery conditions suit them best, where tree roots do not compete for moisture, approximating to their natural habitat where they are often found in quite open situations. In cool high-altitude situations rhododendrons need summer heat, but thrive in semi-shade in lower altitudes where summers are warmer. Rhododendrons often 'look best' when grown together rather than mixed with other shrubs.

The Garden in the Wood at Knightshayes Court in Devon was originally carved out of existing nineteenth-century woodland of tall pines, native oaks, limes, beeches and conifers, with judicious felling of trees and high pruning to reduce the deepest shade. Much of the garden today is open enough to convey the feeling of a series of shrub beds in open glades underplanted with flowering plants, which appear in succession as a visitor moves through the garden between alternating deep shade and light. Besides the horticultural interest (and there are plenty of well-grown botanical rarities), it is this carefully orchestrated progression of light and shadow that makes Knightshayes so distinctive. It is a woodland and shrub garden planned to please through the seasons, but also, with horticultural expertise, a garden in which plants of great interest are given environments in which they thrive. The soil is rich and acid, further enriched by organic mulches. The site is sheltered from south-westerly gales by long-established trees, and, although not as mild as gardens in Cornwall, since it slopes to the south,

Knightshayes enjoys a favoured climate compared to many inland counties in the British Isles. With many early shrubs providing low canopies over American and Asiatic underplanting of 'woodlanders', the Garden in the Wood at Knightshayes is at its most colourful in spring, but shrub foliage, green tones of hosta leaves, grasses and ferns make garden visits later in summer quieter but unforgettable.

From 1950 the whole of this garden area was annexed at a rate of two or three acres/about 0.8 hectares a year and now covers some thirty acres/twelve hectares. Rhododendrons and shrub roses line the first alley, underplanted with drifts of electric-blue omphalodes, hardy crane's bill geraniums and pulmonarias filling the spaces between wide drifts of earlier-flowering hellebores. Specimen magnolias are a feature, with massed underplanting of shade-tolerant bulbs and/or perennials. Clerodendrons, hypericums, hydrangeas, clethras all enjoy the soil and microclimatic conditions. Further on beds of acid soil supported with peat blocks are colonized with ferns, mosses, different wood anemones and American trilliums,

(Above) Deeper in the wood at Knightshayes, but in an open glade with plenty of light, *Persicaria bistorta*, pink-flowered *Geranium macrorrhizum*, *Lamium orvala* and a tender libertia from New Zealand, with white panicles carried in umbel-like clusters, grow under and beside the light foliage cover of Japanese maples (*Acer palmatum*).

This sort of shrubbery planting could be the pattern for a whole garden scheme, with plants attuned to similar conditions performing for many months of the year, with perennials covering the ground used more extensively than the woody plants. Many shrubberies are spoilt by allowing shrubs to shade out the colourful lower planting.

(Above) Looking back towards the house at Knightshayes from the first ride in the wood. Pacific Coast irises (*Iris douglasiana*), a beardless rhizomatous iris from the west coast of North America, with flowers in tones of lavender-blue, red-purple and cream or white and untidy grassy foliage, thrive in situations where overhead canopies of

trees or a middle layer of deciduous shrubs give some winter protection. They enjoy the relatively mild Devon climate of Knightshayes. Planted in wide groups, they mix in well with shrubs such as potentilla and other low-growing, bushy plants such as hardy cranesbill geraniums to flower in late spring and early summer.

erythroniums and woodland phlox. Under and between shrubs euphorbias (mainly shade-tolerant forms of *Euphorbia amygdaloides*), *Tellima grandiflora* (like *Alchemilla mollis*, a prolific seeder), *Arum italicum* 'Marmoratum' with decorative winter foliage, and little sweeps of Bowles' golden grass (*Milium effusum* 'Aureum') give colour; in later summer drifts of Japanese-type anemones light up darker recesses, while autumn cyclamen (*Cyclamen hederifolium*) flowers in swathes of pink and white around the base of tall trees. Mahonias are mainly winter- and spring-flowerers, often opening at the same time as *Cyclamen coum* and *C. repandum*.

changeable 'stop-go' climates immature shrubs such as hydrangeas are particularly vulnerable to spring frosts when stems are still soft and the root system is inadequate to provide a back-up if young shoots are damaged, but are able to withstand spring frosts and freezing winds better as they grow older and have sun-ripened bark. After warm spells in which sap has risen, shoots are easily killed, but an overnight covering of newspaper, fleece or netlon, when frosts are threatened – similar in effect to a protective tree canopy – will prevent frost damage. Getting shrubs through their first few years is part of the gardener's skill and taking this sort of trouble does not mean that unsuitable plants are being grown.

Most shrub beds are likely to include a mix of evergreen and deciduous shrubs and whatever the soil or aspect, these will be treated with more respect than they would get in a wilder woodland situation. Besides pruning to encourage vigour, many can have their heads raised and their crowns thinned to ensure light can enter to improve the growing prospects for plants at their base.

Certain shrubs, such as daphnes, are not really suitable for shrubberies, disliking being jostled by nearby plants. Rhododendrons positively dislike small plants growing over their roots. Shrubs with suckering root systems, such as lilacs, sumach (*Rhus typhina*), sea buckthorn (*Hippophae rhamnoides*) and innumerable roses (rugosas on their own rootstock, *pimpinellifolia* types, *R. virginiana* and others), are unsuitable for growing with other shrubs or low-growing plants. Because of their density (and many of these have prickly stems as well) these shrubs may not be good companion plants, but make effective thickets and barriers for perimeter planting; as informal hedges, they link the garden more naturally with the surrounding countryside rather than separating it with the continuous line of a hedge or fence.

Evergreen shrubs form the permanent structure, contrasting in winter with the bare framework of leafless branches of their deciduous neighbours.

In Britain's temperate climate there is wide range of broadleaved evergreen shrubs that flourish and flower in sun and shade. This is also true for American gardens in the Pacific north-west, but on the east coast and in the Midwest few broadleaved evergreens will survive the much colder winters. Exceptions are lime-haters such as some rhododendrons, mountain laurel (*Kalmia latifolia* Zones 5–9), which flowers in June, and the smaller narrow-leaved sheep laurel (*K. angustifolia* Zones 2–7), hardy to the far north. Also extremely cold-tolerant is the creeping bearberry (*Arctostaphylos uva-ursi* Zones 3–7). Inkberry (*Ilex glabra* Zones 5-9) with stoloniferous roots grows from Nova Scotia to Florida in moist acid soil. The new American 'blue' *Ilex* x *meserveae* hybrids (Zones 5–8) have been bred for the equivalent of a continental climate, and are less fussy about soil.

Many of the evergreens for the British climate are at their most decorative during the winter, making up for the fact that their dense canopies prevent smaller plants growing under them. It was the exclusive use of hardy evergreen shrubs in Victorian shrubberies that earned them a name for dreariness. Robinson criticized their design in *The Flower Garden*: 'Unhappily the common way of planting shrubberies has robbed many grass walks of all charm ... the common mixed plantation of Evergreens means death to the variety and beauty of flower we may have by grass walks in sun or shade. The shrubs are frequently planted in mixtures, in which the most free-growing are so thickly set as soon to cover the whole ground, Cherry laurel, Portugal Laurel, Privet, and such common things frequently killing all the choicer shrubs and forming dark heavy walls of leaves.'

However, when mixed with deciduous shrubs that flower in summer, a proportion of evergreens gives interest and structure to a border. Those evergreens that will flourish in light shade in a north-facing bed or the back side of a shrubbery can be controlled so they do not grow together. They include large shrubs with contrasting foliage textures – *Arbutus unedo*, aucubas, bamboos, camellias, choisyas, cotoneasters, elaeagnus, euonymus, autumn-flowering fatsias, winter-flowering mahonias,

April-flowering osmanthus, phillyreas, cherry laurel, Portugal laurel, rhododendron and evergreen viburnums; their companions on a lower plane include more compact-growing box, *Danae racemosa*, leucothoe, pachysandra, *Rubus*, January-flowering sarcococcas and spring skimmias. Of these camellias, leucothoes, pachysandra and rhododendrons are lime-haters; arbutus will grow in shallow alkaline soil; aucuba, choisya and phillyrea thrive in heavy clay once well established, the latter also doing well on chalk. Some of these real woodland plants, coming from habitats in woods or on north-facing slopes, have been discussed in more detail in Chapter Three.

The larger cotoneasters are useful windbreaks at the back of a border: *Cotoneaster conspicuus* and its many forms (with berries neglected by birds), yellow-berried *C.* 'Rothschildianus', and cultivars of *C. salicifolius*. They all have an open habit, allowing sunlight and light rain to penetrate to smaller plants below. Mahonias from Asia, which flower in winter, prefer a neutral to acid soil. These include the scented *Mahonia japonica* with bold pinnate spiny leaves, tender *M. lomariifolia* and their joint seedling hybrids 'Lionel Fortescue', 'Charity' and 'Buckland'. Portugal laurel (*Prunus lusitanica*), described by Robinson as 'a noble evergreen rarely seen in its full beauty, because it is nearly always choked with other things in the shrubbery', needs air and light to produce masses of scented white flowers in April and May. Sarcococcas and skimmias are at their best in full or part shade, providing underplanting to taller-growing deciduous shrubs. More tender cultivars of *Viburnum tinus* (the best are pink-budded 'Eve Price', 'Gwenllian' – the latter's autumn flowers often coinciding with light blue berries – and 'French White'), preferring alkaline soil, flower in the depths of winter. Coming from sheltered oak woods near the Mediterranean, they can be severely damaged in a cold winter. Mexican orange (*Choisya ternata*), with glossy leaves and scented white flowers in spring and again in late summer, will grow in half-shade but flowers better in full sun. *Viburnum davidii* from Asia, with a tabulated habit and not fussy about soil, carries its bright turquoise berries (at least one male plant is necessary in each group) through to Christmas. English holly (forms of *Ilex aquifolium*) will tolerate shade and both acid and alkaline soils as long as drainage is good. Another shade-tolerant evergreen is fast-growing buckthorn (*Rhamnus alaternus*), from Mediterranean limestone woodland maquis, in its variegated leaf form 'Argenteovariegata' described by Robinson in *The English Flower Garden* as 'the best [of the buckthorns], being that in which the leaves are broadly edged with silver'. Like many fast-growing trees and shrubs, it may need staking if given richer garden soil than found in its own stony habitat. Others of the shade-tolerant evergreens have cultivars with variegated leaves and lighten the winter scene; forms of *Osmanthus heterophyllus* from Japan, plenty of hollies and Portugal laurel as well as buckthorn have varieties with leaves decoratively marked or edged with silver or gold. Most of these shade-tolerant shrubs are equally happy in the moderate sun of a temperate climate as long as their roots can be kept cool, but will certainly need a position in shade where summers are hot.

There are more evergreens available for the sunnier side of a shrub border and for sheltered but cool sites. In the mixed shrubbery appropriate evergreens help establish architectural structure and ensure winter interest, the more winter-tender needing severe pruning in spring to keep them shapely and contained, to prevent them encroaching on the more seasonal soft-stemmed plants. Among sun-lovers are Mediterranean shrubs such as *Bupleurum fruticosum*, lavenders, *Myrtus communis* and *M.c. tarentina*, phillyrea, Jerusalem sages (forms of *Phlomis*), rosemaries and *Teucrium fruticans*, all thriving in stony well-drained alkaline soil, and used to hot summers and rain in winter – their natural growing season. Companion plants hiding under their canopies are drought-loving cyclamen and in the more open spaces early spring bulbs, alliums, South African kniphofias, and thistle-like plants, onopordons,

galactites, echinops and eryngiums. These can all be an addition to Californian gardens, while relatively few sun-loving Californian shrubs do well in the changeable British climate. Some, such as Californian lilac (*Ceanothus* species and cultivars), the matilija poppy (*Romneya coulteri*), the endemic *Carpenteria californica*, fremontodendrons and coastal silk tassel *Garrya elliptica* (particularly the form *G.e.* 'James Roof') which flowers in late winter, do well in warm, sunny well-drained protected sites in Britain. All these plants grow at the Hillier Arboretum in Hampshire in an area with dry, sandy acid soil. At Ventnor on the Isle of Wight conditions are so mild that the Californian range, besides Australian, New Zealand and South African plants, can be extended. Most of these plants do not need rich soil, rapidly becoming woody if given too many nutrients. If Mediterranean-type evergreen shrubs perish in a hard winter, it is often not because of cold, but because they

In Beth Chatto's garden, thicket-forming dogwood with bright red stems,spectacular in the winter scene, is undercarpeted with low-growing bamboos (*Sasa veitchii*) with leaves edged in white. Shrubs that grow so densely do not make good hosts to smaller plants, but are used in association with neighbouring groundcover. The leaves of the cornus are quite heavy during the summer months, controlling weed germination under their canopies, and turn pale yellow in autumn. Like willows, these dogwoods need stooling or pollarding to induce production of bright young shoots. Some people prefer to cut back half the bush every other season.

have been grown in too-rich soil, which has encouraged too much vulnerable new growth. They often suffer from insufficiently well-drained soil, allowing water to freeze around their roots, which, combined with dry freezing winds, will prevent replacement of water lost by transpiration. Evergreen abelias from China, from relatively low altitudes, flower in late summer and need full sun in Britain, but shade in hotter climates such as Texas. Many are frost-tender but most generally grown is the hybrid *Abelia* x *grandiflora*, which thrives in any well-drained soil. Its more prostrate form is useful groundcover for shade in southern states of America, surviving hot nights. Holly-leaved *Itea ilicifolia*, also from west China, with honey-scented tassels, thrives in a warm border. Australian acacias and eucalyptus flourish in Californian heat, but are mostly too tender for all except the milder counties in the British Isles. Among evergreen shrubs for the areas washed by the warm Gulf Stream are some from southern Chile and Argentina, preferring a moist cool atmosphere, well-drained but moisture-retentive soil and a hot wall to help ripen summer wood. Tall semi-evergreen abutilons with wide mallow-like flowers, vanilla-scented azaras, *Drimys winteri* (usually recommended for acid soils only, but often seen on neutral to alkaline soils) with umbels of scented white flowers in May, escallonias (particularly good for coastal gardens and usually regenerating from the ground if hit by hard frosts), cinnamon-barked *Myrtus luma* (now *Luma apiculata*), as well as lime-haters such as *Desfontanea spinosa*, crinodendrons and eucryphias are all possibilities. *Drimys lanceolata*, with aromatic leaves, cinnamon bark and greenish flowers in autumn, from damper mountain-sides in Tasmania and south-east Australia, requires very similar cool situations in a favoured locality. Some New Zealand and Tasmanian shrubs, already adapted to salt-laden winds, thrive in milder counties of the British Isles, especially those exposed to the humidity and warmth of the Gulf Stream. Brachyglottis, corokia, griselinias, hebes, hoherias, leptospermum, daisy bushes (*Olearia*),

pittosporums and ozothamnus are all good seaside shrubs for coastal areas, with *Brachyglottis* 'Sunshine' (syn. *Senecio* 'Sunshine') most commonly seen even in colder gardens, and forms of New Zealand flax (*Phormium*) from damp areas in the South Island.

Deciduous shrubs are not only beautiful in themselves but create the microclimates for a host of ground-covering companion plants. Although providing all-year interest, the dense canopies of most of the evergreens make it difficult to grow bulbs and perennials, which need light and moisture during the growing season, at their base. Deciduous shrubs leaf out after the earliest bulbs have flowered, providing dry shade for aconites, chionodoxa, cyclamen, erythroniums and scillas during their summer dormancy. Many of the genera have species or cultivars for both sun and shade situations, and often distinct species inside the genus, which require acid or alkaline conditions. Most calcifuge shrubs will not grow on alkaline soil, while lime-tolerant shrubs often do quite well in a lower pH, although roses and many viburnums do distinctly better on lime.

Among the deciduous woodland shrubs that are tolerant of light shade are white-flowered *Rhodotypos scandens* from Asia, sorbarias, American symphoricarpos and *Rubus* 'Benenden', all of which thrive in north-facing shrubberies. Most dogwoods (*Cornus*) tolerate light or dappled shade: a few have definite soil preferences but most grow easily in any good soil covering a range between quite large trees, flowering and fruiting shrubs, to suckering shrubs distinguished by their shimmering red, yellow or green bark in winter. Acid-loving *Cornus florida* from the American east coast has few rivals, growing naturally in woodland from Maine to Florida and south-east to east Texas, while *C. nuttallii* comes from the Pacific north-west. Both need summer heat to give of their best, seldom flowering in the British Isles. For English gardens the equivalent is *C. kousa* from Japan or, for more alkaline soils, its form *C.k. chinensis*, flowering in May or June. Both of the

ROBINSON'S RECIPE FOR SATISFYING SHRUBS

The English Flower Garden was first published in 1883 and ran into fifteen editions, the last one two years before Robinson's death in 1935. In a chapter on flowering shrubs and trees in the eighth edition of 1900 he describes the desirability of having flowering evergreens near the house, in the 'most precious of flower beds ... often ... in winter as bare as oilcloth. What beautiful groups of flowering evergreens we might plant in them. Mountain laurels (Kalmias), Japan and American Andromeda, Azaleas, choice evergreen barberries, alpine Cotoneaster, Evergreen Daphne, Desfontanea, in the south; the taller hardy heaths, Escallonia, Ledum, alpine and wild forms of Rhododendrons, sweet Gale, star bush and various Laurustinus, leaving out not a few which thrive

(Above) On the upper bank above the west lawn camassias from North America spread in open situations between the scented yellow azaleas, beside dark-flowered biennial honesty. Robinson also planted starworts, forms of aster, between the shrubs for a late summer display. In his Gravetye Manor manuscript – a description of work in the garden from 1885 to 1898 – he wrote, 'Some years ago Starworts were rarely seen except in bundles in botanic gardens ... as soon as the heavy ground work round the house allowed of planting belts and groups of flowering shrubs, I dotted a few of the best Starworts through these, to furnish the bare ground between, and flower in due season.'

(Above) At Gravetye terraces of mixed shrubs and flowers rise above the horizontal west garden – which has now been put down to lawn. In Robinson's day, stone-edged beds provided a colourful display for the whole summer, but their excellent drainage also allowed more tender plants to survive throughout the winter. Many of the shrubs flower in spring, allowing the smaller plants to steal the limelight later in the year. Moroccan broom (*Cytisus battandieri*) with pineapple-scented yellow blooms, red shrub roses, persicarias, feathery *Aruncus dioicus*, magenta *Geranium psilostemon* and foxgloves can be seen performing in the foreground.

Robinson liked to plant shrubberies 'in bold beds to screen rather steep and awkward banks, and at the same time to give a home to many fine things that would not be very well placed in the flower garden: – Bay, Pampas Grass, Barberry, Venetian Sumach, and many choice flowering shrubs planted in November. Planting of tall flowers and Lilies between to go on all the Winter.' The main view, in spring, of the shrubbery beds to the west of the house shows massed azaleas with mixed flower planting in between shrubs: foxgloves, comfrey, sedums, groups of spiky iris in full sun and white-flowered *Allium neapolitanum* and *Iberis sempervirens*.

only in the warmer districts. Charming gardens might be made of such bushes, not lumped together, but in open groups, with the more beautiful American hardy flowers between them, such as the Wood lily and Moccasin Flower, many rare Lilies, and beautiful bulbous flowers of all seasons.'

We might add deciduous shrubs to his evergreens, but as a prescription for shrubbery beds – especially advocating open groups of shrubs with flowers between – Robinson gives the best advice. Any of these combinations, with care given to associating plants appropriately so that all need the same soil and situation, will turn the often-neglected shrub borders into flowering delight, with light and shade, and valleys of low plants between the taller shrubs. As he says, 'the plan would be a permanent one as it would tend to abolish the never-ending digging in the flower garden'. It features woody plants accompanied by an understorey of flowering plants, in mutual dependency. This sort of arrangement in shade or sunshine has become the backbone of many gardens today; unfortunately, the shrubs are often allowed to grow together or into thickets, so that

the perennials and bulbs that breath life into the arrangement get grown over and cease to have enough light to flower. Shrub or 'mixed' borders need looking after. Shrubs may need to be pruned annually to keep their shape and their allotted space.

As Robinson says, 'If one tenth the trouble wasted on "carpet-bedding" plants and other fleeting and costly rubbish had been spent on flowering shrubs, our garden would be all the better for it. There are no plants so much neglected ... and even when they are planted they are rarely well grown, owning to the "traditions" of what is called the shrubbery. The common way is to dig the shrubbery every winter ... much harm is done by mutilating the roots of the shrubs. The labour and time wasted ... if devoted to the proper culture of a portion of the ground each year, would make our gardens delightful indeed ... many shrubs ... have been destroyed by the muddle "shrubbery".' At his own home, Gravetye Manor, the beds near the house, some of them on terraced slopes at right angles to the main building, are arranged in this fashion as part of the superb restoration undertaken by Peter Herbert.

These should be cut or 'stooled' every two years, cutting half a bush at a time.

Deciduous shrubs grown for their winter outlines and/or barks and attractive summer foliage tend to be less suitable for the north-facing border or for the shady side of a shrubbery. Many deciduous shrubs will not flower unless grown in partial sunlight, but winter-flowering viburnums (*Viburnum farreri* and *V.* × *bodnantense* 'Dawn') will perform well even in shade, producing a succession of flowers from autumn to spring as frosts come and go, in spring surrounded by carpets of Apennine anemone, leaving space for summer-flowering viburnums in more open places. Winter-flowering honeysuckles, of which the best is the hybrid *Lonicera* × *purpusii*, deserve a place in sun or shade, making a winter companion for lower-growing winter-flowering sarcococcas. Corylopsis species, all from Asia, with drooping racemes of fragrant primrose-coloured flowers in spring, are among the most valuable shrubs for half-shade, leafing out to make a light canopy under which many bulbs and perennials will flourish through the summer months. Most thrive in acid to neutral soils.

Magnolias, tree or bush forms, are among the most desirable of all shrubs, but their frost-tender flower-buds are liable to be caught by late frosts in a temperate climate. Planting at the top of a slope so that frost drains away gives them the best chance of succeeding each spring; they revel in deep loamy acidic soil, although forms and hybrids of *Magnolia* × *soulangeana* perform well in neutral and a slightly alkaline soil. Viburnums, kolkwitzias, spiraeas and deutzias all make excellent companions to perennials, flowering before the June flush of shrub roses. Philadelphus and shrub roses are a mainstay of shrubberies in June and early July, when most of the spring-flowerers are over.

Most hydrangeas will grow in cool soil in shade; in areas with hot summers they require adequate shade. Some, such as the cultivars of the mop-headed *Hydrangea macrophylla*, *H. serrata* and *H. paniculata*, all

Golden variegated dogwood (*Cornus alba* 'Spaethii') with a broad yellow stripe to its leaves and *Astrantia* 'Shaggy' both like rich moist soil and look right together growing in Sheila McQueen's garden. Astrantias quickly droop in periods of drought. Shrubbery planting should, to be natural, depend on establishing a pattern of growth for both the woody plants and for the perennials and/or bulbs. The natural shrubbery will be planted with semi-wild plants, those native to the region or resembling natives, which do not give too sophisticated a vision and which will thrive in the open and in the light shade cast by the shrubs. Chosen appropriately, the mixed shrub border should give a very long season of interest.

'wedding cake' dogwoods, *C. alternifolia* from America and, for a larger garden, giant Asian dogwood (*C. controversa*), are architectural plants for corners or focal points; usually the variegated forms of both are a popular and striking choice. The former casts little shade, looking best if underplanted with flat massed buglossoides or *Brunnera macrophylla*, while shade-tolerant bulbs such as erythroniums and perennial blue-flowered comfrey, omphalodes, *Trachystemon orientalis* and hostas thrive under the larger specimen. Hardy suckering dogwoods, good forms of *Cornus alba* from Siberia and China and of red osier dogwood (*C. stolonifera*) from North America are most useful in wild shrubbery situations, preferring damp sites but not fussy about soil. Variegated forms of *C. alba* give pleasing foliage colour in the garden, especially when combined with green or purple-leaved shrubs. They have splendid autumn tints and bright crimson, yellow and green stems in winter.

from Asia, will only tolerate lime-free soil. Others thrive in alkalinity and even chalk. Both the American hydrangeas valuable in gardens, *H. arborescens* (Zones 4–9) and oak-leaved *H. quercifolia* (Zones 5–9), come from a wide geographical range, and perhaps therefore not surprisingly are ready to thrive in any soil, if given a cool root-run. The former, found in woods from Florida to Louisiana and from New York to Iowa, has many good forms, the best of which is *H.a.* 'Grandiflora', with large rounded heads of snowy creamy flowers, suckering freely in a loamy soil. *H. quercifolia*, a native of the southern states (Alabama, Florida and Georgia), will colour less well in the autumn in shade than it will in an open situation. Both Americans are much hardier than the popular macrophylla mop-headed hortensias or lace-caps from the Far East, suitable for maritime climates and flourishing in protective light-canopy shade in mild Cornish, Scottish and Irish Gulf-Stream gardens in the British Isles. In more continental climates they survive to Zone 6. Lacecaps, with infertile ray-florets surrounding the flat fertile heads, are generally hardier than the mop-headed hortensias with heads entirely formed of sterile flowers. Shade-tolerant toad lilies (*Tricyrtis*) and arching willow gentians make perfect companions to these hydrangeas. *H. sargentiana* (Zone 7, to 5° F/–15° C), introduced by Wilson from West Hupeh in 1907, is easily damaged by spring frosts and needs shade from protective tree canopies or from a wall. Its upright habit allows smaller plants to grow in close association around its base. Not all hydrangeas fuss about soil. In the famous chalk garden at Highdown in Sussex the best hydrangea species are *H. villosa* and the old Japanese garden form of *H. involucrata*, *H.i.* 'Hortensis'.

A shrub bed need only be dug when it is first prepared for planting: but then it should be well done; as Robinson says, 'nobody will begrudge a thorough preparation of the ground at first'. Deep double digging, incorporating manure and adding a mulch, are all essential tasks. In the following seasons all the soil requires is

At Newby Hall in Yorkshire a magnificent flowering dogwood (*Cornus nuttallii* 'Eddie's White Wonder', a hybrid of *C. nuttallii* and *C. florida*), which needs an acid soil, flowers in a mixed border. Its blossoms, weighing down the branches, overhang smaller spring-flowering plants, with a line of irises growing in full sun across the path, near the profusely flowering roses. The Chinese form of the dogwood (*C. kousa chinensis*) is most comfortable in alkaline soil. In some shrubberies a few appropriate large shrubs will look more natural and be more effective than a greater number, leaving space between them for a whole scheme of perennials, biennials, annuals and bulbs.

a frequently applied top-dressing of mulch on bare areas; this will keep the ground in good heart without more digging (which may well damage surface roots). Decaying leaves from the shrubs and other plants will also play their part in providing a natural mulch, although in the autumn it is important to make certain that leaves do not smother the shoots of small bulbs or make dense mats over crowns of perennials, causing them to rot. In *The Wild Garden* Robinson deplored 'the custom of digging shrubbery borders', which prevailed in almost every garden: 'there is no worse custom ... we need plant beauty instead of garden-graveyards'. Whether through Robinson's influence or through an

improved sense of what works best, his advice is followed today in most gardens.

Robinson's advice to make the edge of your shrub planting 'broken and varied', creating patterns of light and shade at different heights and on different planes, allows the gardener to carpet the ground with attractive smaller plants: 'Let hepaticas and double and other primroses and rockfoils and golden moneywort and stonecrops and forget-me-nots, and dwarf phloxes and many similar plants cover the ground among the taller plants ... at the back as well as at the front.' The surface of the soil between the main shrubs can be planted with free-growing hardy plants and/or dwarf evergreen shrubs, designed to complement and/or to contrast in shape and form with the main shrub planting. Changes in the growing conditions, as shrubs encroach on the available space, will put pressure on the smaller plants and it will be up to the gardener to decide whether shrubs are suitable for cutting back or whether the range of low-growing plants should be reduced. As a planting scheme matures, shrubs tend to grow together, more aggressive perennials overcome others that may be abandoned, and fewer different varieties will survive.

Perennials to complete the border picture must be chosen partly to suit soil conditions, but in general fewer perennials have such definite soil preferences as shrubs. When they do, it is better to work with the soil than try to alter its fundamental character. As with shrubs, many lime-tolerant perennials will grow in acid or neutral soil,

while definite lime-haters must have acid soil. Lime-lovers include campanulas, dianthus, bearded irises, scabious, knautias, euphorbias and others. Real lime-haters are listed on page 112. But unlike shrubs, which will ultimately send their roots down into the original earth and so should be chosen for their affinity with it, perennials and bulbs can grow successfully in the top layer of worked soil, which will improve each year as humus-making mulches are added. Most important is soil texture, workability and drainage. All soils can be improved, but heavy clay is the most difficult to work – although as its texture improves with the addition of grit, organic manure and gypsum (a clay-breaker), it is usually found to be very fertile. Ideally nothing should be planted until the soil's condition is improved. After planting, frequent organic mulches combine with decaying leaves to continue to improve its workability and often to lower its pH. But how the perennials will do also depends on many other factors: the climate, pockets of favourable or unfavourable microclimate, their suitability as neighbours beside the shrubs and the patterns of light and shade created by the shrub branches.

Among perennials suitable for sharing a shrubbery in an open situation are asters, aconitums, astrantias, boltonias, bleeding heart (*Dicentra spectabilis*), euphorbias – not the sun- and drought-loving kind, but species such *Euphorbia griffithii* and *E. sikkimensis*, evening primroses, hardy cranesbill geraniums and heucheras, eupatoriums, hemerocallis, hostas and lilies. Self-seeding columbines (*Aquilegia vulgaris*), forget-me-nots and small violas can drift between sun and shade, with lady's mantle and forms of Jacob's ladder (*Polemonium*) choosing the open ground in which to germinate. Perennials that prefer alkaline soils include self-seeding cowslips (*Primula veris*), graceful Solomon's seals (*Polygonatum* x *hybridum* and *P. odoratum*) and yellow foxgloves (*Digitalis grandiflora*, which are longer-lived than the usually biennial *D. purpurea*).

An alternative effect is created by having only one sort of groundcover running in and out between the shrubs

The most successful mixed borders have more perennials than shrubs, with the latter giving structure, height and shadow effects and the lower-growing soft-stemmed plants providing colour nearer ground level. At Kiftsgate in Gloucestershire *Rosa* 'Cerise Bouquet' provides a vivid backdrop to the whole scene, with thick underplanting of perennials. On the opposite side a graceful weeping escallonia trails above purple-leaved sage (*Salvia officinalis*) without creating deep shade. Burning bush (the purple-flowered form of *Dictamnus albus*), hardy geraniums and variegated brunnera are repeated along the beds.

along the whole shrubbery or the length of the border. This, once established, will require little maintenance compared to more species-rich schemes. In alkaline soil blue gromwell (*Buglossoides purpurocaerulea*) with bright blue flowers in May has long rooting stems, which quickly spread to carpet under vigorous shrubs. Bugles, forms of *Ajuga reptans*, cranesbill geraniums of one variety – such as *Geranium endressii*, *G. macrorrhizum* or *G.* x *magnificum* planted *en masse* – would be equally appropriate, or mauve-flowered *G. nodosum*, which thrives in sun and shade and seeds very freely. Creeping Jenny (*Lysimachia nummularia*, Robinson's moneywort) is a discreet almost flat spreader, easily weeded out if too vigorous, but, particularly in the gold-leaved form, shining through the winter months. The semi-shrubby rose of Sharon (*Hypericum calycinum*), with yellow flowers in summer, has rooting branches and spreading roots to thrive in dry soil in shady places. Comfreys (particularly *Symphytum grandiflorum*) *Vinca minor* and *Rubus tricolor* reject all invaders, although the bramble may also smother the lower-growing shrubs. For the north-facing beds with more pervasive shade, different cyclamen species, coming from areas with mild winters and hot summers, will provide attractive flowers or leaves for most of the year in dry or slightly moist shade. Most originate in a limy humus-rich soil. Their corms will grow large wedged between matted tree or shrub roots. For a warm climate the false strawberry (*Duchesnia indica*) spreads by runners, rapidly colonizing under shrubs in alkaline soil. Lily-of-the-valley (*Convallaria majalis*) thrives in soil that is alternately moist and dry and soon spreads to make a mat of leaves and roots in the shade of the back of a border. In a mild climate the old cottage-garden plant mother-of-thousands (*Saxifraga stolonifera*) with its beautiful veined leaves and white flowers will also do best at the back. Bergenia, with leathery leaves and pink or white flowers in spring, seeding *Tanacetum parthenium*, with green or golden leaves, foxgloves, comfrey and nettle-leaved bellflowers (both *Campanula trachelium* and

creeping *C. rapunculoides*), toad lilies (*Tricyrtis hirta* and *T. formosana*) and the perennial golden hop, scrambling up through the shrub branches, all thrive in fairly deep shade. Most of these plants will succeed in alkaline or acid soils, but some that come from the North American woods – phloxes (*Phlox divaricatus* and *P. stolonifera*), *Dicentra eximia* and *D. formosa*, and trailing arbutus (*Arctostaphylos uva-ursi*), trilliums and blood-root (*Sanguinaria canadensis*) – only thrive in a moist rich loam with pH below a neutral 6.4. Graceful willow gentians (*Gentiana asclepiadea*) from Europe are said not to be fussy about soil, but perform better in a humid climate and in acid conditions, as does the evergreen creeping *Rubus pentalobus*. All these should not be grown as single specimens or even small groups of three or five but, as Robinson says, 'rightly we must group and mass as nature does' making colonies of one or two kinds in any spot between the shrubs so that – apart from looking much better and more natural – each drift can be provided with exactly the sort of environment the plants require.

Another idea for a shrubbery or shrub bed is to be selective about which of the small perennials you plant with the shrubs. Instead of choosing quite ordinary plants, which will thrive in between shrubs in a particular aspect, it can be exciting to choose 'difficult' plants, also suitable in having the same requirements, but less easy to grow successfully and needing extra care and attention. This might be the specialist plantsman's approach. They can still look natural. Among them are perennials, which either come up very late in spring, thus often being overlooked or damaged by the gardener during spring work, or endangering their survival by disappearing after flowering and being overrun by competing plants during the rest of the season. Among the more specialist perennials suitable for extra attention, shoots of which appear late in spring, are the tender *Begonia evansiana* (syn. *B. grandis*) from Asia, hardy in most English counties, with glistening leaves red-tinted on their undersides; angular Solomon's seal (*Polygonatum odoratum*) and its variegated form; the rare roscoeas, and the similar *Cautleya lutea* and *C. robusta* from China and the Himalayas. Shooting stars, species of *Dodecatheon*, die down immediately after flowering, as do blue-flowered *Corydalis flexuosa* and Virginia bluebells (*Mertensia virginica*). (Hansen points out that *Dodecatheon meadia* from eastern North America has two distinct ecological forms, one of which prefers forest habitats, the other open prairie, but both enjoying damp acidic soil.) Among the more difficult-to-grow perennials I include snow poppy (*Eomecon chionantha*) from China with strong questing fleshy roots, blue poppies and other *Meconopsis* from Tibet and Nepal, which need a dew-drenched atmosphere. All Liriopes (various species) do best in shade, and in hot climates shade is essential for them to flourish (unless there is an irrigation system). *Saxifraga fortunei* and *Kirengeshoma palmata* from Japan prefer an acid soil and cool conditions. Among American plants requiring star treatment are *Shortia galacifolia*, the pick-a-back plant (*Tolmiea menziesii*), celandine poppy (*Stylophorum diphyllum*) and *Galax aphylla* – all of which require humus-rich, well-drained lime-free soil. The slipper orchid (*Cypripedium calceolus*), now rare in Europe but more common in American woods, and twinleaf (*Jeffersonia diphylla*) prefer a rich alkaline loamy soil.

Shrub borders, particularly against walls, generally have their main flush of flower in spring. William Robinson suggests growing scrambling and sprawling plants as well as perennial climbers through their branches to flower later in the season: 'There are few things in plant life more lovely than the delicate tracery of low-climbing things wedded to the shrubs in all northern and temperate regions.' Throwing 'a delicate veil of some pretty creeper' over a group of shrubs, as he suggests, extends the interest considerably. Many late-flowering small-flowered clematis clamber naturally towards the light through the more vigorous shrubs and roses. Forms of *Clematis viticella* and *C. texensis* are admirable for this purpose, filling the late shrubbery

borders with colour. Herbaceous clematis, which make prodigious growth in one season, without rooting stems or spreading rhizomes, grow below and through shrubs. But there are also perennial sweet peas (forms of *Lathyrus latifolius*) with pink or white pea-flowers, and twining perennial hops – the golden-leaved form is good in a dark corner. In north-facing borders the Scotch flame flower (*Tropaeolum speciosum*) from Chile, enjoying moisture-retentive acid soil and a cool situation, carries scarlet nasturtium flowers followed by indigo berries, decorating the green leaves of the shrubs. In more open situations the annual canary creeper (*Tropaeolum peregrinum*), with pale yellow flowers, scrambles rather than climbs through lower shrubs and over the stems of earlier-flowering perennials, self-seeding *in situ* to perpetuate itself.

At Stone House Cottage near Kidderminster the Arbuthnotts have mainly mixed planting in their borders in the walled garden. With tabulated spreading branches *Viburnum plicatum* has such dense foliage during the summer months that there is very little moisture or light for other plants to survive under the canopy. The taller roses and the Moroccan broom (*Cytisus battandieri*), trained flat against the wall, create much less shade under their branches, making it possible to grow companion plants. Shrubs, especially if space is limited, can often have their heads raised to let in more light.

SHRUBS IN MIXED BORDERS FURNISH GARDEN ROOMS

In the Red Border at Hidcote purple-leaved small trees and shrubs provide the foliage colour and structure, with red-flowered perennials and annuals heating up the border appearance by midsummer. Purple hazel (*Corylus maxima* 'Purpurea'), *Prunus spinosa* 'Purpurea', with purple-leaved *Salvia officinalis* Purpurascens Group, phormiums and berberis, provide the background to flowers in orange, scarlet and deep red. Sultry day-lilies, *Geum* x *borisii* (syn. *G. coccineum*) and *Fuchsia* 'Koralle' combine with dark red dahlias. Over many years the shrubs in the Red Border have grown too large, leaving little space for the later summer flowers.

The garden at Hidcote Manor in Gloucestershire is well known for its series of garden rooms, planted in cottage-style, with shrubs, bulbs and flowers packed tightly together so that the results are not only naturalistic and casual but, with plants covering the soil between the woody specimens and so preventing weed germination, maintenance is reduced. This sort of planting owes much to William Robinson and Gertrude Jekyll, who invented the 'mixed' border, drawing their inspiration from natural groupings in the wild as well as from the simple planting in Victorian cottage gardens. Romantic informality is the Hidcote keynote, with shrubs, climbers, self-sowing perennials and bulbs all spilling over in an apparently very carefree fashion, albeit in a tightly controlled geometric overall design, which unites the whole garden. One of the great advantages of gardening informally inside formal constraints is that the actual contents of the flowerbeds can be chosen for the most naturalistic effects, with companion plants with similar requirements growing cheek by jowl. Of course, annuals may be added each year to give an increase in flowering appearances, as is done in the Red Border at

Hidcote, but the mixed border will only work as intended if the permanent plants come from the same sort of habitats and all thrive in the same sort of conditions.

Deciduous shrubs and shrub roses extend the possibilities of associated bulbs and perennials, as both the last two can flower while the shrubs are still leafless in spring and, if well chosen, will enjoy the relatively dry shade of the rest of the summer. Evergreen shrubs, on the other hand, although often giving vital winter structure, seldom make such good companions for lower-growing plants. At Hidcote evergreen shrubs such as yew, Portugal laurel and box tend to be used as plant architecture and as hedges to give protection against wind, and the borders are mainly composed of deciduous flowering shrubs and roses. Smoke bushes, hazels, berberis and hydrangeas ring the changes through flowerbeds and in the more shaded stream walk and woodland. In summer shrub roses stretch gracefully over pools of penstemons, lupins, dianthus and purple sage, and in the Red Border tall purple and bronze-leaved shrubs are a foil to day-lilies, scarlet salvias and heuchera.

(Top left) Lacecap forms of *Hydrangea macrophylla* and the species *H. arborescens* with rounded greenish-white flowers mark the corners of a meeting point by the stream path at Hidcote. Hydrangeas are found in the wild in Asia and North and South America, and are useful shrubs in a late mixed border (many good shrubs flower early in the season), grown in moist but well-drained fertile soil in sun or partial shade, and protected from drying winds. Small bulbs, wood anemones, scillas and chionodoxa grow happily at the base of hydrangeas, which leaf out late in the spring.

(Top right) Along the shaded streamside at Hidcote, skunk cabbages, darmera, *Iris pseudacorus* and little violas, with astrantias and hostas lining the stone pathway, fill in under the canopies of a chestnut in a very natural way. Trees and shrubs provide the form and structure to shrubbery planting but the small perennials and bulbs, growing between them, must be planted in big groups in order to make their flowering effects most telling. Planting very closely also eliminates the possibility of weed germination. Any bare earth should be thickly mulched in spring and possibly again in the autumn to help prevent weeds seeding and also to conserve moisture in the beds.

(Right) In a sunny area around the watertank at Hidcote, shrub roses (including *Rosa glauca* and various rugosas) provide a frame for heat-lovers: sculptural agaves in pots (overwintered in the greenhouse), cistus, santolina and lavender, all thriving in full sun and requiring adequate drainage. It is always difficult to combine plants with different requirements – in this case roses need rich feeding, while the Mediterranean-type plants thrive in poor stony soil, growing too fast and lush if the soil is too fertile and then succumbing to a harsh winter. In a more natural gardening scene, replacing the roses with other drought-lovers might reduce the workload.

OPEN GROUND

*I*N GARDENS 'open ground' is a blank canvas on which the gardener can impose a style at will, uninhibited by existing features such as woodland or other specific environments that ecologically dictate the sort of gardening done. This open ground is predominantly sunny, possibly windswept and – apart from any decisions to build walls or plant hedges (for windbreaks or design purposes), create paths or in other ways break up the space by design measures – the gardening in it is concerned with horizontal space. Conventional gardeners fill the space with mown lawns, borders and sometimes island beds. In the more natural garden, grassy areas can become fully fledged meadows or at the very least grass-cutting is restricted so that only pathways have a regular cutting programme in summer, leaving large areas, possibly wrapped around by paths, where seldom-mown grasses reveal all the interest of their different colours and textures, and their swaying beauty as they come into flower and seed. The longer grassy areas can become wild-flower 'flowerbeds', or rich meadows planted with mixed natives and exotics, either on a permanently developing basis in which certain plants come to dominate over the years, or by annual rotavation and resowing with flowers and a matrix of grass. In natural gardens, borders – instead of being formal in outline and planted with isolated blocks of plants – become new man-made, evolving plant communities in which plants, selected specifically for the site, grow together in more natural ways, making their own interrelated abstract shapes.

Oranges and yellows are used informally in Ton ter Linden's garden in northern Holland. As a painter Ton ter Linden composes canvases, but as a plantsman with a strong feeling for nature and native planting, he combines his talents to create these semi-spontaneous garden compositions, which owe less to self-conscious colour planning than Gertrude Jekyll's carefully orchestrated schemes. One of the reasons for their success is that he does not rely on colour blocks, rather encouraging weaving colours, demonstrated by the purple-leaved orach (*Atriplex*) in the bed, to make a tapestry of interacting threads. In the final analysis colour effects are subjective and it is the gardener's or artist's eye which makes the ultimate choices.

In spring at Forde Abbey in Dorset daffodils grow in clumps through the garden, in open areas or at the edge of tree canopies, following on after snowdrops and crocus. To get natural effects bulbs are scattered by hand and planted where they fall rather than arranged in symmetrical lines. Many daffodils are easily naturalized in grass but their dying foliage must not be cut until four to six weeks after flowering. The smaller species, except for the native Lent lily, *Narcissus pseudonarcissus* and the Tenby daffodil, *N.p. obvallaris*, grow best in cultivated soil.

These 'new' perennial beds, with self-seeding, self-perpetuating plants, occupy a sort of halfway stance between the old-fashioned military-style border, with every plant in its allotted place, and actual meadows, where grass provides a background and underplanting to a rich plant tapestry. Another less 'wild' planting for open ground involves the cottage-style mixed borders advocated by William Robinson and Gertrude Jekyll, where seemingly unplanned luxuriance is achieved by planting very close together in informal drifts. A further extension of this is to soften the distinction between actual bed and neighbouring grass, paving or gravel, letting plants choose where to make the uneven flowing edges of the design.

In gardens open ground can be adapted in many ways – not excluding true xeriscapes, gardens designed for drought-tolerant plants that seldom if ever require watering, and where the more natural approach ceases to be so much a matter of taste and style as a determined intention to work with nature and in sympathy with the existing environment.

The Lawn and its Variations

The concept of the smooth green lawn is ingrained in most gardeners who inherit western cultural ideas: the well-kept lawn is as much a traditional design element as any border planting or elaborate parterre layout. Even before lawnmowers were invented in 1830, short grass – cut by scythes or grazed by sheep – created the frame and setting for English and European gardens and garden features. And lawns are not only an ambience, but are also functional. Tight turf grasses with horizontal spreading shoots control erosion, create places for walking, sitting and recreation, and remain cool in summer. Lawns have an evocative appeal: even the smell of newly cut grass has been one of summer's pleasures, though diminished now by the persistent drone of mowing machines.

Today many owners and designers have begun to question the desirability of the conventional lawn with its unnatural 'golf-course look' for a number of environmental and maintenance reasons. During the growing season most British lawns are cut once a week, more if a fine turf is desired; the average manicured lawn is cut about thirty times a year and has fertilizers and herbicides applied in spring; irrigation is necessary in hot summers. In North America lawns need cutting twice a week in spring, plus frequent watering if they are to be kept green in summer. Increasingly American gardeners join with the environmentalists in deploring the distinctly unecological use of scarce water for lawn irrigation, as well as the costly maintenance, mowing, feeding and application of selective weed-killers (which pollute the natural water table). As water becomes scarcer in the British Isles, so here also gardeners seek satisfactory alternatives to lawn.

The first English lawns, both open spaces between trees and flowers and settings for cricket and lawn tennis, belonged to estates and suburban villas rather than to cottages, where useful vegetables and flowers occupied all available ground. It is only comparatively recently that lawns have become so popular in all income groups, partly because their maintenance is regarded as requiring less skill than looking after other types of plants (and partly because so many more people now have the space for a garden). In America lawns were included in the 'gardens of taste' advocated in his *Treatise* of 1841 by Andrew Jackson Downing, the first popular American writer on landscape gardening, but the idea of the traditional unfenced front-garden lawns, uniting whole neighbourhoods and reflecting democratic instincts, was first implemented in plan form by Frederick Law Olmsted in 1868. In his development for the Riverside community in Chicago, Olmsted – a pioneer in saving natural landscapes and providing city dwellers with green parks for pleasure and recreation – advocated houses being set back thirty feet/some ten metres from the road, with a few specimen trees set in rolling grass, which would flow seamlessly into the neighbours' property and on beyond to create a park-like impression. This theme was taken up by Frank J. Scott in *The Art of Beautifying Suburban Home Grounds* (1870) – 'A smooth, closely shaven surface of grass is by far the most essential element of beauty on the grounds of a suburban house' – who elevated the unfenced lawn into an institution of democracy, as it has remained for more than a hundred years. Neighbourhoods have only recently accepted partitioned front yards laid out as flower gardens or in 'meadow' style. Some suburban areas issue 'weed ordinances' banning lawns over a certain height. In 1989 Michael Pollan discovered from the Lawn Institute in Tennessee that America had 50,000 square miles of lawn under cultivation, regardless of climate and water requirements, involving $30 billion a year in maintenance costs. Mown lawns in America can still, in contradiction of the movement towards naturalism, be redolent of high morality and the pioneering spirit, reflecting earlier needs to keep nature at bay.

In nature, open landscape in temperate zones is dominated by grass (although, as we have seen, this will quickly revert in a slow process of regeneration from weeds and wild flowers through scrub to forest unless woody seedlings are checked by mowing, grazing, burning or drought). In Great Britain untended grassland, especially if the soil is fertile, becomes infested with rank weeds like nettles, brambles and thistles, but there are many intermediate stages of maintenance between so-called 'set-aside', where nothing is done, and the traditional English lawn of velvet close-knit smoothness, its success assured by frequent mowing and regular applications of fertilizers and herbicides.

The character of any grassland – lawn, meadow or prairie – is dependent on the grasses of which it is composed. The grass family includes many economic crops – corn, oats, wheat, rye, rice and barley – as well as clump- or tussock-forming ornamental grasses (and bamboos), but the turf grasses most suitable for garden lawns are those that form tight mats by sending out horizontal shoots. They have an efficient metabolism which allows them to exploit all available light, moisture and nutrients in the soil and survive frequent cutting. (Physiologically grasses differ from other flowering plants in that their region of active growth is at the leaf base, near where it joins the stem, not at the tip.) Some of the turf grasses are cold-tender, turning brown or even dying in cold winter climates; others dislike prolonged heat and need constant irrigation in hot countries and in periods of drought in temperate climates. Most do not naturally tolerate shade, although new, more shade-tolerant cultivars are being introduced.

The turf grasses suitable for making lawns in temperate climates – the cool-season grasses – include fescues, bents, meadow grasses and the most resistant-to-wear perennial ryegrasses. In North America summers are too hot for good performance of the temperate-climate 'cool' grasses used for the European lawns, and, in many areas, winters are too cold for the warm-season turf grasses, often of tropical or subtropical origin, to

119

At the Bloedel Reserve on Bembridge Island, a ferry's ride from Seattle, Douglas firs are silhouetted against the skyline, while manicured lawn – cut in traditional broad stripes – and surrounded by thicker longer grass, makes a dramatic foreground to Puget's Sound. Grass, cut at different levels, gives a combination of gardening formality and beautiful naturalistic effects, and maintenance costs of regular mowing of the whole area are reduced. In Seattle with rainfall an average of 34in/850mm, and the Japanese current moderating extremes of climate, the lawn seldom needs irrigation.

survive. Warm-season grasses include the invasive Bermuda grass (*Cynodon dactylon*) and zoysia (*Zoysia japonica*), which turn brown in winter and do not 'green up' again until trees leaf out in spring. Hardier grasses include Kentucky bluegrass (*Poa pratensis*), originally from Africa and Eurasia, which survives low temperatures and thrives on damp limy soil; it is often used for lawns in the Midwest. In the hot summers of continental-climate areas in central Europe and in most of the United States, conventional lawns need constant irrigation and mowing at least twice weekly; in the USA none of the grasses suitable for lawns that stay green in winter is native. Roberto Burle Marx followed a different tack in Brazil: he used the green and variegated forms of *Stenotaphrum secundatum*, a rhizomatous, ground-hugging subtropical grass, to make elaborate groundcover patterns lasting through the year.

Most (if not all) of the grasses recommended for lawns grow only in sun, as many lawn-loving gardeners in small shady city gardens have found to their despair, although today there are recommended varieties of many grasses naturally adapted for more shady situations: wood meadow grass mixed with rough-stalked meadow grass survives moist shade, though it will not survive close mowing or much walking on. Native American grasses require less water, less frequent mowing and fewer nutrients, but most of them, such as blue gramma grass (*Bouteloua gracilis*) and buffalo grass (*Buchloe dacty-*

loides) do not stay green in winter. The blue-grey buffalo grass comes from the Great Plains, its range from Minnesota to Montana and then south into Mexico. Although never achieving the velvet smoothness and density of an English lawn, its use as a lawn alternative in the United States is becoming synonymous with low maintenance; it and some of its varieties are widely used from California eastwards. Like all grasses it prefers full sun; it needs little water or fertilizers even in the hottest regions, and adapts to most soils except those that are too sandy. In warm climates it retains its grey shaggy appearance even in winter, but in the colder regions it bleaches to tones of beige, which have their own attraction: as the environmentalist Darryl Morrison said in 1990, 'People need to adapt their aesthetic sensitivities to see beauty in colors other than green – golds, tans, russets...' Another environmental concern now freely expressed in both Europe and America relates to the over-use of pesticides and fertilizers, for lawns as well as in gardening in general. New products go through more stringent testing, and slow-release fertilizers release nutrients at the rate plants use them, controlling the amount of excess nitrates seeping into natural groundwater.

However well tightly spreading grasses respond to cutting – in the same way that they do (or did) to grazing – lawns create a very artificial environment; faced with the stress of frequent cutting, these grasses need constant applications of nutrients and chemicals and water in dry summers to remain green. Plants under stress need much more help and are much more disease-prone. Having fed and encouraged healthy grass, the gardener mows it back again as soon as it starts to grow. The constant mowing programme is a reversal of most other gardening activities, which involve encouraging plants to grow tall. Can designers, used to featuring high-maintenance manicured lawns in their proposals, persuade clients and the public to adopt more natural approaches – either allowing lawns, mixed with flowers, to grow longer, or substituting suitable low-growing plants, paving or gravel for the lawn's ordered greenness?

Already in 1881 Robinson decried the monotony of the smooth, weedless lawn: 'Who would not rather see the waving grass with countless flowers than a close surface without a blossom?' Anticipating more natural approaches, he recommended making lawns less feature-less by cutting grass at different levels to give variety and save labour. Other more colourful effects could be achieved by growing flowers in the grass so that they resembled Swiss mountain meadows in June, or the romantic conception of medieval 'flowery medes'. He advocated planting bulbs and flowers, both hardy and exotic, in the grass to make more natural-looking scenes, timing cutting to take place after the flowers had seeded and perhaps once in the year thereafter. His flowery meadow was a metaphor for the real thing and not exclusively of 'wild flowers' native to the region.

Other groundcovering plants can be considered for places where lawn grasses do not grow well. Where open lawns are shaded with specimen trees, low-growing evergreens, instead of grasses, can extend the lawn as it drifts back under the tree canopies. Flat groundcovers of evergreen comfrey, ivy, vinca, ajugas or exotic acid-soil pachysandra from Japan, invasive petasites, or even woody plants such as *Cotoneaster dammeri* are all possibilities. These need less upkeep, look quite natural, and can be mown into to make a crisp edge with the grass. In sun or half shade *Geranium macrorrhizum* and St John's wort (*Hypericum calycinum*) can be massed for similar effects. Of course, none of these makes such an appealing surface as grass for walking or sitting on. In appropriately damp and humid situations of very deep shade, such as that under conifers, a brilliant alternative to lawn is to copy the Japanese and use green or grey mosses. In the American south coarser-leaved shade-tolerant ophiopogons and liriopes from Asia, which withstand alkaline soils and high temperatures, take the place of grass under shade trees, giving an almost natural look and needing much less water. Both need a sunny situation in England or in other climates with cooler summers.

THE MYTHICAL FLOWERY MEADOW

In *The Well-Tempered Garden*, published in 1970, Christopher Lloyd introduced the reader to 'Wild Gardening in Grass' – what is today most frequently called Meadow Gardening. 'One of my favourite branches of gardening, in rough grass, has the peculiar attraction that you can give it as much or little attention as you feel inclined. The only essential is to cut and pick up the grass two or three times a year.' Although plenty of literature has been written about the natural meadow – especially in the last decade or two – unless you are an expert like Miriam Rothschild or Christopher Lloyd, meadows are extraordinarily difficult to do well; and even experts do not attempt one unless they have appropriate terrain. Meadows may be of wild flowers or of wild flowers combined with exotics, plus carefully chosen grass species. A meadow, especially one made where there is fertile soil, all too easily becomes infested with mat-forming invasive grasses, which prevent flower seedlings from germinating; rich soil also encourages colonization by opportunists like nettles, thistles and creeping buttercups, which spread more quickly than the desirable plants, so that the whole effect becomes unacceptably unsightly. In the right conditions, where soil is relatively nutrient-poor, meadows can be established in the most simple way: just stop mowing and wait for the native flowers to seed in. Alternatively, the whole ground can be treated with weedkillers and rotavated; then plants put in and/or seeds sown. You may choose annuals only, sown in a matrix of grasses. Sometimes the best course of action is to scrape off the whole nutrient-rich turf layer with its roots and work with the poorer fresh soil below.

The meadow at Great Dixter, which is on heavy soil, was made from existing grassland. Christopher Lloyd advises beginning by mowing very tightly for at least a season, always removing the mowings. After that plants that may appear spontaneously can include three species of buttercups (*Ranunculus bulbosus*, *R. repens*, *R. acris*), red clover, hawksbeards (forms of *Hieracium*) and ox-eye daisies (*Leucanthemum vulgare*). Earlier in the season there are celandines, dandelions and lady's smock (*Cardamine pratensis*), the latter for the damper places. Bulbs, which once established should self-seed and colonize, include crocuses, muscari, scillas, narcissus species such as *Narcissus pseudonarcissus*, snakeshead fritillaries, Apennine anemones and camassias. The small species *Tulipa sylvestris* and Spanish bluebells succeed in grass in light shade.

Tulips, grown in pots the previous year, peonies and oriental poppies can be added.

At Dixter the meadow seasons start early, in January, with snowdrops and crocuses, then narcissus, then early purple orchids (*Orchis mascula*), camassias and *Fritillaria meleagris*. Moon daisies and *Dactylorhiza maculata*, the heath spotted orchid, flower in July. The meadow at Great Dixter has three annual cuts: the first in July after the early flowering bulbs and other flowers and orchids have seeded, the second at the end of August just before colchicums start flowering, and the last late in the year, before daffodil tips have started to appear.

(Opposite) At Great Dixter, Christopher Lloyd's garden in East Sussex, orchids such as the early purple, *Orchis mascula*, grow in the rough grass with an assembly of other plants such as camassias and snakeshead fritillary (*Fritillaria meleagris*). Earlier, snowdrops and crocus start the season, followed by narcissus. Later flowers include the heath spotted orchid (*Dactylorhiza maculata*) and moon daisies. After the spotted orchid has seeded, the meadow, by now shaggy with long arching grass seedheads, is cut and cleared of mowings. Meadow gardening provides an attractive alternative to the labour-intensive lawn, requiring no use of fertilizers or pesticides, so much more ecologically friendly. Wild flowers or even exotics planted in long grass do best if the soil is poor, encouraging less competition from grasses, nettles and thistles.

(Above right) In May quamash, different camassias, are in flower in the flowering lawns in front of the house at Great Dixter. Now so full of flowering plants, performing from early in the season with snowdrops, crocus and narcissus, a colourful tapestry set in the grass, it is almost impossible to add any more without damage to those existing; instead many plants gradually increase by enlarging their clumps or by seeding. March and April-flowering native narcissus (*Narcissus pseudonarcissus*, raised from seed by Christopher Lloyd's mother) are followed by *Camassia cusickii* from north-east Oregon, with flowers varying between pale and darker blues. The grass is first cut in July when camassia seed is ripe, and grass cuttings are removed to prevent the soil fertility from being increased as they rot down.

(Bottom left) Perennial oriental poppies (*Papaver orientalis*), which bloom in early summer, can be planted in rough grass rather than in conventional borders, where their unsightly fading leaves need disguising with later flowerers. In a meadow strong-rooting perennials such as oriental poppies and peonies can compete with mat-forming

grasses, which may prevent seeds from other plants, such as the annual field poppy (*Papaver rhoeas*) and ox-eye daisy (*Leucanthemum vulgare*) from germinating for regeneration. Tulips also naturalize in grass, especially the late-flowering Darwins, although each successive season their flowerheads will become smaller.

(Bottom right) By the Lutyens steps which lead down to the lower meadow the little daisy, *Erigeron karvinskianus*, a prolific seeder in stone cracks and walls, curtains the low wall with its delicate pinkish-white yellow-centred daisy flowers and charmingly natural habit. Ox-eye daisy joins the erigeron, having seeded from the meadow below.

In natural gardening self-seeding is encouraged, demonstrating that the plant is happy *in situ*. Careful and skilful editing of germinating seedlings each spring keeps them in the required locations, just as restraining and augmenting perennials in other parts of a wild garden is necessary to keep the final picture aesthetically and ecologically in balance.

At Holker Hall in Cumbria, with views to the hills of the Lake District, the meadow of ox-eye daisies and yellow *Chrysanthemum coronarium* has annual Flanders poppies (*Papaver rhoeas*) and purple cornflowers and corncockles as spots of pointillist colour among the flowers and grasses. In a wild-flower planting certain species usually come to predominate, while others, such as the ox-eye daisy, flower well for a few years and then, unable to regenerate by seed because the grass has become too matted with roots, begin to fade out. In natural circumstances such as the wild-flower meadows of Switzerland or the mountains of South Africa the native flora do not flower every year. Wild-flower performance can depend on the weather cycle, some plants needing more sun to set seed and others needing moisture at specific times in their growth pattern.

The Flowering Meadow

While there is much to be said for close-cut grass as a setting or 'frame' for other garden features, grass cut at different times and at different heights can have its own attractive textural variety. The more naturalistic approach is to make meadow flowerbeds of the grassy areas where there is no need to tread. Mown grass can be kept where it has a functional and directional purpose, providing paths and linking areas of the garden, or where it forms a real design feature, with narrow paths opening out to wider spaces and narrowing again, and surrounded by longer grass with flowers. Grass can be a combination of manicured lawn with some rougher areas of simple meadow, not cut until well into June, in which spring daffodils, fritillaries, ornithogalum and other bulbs grow; the coarser surface for the rest of the season makes a welcome contrast to the mown smoothness.

For any plantings in full sun there is a limitless palette of soft-stemmed plants, which can extend the meadow effects right through the summer season – bulbs, perennials (including tall-growing grasses), biennials and annuals – and a number of different stylistic ways in which they can be associated in these new kinds of 'flowerbed'. These meadows can be on the flat and just part of a much wider lawn, or on steep slopes and banks that are difficult to access regularly with mowers. A matrix of turf grasses is interplanted with a mixture of suitable hardy soft-stemmed flowering plants and clump-forming grasses. There are different sorts of meadow and different ways of managing them, but all meadows are essentially a form of grassland and need at least six hours of sunshine a day to achieve the ideal of a natural confusion of flowers and waving grasses, recalling the paradise gardens of Islam and making pictures of pointillist colour.

These meadows can be on any scale – a small pocket of grass and flowers, or waving fields surrounding orchard trees that cast little shade. They are only 'managed' at certain times of the year, but mown grass paths cut as

swathes through them and surrounding them give contrast and definition and demonstrate that the meadow is part of an overall garden design scheme and not just part of a natural development. Unlike a traditional herbaceous border, in which plants are kept in their allotted place by the gardener, there is nothing static about a meadow. Native or introduced flowers become established, last a few seasons and disappear. Many seeders, such as ox-eye daisy (*Leucanthemum vulgare*) and wild carrot (*Daucus carota*), may thrive at first and then disappear, depending on seasonal weather variations and the density of the ground vegetation, which may prevent germination. A meadow, as opposed to a conventional border, is in a constant state of flux as plant communities thicken up or fade away. The most successful meadows are those in which plant combinations resemble as closely as possible their communities in nature; even so, alien grasses and weeds from neighbouring land will always attempt to seed in, altering relationships, influencing future development and calling for the gardener to be vigilant.

Robinson continually stressed the importance of knowing the nature of the soil and other circumstances before embarking on any sort of natural gardening. Fertile nitrogen-rich soils favour vigorous competitive plants (some of them undesirable weeds) and meadow grasses. Slow-growing stress-tolerant plants flourish in problem places (including shade), where the climate may be harsh and the soil poor and dry. Some plants, known by ecologists as disturbance tolerators, move in as soon as there is any bare soil. They may germinate from seed already present (field poppies and mulleins in open ground, foxgloves and epilobiums in shady areas), blown in or brought by birds. As usual other factors besides soil need to be considered in selecting plants for a particular environment; the altitude and latitude and general aspect of the garden will all influence the choice of plants that will coexist well together, more or less maintaining their relative group sizes without swamping each other. The creation of plant communities in garden

circumstances is an artificial version of natural eco-systems but in meadow gardening the gardener must expect to stand back – after allowing a period of weeding and general establishment – and allow the scheme to evolve, not only to give a natural look, but also so that plants in groups or singly thrive in a natural way because they have the situation that suits them.

These open flowerbeds can simply be grass with flowers in them, true meadows on poor soil with a mix of suitable grasses and perennials, or, as often seen in North America, late-flowering prairie-type meadows made in rich fertile soil in which robust perennials and grasses, both native and foreign, with deep roots searching for moisture, can be grown. The true prairie meadow will consist of plants only from the American Midwest, in which many of the plants suitable for an ornamental garden have golden flowers, buff stems and black seed-heads evoking the colours and atmosphere of the late season. Other sorts of meadow can be established in bogs and marshy ground where large-leaved moisture-loving plants from naturally wet habitats (many from the Far East introduced to Europe towards the end of the nineteenth century) will fight it out with invasive weeds and grasses. All these different schemes can, up to a point, be managed for different seasonal performances, but all need some skilled gardening input – a lot during the first years, but less in the succeeding years if preparation and plant choices have been right for the aspect.

Maintenance includes planning a suitable mowing regime – infrequent, but judiciously timed. Mowing must be done at least once a year, at the end of the season if not before. In some schemes mowing can take place after the leaves of early flowerers have died down and seed has set. In late-flowering schemes the meadow may advantageously be cut in early spring, the grasses 'topped' to delay their seeding while late-flowering perennials have hardly begun to grow. A midsummer cut will substantially delay, but permit, flowering of some later perennials (and bulbs such as autumn crocus, colchicum and sternbergias). If properly planned and appropriately planted, working with nature rather than in defiance of it, these meadows, although difficult to establish, should in the long term be low in maintenance. As well as in garden areas where close-mown lawns are not necessary, meadow effects can be created in waste areas and on roadsides.

Meadows *can* sometimes be established simply by stopping mowing existing grass and allowing natural flora to develop unaided, with or without the addition of suitably chosen other hardy plants. A potassium- and phosphate-rich fertilizer will encourage flowering, but no nitrates should be added. Much of the success of this will depend on soil conditions and type. It will work best and be easiest to maintain if the soil is already starved of nitrogen. In Britain the limited native flora (after the last Ice Age the English Channel provided a barrier for plants) makes wild-flower meadows, although in vogue for other ecological reasons and for the promotion of wildlife, rather dull. Many of the most interesting British native flora thrive on the chalk or limestone downs, grazed by sheep and rabbits, where soil is thin and alkaline. In these sorts of conditions – where the soil is dry in summer and where grasses are not too competitive – native bulbs and flowers, augmented by some suitable introduced species (probably most successfully brought in as plugs or plants, available today for different soil types and conditions, rather than as seeds), will soon make a colourful display. Exotics include those that flower early in their own habitats, where summers are hot. Asphodeline (and asphodels if drainage is good enough) and Byzantine gladiolus from Greece, alliums, carline thistles, catmints, centhranthus, the more drought-tolerant meadow cranesbills such as *Geranium sanguineum*, *Linum perenne*, muscari, *Narcissus poeticus*, *Prunella vulgaris*, pulsatilla and meadow clary (*Salvia pratensis*). If the meadow is not cut until the end of the season some later-flowerers can be added such as *Aster amellus*, chicory (*Cichorium intybus*), knautia, scabious, *Sedum telephium*, and selected mulleins, as well as attractive

grasses. Arching feather grass (*Stipa gigantea*), *Achnatherum calamagrostis* with fluffy flowerheads and the invasive blue-leaved *Elymus arenarius* (now *Leymus arenarius*) all grow in poor, well-drained alkaline soil. In England foliage plants such as acanthus (*Acanthus mollis* Latifolius Group) will still be decorative through the summer but go dormant under hot sun, as in their own Mediterranean habitat, until reviving as the weather cools. Delaying cutting the meadow until after the plants have set seed allows them to germinate *in situ* in the poorly covered soil, which they will not do in more closely knit fertile grassland.

In moist to moderately dry meadows there are other suitable, but less stress-tolerant, species: yarrow (*Achillea millefolium*), kidney vetch (*Anthyllis vulneraria*), clustered bellflowers (*Campanula glomerata*), knapweeds (*Centaurea*), ox-eye daisy, cowslips, polemonium, meadow clary (see above), salad burnet (*Sanguisorba minor*), red clover (*Trifolium pratense*) and meadow geranium (*Geranium pratense*). Conditions at

At Winterthur blue and white camassias grow in an open situation on the edge of the woodland garden. Camassias, bulbous perennials from damp fertile meadows in North America, spread by increasing their clumps and, if the terrain is suitable, by seeding. They are admirable plants for naturalizing in grass in the wild garden, but produce the richest spikes if in well-cultivated soil in sun or part shade. They do not thrive in water-logged soil. The bulbs of *Camassia quamash* were once used as a food source by American natives.

the opposite extreme – rich, heavy clay with vigorously competitive turf grasses spreading sideways (the worst is probably perennial ryegrass) – are more difficult to keep going. The grasses and weeds will compete with the desirable plants. Relatively few flowers will already be growing in the grass and those added will soon be threatened; grasses will ultimately dominate as germination of flower seedlings is almost impossible. Along with other more acceptable flowers such as buttercups, celandines and dandelions, competitive nettles, thistles, docks and couch grass will quickly take over once mowing ceases. Best results will come from having two distinct periods of flowering in two locations, one for early summer flowerers, after which the meadow is cut, and the other for late-summer and early-autumn flowerers, which can be topped in early spring. In Christopher Lloyd's lower meadow at Great Dixter, in moist soil, dandelions and hawkweeds are among the flower 'crop' in May. Plants that are naturally thuggish and able to compete, such as many of the plants from moist habitats and American prairies, can be planted straight into grass. This is best done in August or September after the grass has been cut short to give them a chance to establish their roots before cold weather. Early-flowering aquilegias, lady's mantle, spreading yellow-flowered *Thermopsis montana*, ox-eye daisy, meadow cranesbill and many other of the hardy geraniums, herbaceous peonies and oriental poppies should all be planted in autumn. Bulbs such as robust narcissi and camassias are a welcome addition for spring and early summer. All these will enjoy their environment if the meadow is mown after the plants have flowered and seeded, probably in July, although if native heath spotted orchid (*Dactylorhiza maculata*) and bee orchid (*Ophrys apifera*) are included, the first cut should be later, sometime in August. Flowers for a late-summer performance towards the end of July include campanulas such as *Campanula lactiflora* and *C. rapunculoides*, day-lilies, autumn meadow performers such as persicarias (*Persicaria polystachya* and *P. amplexicaulis*) and macleaya, as well as

some of the really vigorous miscanthus grasses, and some American prairie plants, which will grow tall and flower in September. These prairie plants are accustomed to growing with all sorts of grasses, including tussock grasses and turf spreaders. Flowers from the prairies for the rich meadow include a selection of tall composites: asters, eupatoriums (*Eupatorium purpureum*), helianthus and vernonias. An early-spring cut, timed to take place before leaves of most of these plants appear, can prevent seeding of some of the competitive grasses and in general weaken their capacity to spread.

In these richer soils (and especially if the grass is already filled with undesirables), establishing a long-lasting meadow will be more successful if it is tackled much more radically and scientifically. It may be helpful to reduce fertility by stripping off all the topsoil and starting from scratch, planting suitable grasses and plants straight into the undisturbed subsoil. By doing this growth rates, plant habits and flower colours can be carefully assessed. Most of the worst weed seedlings will have been removed in the topsoil, and the subsoil may turn out to be a natural seed-bank of desirable Flanders red poppy (*Papaver rhoeas*) and mulleins, which will germinate and flower in the succeeding seasons – eventually to die out as other plants get established, a common occurrence on new verges after road-making. Before stripping the ground, all the existing grasses and the deeper-rooting perennial weeds such as docks, creeping buttercup and ground-elder should be eradicated, if necessary by using a herbicide. Using this method means that seeds from colourful annuals (as proposed for annual meadows on page 132), which will flower in the first season, can be scattered in around the new plants. They will help to keep down the germinating weeds during the first year, as well as improving effects while slower-maturing perennials and grasses reach full size. Even on quite heavy clay soils Californian poppies, red-flowered *Linum grandiflorum* and marigolds will flower and seed and flower again before dying

At Doe Run in Pennsylvania, Flanders red poppies (*Papaver rhoeas*) are annuals at the edge of the meadow garden. Seeds of these poppies often lie in soil for many years, only germinating and flowering when the ground is disturbed. They are often seen by the sides of new roads, a fertile site for other plants of botanical interest. Annual meadows are rotavated and resown each year, using annual grasses amid the flowering plants.

out. To these might be added varieties of love-in-the-mist (*Nigella damascena* and the more beautiful darker blue *N. hispanica*). In gardens with hotter summers than Britain calliopsis (*Coreopsis tinctoria*), butterfly weed (*Asclepias tuberosa*) and gomphrenas, which seldom perform in more temperate climates, will also thrive and flower. Where the soil is waterlogged clay, it will benefit from drainage, and by adding gypsum, a clay-breaker and soil conditioner, the range of plants that will tolerate the site can be extended.

If the soil is naturally infertile, no topsoil needs to be removed. After the herbicide is used, plants can be planted straight into the matted turf, without disturbing or digging, although just skimming off the top layer where the grass is dead will make planting much easier and reduce fertility a little more. Rotavating the topsoil only exposes a seed bank of perennial and annual weeds, which will germinate in spring and may have to be poisoned or hoed off before it is safe to add the more desirable meadow flowers.

PRESERVING THE PRAIRIE AND ITS PLANTS

(Left) Given similar conditions to their own specific habitats, many prairie wild flowers make excellent garden plants, needing infrequent watering and little fertilizing if given the deep, moist, slightly alkaline soil found in their own regions, and an open sunny situation. Tallgrass prairies are most suitable for 'copying' in a garden but vary depending on site. The dominant tall grasses include bunch grasses such as the bluestems and the tuft Indian grass (*Sorghastrum nutans*). Indian grass (*S. avenaceum*) reaches well over 7ft/210cm in its native habitat. Often mixing with other grasses such as big bluestem (*Andropogon gerardii*), it is common in mesic prairies that remain moist through most of the season as well as in dry prairies, pastures and open savannahs. Here it grows with golden rod, in one of the man-made prairies at the Chicago Botanic Garden.

Today there is almost nothing left of the original tallgrass prairie, known as true prairie, where it once stretched from southern Manitoba in Canada to northern Texas, and westwards from the Appalachians to the Rockies with periodic fires, grazing and drought keeping the forests at bay. Millions of acres have been converted to agriculture, much more intensive stock-grazing or development. Any remaining grassland is threatened by fire-suppression, altered water-cycles, or other forms of human intervention (including introduced plant species). Given enough moisture woody plants, seeding from nearby forests to east or west and from wooded valleys, will rapidly invade unless continuously deterred.

The tall grasses, a mixture of turf- and clump-forming species, with the latter tall enough by July to conceal a man on horseback, have deep questing roots, which help them survive the hot suns and evaporating winds. Between the clump-forming grasses native prairie flowers, low-growing early flowerers as well as those for late summer, of great beauty and value for ornamental gardening, spread and bloom. Adaptation to low rainfall, much sunshine and low temperatures in winter makes them hardy in gardens in most regions of the world. Variations in rainfall, climate, soil and terrain throughout the great grasslands produce an infinite spectrum of conditions in which different combinations (subtly changing over the years) of plant communities will thrive. All perennials need growing conditions which ensure that as well as flowering and producing seed to ensure survival, they also develop their strong roots and the underground buds that produce the following year's growth. Some prairie flowers bloom and produce seed early (the black seeds of blue indigo, *Baptisia australis*, are especially attractive in late summer). Others flower early and spend the season of greatest heat and drought in dormancy. Yet others such as the many composites – golden rod, coneflowers (*Echinacea purpurea*: *E. pallida* flowers earlier), prairie coneflower (*Ratibidia columnifera*), gaillardia species and black-eyed Susan (*Rudbeckia hirta*) – flower in the heat of summer and adapt well to gardens exposed to hot sun and almost drought conditions.

The mesic prairies provide the most showy garden flowers, usually in a ratio of about 60 per cent grass to 40 per cent flowers, with the latter needing the grasses for support as well as to look natural. Over the years the ratio of grasses may well increase. Among the flowers

(Top left) Grasses and sedges are the most common plants in tallgrass prairies, but plant associations are localized depending on growing conditions, particularly moisture levels. Here little bluestem (*Schizachyrium scoparium*) combines with *Solidago speciosa* at the Chicago Botanic Garden.

(Left) In an autumnal view of the prairie demonstration area at the Chicago Botanic Garden prairie flowers and grasses have a more garden appearance. Asters, golden rods and grasses, separated by wide swathes of mown grass paths, grow as they would in a garden flowerbed. In most prairie 're-creations' the gardener is dealing with a defined garden space rather than the almost limitless plains which originally stretched to the horizon and, in most cases, a wider variety of different plants and grasses are used than would have been found in a small area in natural conditions.

(Above) In Neil Diboll's seed nursery for prairie flowers in Wisconsin, coneflowers (*Echinacea purpurea*) and golden rod make an impressive appearance. Today ecologists and gardeners are deeply interested in re-establishing prairies with their original flora, following the teaching of Jens Jensen, the first environmentalist to worry about their disappearance under the plough. Gardeners find that, even on quite a small scale, wild-flower meadows based on prairie plants give immense satisfaction and although 'aliens' (woody plants and soft-stemmed grasses) have to be weeded out constantly, the extra effort brings its rewards.

most suitable for garden cultivation are butterfly weed (*Asclepias tuberosa*), queen of the prairie (*Filipendula rubra*), blue and white wild indigo (*Baptisia australis* and *B. alba*), purple poppy mallow (*Callirhoe involucrata*), Joe Pye weed (*Eupatorium maculatum*), indigo bush (*Amorpha fruticosa*) and lead plant (*A. canescens*), prairie blazing star and marsh blazing star (*Liatris pycnostachya* and *L. spicata*), showy evening primrose (*Oenothera speciosa*), as well as various helianthus and other composites mentioned above.

Fortunately prairies still survive in a few nature reserves. By the start of the twentieth century the 'vanishing' prairie already had a strong advocate in the designer Jens Jensen, who encouraged the restoration of prairie landscapes with their original native flowers. He made people in the Midwest aware of how quickly a whole environment was disappearing under the plough or for city development. The first of the tallgrass prairies to be re-established was at Madison, Wisconsin, in 1934.

In adequately prepared soil perennial meadows can be established by seed. Suitable mixtures of wild and/or exotic flowers and the less invasive grasses are sown in autumn or spring. These can be obtained for each different soil type: chalk grassland, alkaline soil (pH above 7), acid soil (pH 4–5.5), sandy coastal sites, heavy clay soils and fertile loams, as well as especially prepared mixes for emphasis on wildlife, butterflies, etc. On the whole seed-grown meadows are difficult to establish and often disappointing in their result, with alien grasses and other weeds competing too successfully with the wanted plants.

Annual Meadows

In many ways, if you can afford the annual expense and effort of raking or rotavating and buying in seeds (although after the first year many can be collected or will fall to the ground and germinate), a meadow composed only of annuals is one of the easiest to make. It can also be among the most beautifully romantic, although it is less truly 'natural' than the schemes mentioned above. It is man turning nature into art, and the annual meadow, spangled with bright flowers set in a matrix background of green grass, is the ideal of nature's possibilities, although probably little to do with ecological conceptions involving 'socially thriving' plant communities. Annuals are often treated as second-class plants; perhaps their willingness to flower and reproduce themselves all in one summer season leads gardeners to suppose they will tolerate anything, but almost all are sun-lovers and need light and space, even among their neighbours, to develop properly. William Robinson's teaching is recognized as mainly concerned with hardy plants that look after themselves, but he devoted plenty of thought to growing annuals and biennials. Both he and Gertrude Jekyll were against their being used in the expensive and monotonous bedding-out system current in the second half of the nineteenth century, but not against annuals themselves; they appreciated their qualities keenly, often associating them in combinations with other plants to enrich their border schemes.

Annual meadows in which grasses are dispensed with altogether consist of a tapestry mixture of flowers alone, with their leaves providing the woven green background. In an article in *The Garden* in July 1996 Brita von Schoenaich suggests adding to a mix of annual flowers some annual grasses such as American foxtail barley (*Hordeum jubatum*) and oriental fountain grass (*Pennisetum orientale*), or a perennial fountain grass (*P. setaceum*) – suitable for heavy clay or in cracks between rocks – which can be treated like an annual. These would add that elusive wispy quality so desirable in a wild-flower meadow and 'introduce a natural rhythm to the planting'. Quaking grass (*Briza maxima*) will reappear year after year from self-sown seedlings. Seeds for the annual meadow are easily available either as a 'put-together' mix suitable for different types of soil or as separate seed packets, which can be combined for desired effects in suitable soil; and, of course, exotic flower seeds can be added. A cornfield mix without grass to be sown directly into soil can contain buttercups, campion, centaury, chamomile, charlock, corncockle (*Agrostemma githago*), cornflower, fumitory, forget-me-not, field marigold, pansy, poppies, pimpernel, lesser snapdragon, yellow corn marigold and vetch, the old-fashioned cornfield 'weeds'. Other bought or home-made annual mixes can include exotics such as different love-in-the-mists (*Nigella damascena* and *N. hispanica*), meadow clary (*Salvia pratense*) – which with *Lychnis coronaria* will flower in the first year, *Limnanthes douglasii* and Greek cerinthes.

For the enthusiastic plantsperson more exciting possibilities exist for making mixed annual beds in a meadow style for a semi-natural situation using mainly exotic annuals, some of which can be sown directly into the ground in spring, while others are grown each year under glass from seed or cuttings. Those sown directly into soil will not be flowering until July. It is even possible to add tender perennials, grown as annuals, and biennials (grown from seed the previous year) that will flower in the current season. To maintain the meadow effects the flowers should not have large tropical-looking leaves but be combinations of indigenous flora and 'wild-looking' exotics such as blue salvias from North and South America (*Salvia patens, S.* 'Indigo Spires, *S. pratense, S. farinacea* 'Victoria'). *Verbena bonariensis* and biennial *Salvia sclarea turkestanica*, combine with white- and yellow-flowered nicotiana species, small-flowered *Zinnia angustifoli*a and short-lived perennials such as *Gaura lindheimeri* and spiky-leaved sisyrinchiums, seed *in situ* and will come up to flower the following year in raked ground. Without grass, but with additional seed each year, this 'meadow' will keep going for many years if undesirable grasses and other weeds are removed in autumn, when it can be raked or rotavated. It is equally possible to make your own mix and many serious gardeners will do this, adjusting the proportions of different flowers to suit their taste, but also to suit the expected spread of each flower.

The great advantage of annuals over perennials is the speed of their maturing. Depending on varieties they can be sown in autumn or in spring, and they peak in the summer. With such a short time to grow and flower they are especially floriferous, making as many flowers as possible in order to ensure seeding and reproduction. Most annuals prefer a soil pH close to neutral (about 6.4) and they do best if given a moisture-retentive humus. Clay soils need the addition of grit and sand to make them 'workable'; sandy, quick-draining soils need more organic mulch to make humus, and rich feeding in order to achieve so much in such a short time. Fertilizers should be strong in phosphorus and potassium and relatively low in nitrogen. As soon as the annuals are combined with either grasses or perennials and biennials (which makes annual preparation by rotavating or digging impossible), the annuals will die out as the grasses and other flowers start to cover the ground completely, preventing seed germination. The only problem with the annual meadow remains its bareness in winter. In natural habitats, especially the dry ones with poor thin soil, the native flora includes annuals among the richness of its more permanent plant population, which give natural cover through the cold months.

Groundcover and Xeriscapes

Turning the lawn into meadow is not the only alternative. Where summers are dry, attractive lawn substitutes include low-growing creeping plants. Although not to be sat upon or walked on in quite the same way, low-growing spreaders such as thyme and creeping mint planted in between paving stones laid in sand or directly into gravel will make a fragrant carpet, remaining green or grey-green throughout most of the year and not requiring water or feeding. In fact just the reverse: the plants are provided with just the sort of natural situation they enjoy, and will grow in a very natural way. Apart from some hand-weeding between them, there is nothing for the gardener to do. These paved gardens can be interplanted with self-seeding rock roses, New Zealand acaenas, daisy-flowered *Erigeron karvinskianus*, creeping campanulas, the self-renewing annual seeder *Persicaria capitata*, as well as the flatter thymes and mints. This sort of planting is the English equivalent of the more vital North American xeriscape.

In climates with very hot summers, water conservationists encourage xeriscape gardening, using natives and any drought-tolerant plants to create alternative – although not always green – vegetation. Most of the truly drought-tolerant plants have silver or grey leaves and twisted stems and leaves, which resist the sun's hottest rays. Lawn alternatives such as camomile or thyme used in European gardens since medieval times do not take constant wear, but in warm climates dichondras and cotulas spread luxuriantly in open situations. Cotulas are used for bowling greens in New Zealand. In deserts and very hot climates where lawn grass will not grow it is replaced by small creeping evergreen bushes, their leaves and stems specially adapted to sun-scorch, while succulents (forms of *Lampranthus*), originally from

South Africa, grow in drifts in frost-free coastal areas, colonizing when the habitat suits.

The xeriscape approach developed in North America creates 'no-water' garden landscapes, in which, by planting only totally drought- and sun-resistant plant communities – and making sure any bare earth is mulched with gravel or some other similar product – scarce and expensive water is saved. In a normal year in coastal California the landscape is a lush green from December to May, drying to its golden brown from June through until the first rains. During the yearly natural 'drought' native plants go dormant and any 'greenness' from shrubs and lower-growing plants such as grass is entirely artificial and water-induced. Bermuda and Kikuyu grasses for lawns still need at least half an inch/a good ten millimetres of water each week from early spring until December. Natural xeriscape gardening means gardening with self-adapting plants that replicate the natural environment: regional natives, desert plants that store water naturally and equally drought-tolerant exotics from Mediterranean-type climates, which can all be combined to make an attractive, ecologically sound garden scene. At the Huntington Botanical Gardens in Pasadena a desert garden full of succulents, including agaves, aloes, aeoniums, echeverias, giant and miniature cacti and yuccas makes a living sculpture park of shapely blue-greens, greys and silver, all totally ecologically adapted to their site (see page 37).

Even in Britain drier summers and lower rainfall patterns have become a feature of the last decade, a symptom of climate change throughout the world. Saving water becomes a top priority even in this maritime climate and, in gardening, sprinklers on water-greedy lawns become an extravagance, using in an hour about the amount of water a family of four uses for all their domestic needs in two days, or the equivalent of washing forty-four cars. For gardeners a lawn that looks brown for much of the summer is hardly worth having. Paving and gravel are often advocated by designers, especially for small gardens, but plants other than grass

which actually enjoy drought conditions can be an exciting alternative. A wide range of bulbs, perennials and shrubs can be grown with no additional water beyond natural rainfall, either in paving or alternatively in specially created sites, which, with excellent drainage, have the surface of the soil covered with a mulch of gravel to prevent water evaporation.

There are 'in-between' methods of adapting the lawn area for drought conditions, which still allow an overall 'green' effect, but are neither lawn nor meadow. Low, densely growing perennials and dwarf shrubs can fulfil the visual functions of an ordinary lawn, even if this makes a carpet that cannot be walked upon in quite the same way. Plants selected as lawn substitutes must grow evenly and vigorously over a period. The selection of suitable plants and good drainage are essential. After planting, the ground can be mulched with gravel to conserve moisture during the few years it takes for plants to grow together to make the 'lawn' or lawn-substitute. The gravel also reflects heat and can be trodden without fear of compaction to the soil. Schemes of this sort are easiest to operate in poor soil. In half shade prostrate plants such as *Arabis procurrens*, creeping Jenny (*Lysimachia nummularia* or the golden form *L.n.* 'Aurea') and London pride (*Saxifraga urbium* 'Elliot') will make tight evergreen mats in moist or damp soil; in sunnier situations blue-flowered *Ceratostigma plumbaginoides* can be effectively massed and much larger plants such as dwarf bamboo (*Arundinaria pumila*) will be invasive. If the ground is well-drained, small creeping phlox (*Phlox subulata*), *Campanula poscharskyana* and acid-loving *Dryas octopetala* will make semi-evergreen carpets. As well as using creeping thymes and mints, selected drought-resistant tussock- and hummock-forming grasses, which need no regular mowing and look good most of the year, can provide the matrix. Forms – there are more than a dozen cultivars to choose from – of clumping evergreen blue fescue (*Festuca glauca*, syn. *F. cinerea*) have hair-like blue-green leaves, ranging in height from six to twelve inches/fifteen

In the Nancy Bryan Luce Herb Garden in the New York Botanical Garden medicinal and useful herbs grow in an outer perimeter border with a patterned box parterre in the centre of the area. The garden is open to the sun and wind, as most herbs, many of Mediterranean origin, require maximum light. Herbs grow best in infertile stony ground with adequate drainage, so need few fertilizers and little extra irrigation, even in the hot New York summers. Xeriscapes in hotter western regions of North America are often planted with Mediterranean plants, which retain their looks after flowering, while many natives become desiccated or go dormant.

135

GRAVEL AND GRASS IN 'CARELESS ORDER' AT DENMANS

John Brookes's walled garden is remarkable. Instead of treating it in a conventional way with straight-edged borders underneath the walls, central divisions and patterning, the garden has a much more informal air with large shrubs clothing the walls as well as occupying positions in the central gravelled area as if they were architectural features, like the Greek oil jar. Perennials, mainly self-seeding and self-perpetuating plants, grow under and around the main feature shrubs, giving a very natural air to the whole effect. Alchemilla, verbascum and *Allium christophii*, grow under box and purple berberis with spiky-leaved irises and roses, watched over by the graceful golden-leaved *Robinia pseudoacacia* 'Frisia'.

John Brookes's gardens at Denmans in West Sussex have a rare naturalistic quality. It is achieved by allowing flowing gravel paths to separate planted areas, instead of having conventional flowerbeds. You can almost believe that the planting came first, and that the opening out to areas of gravel or grass (the latter uncut lawns mixed with local flora and what John calls 'more gaudy foreign flowers') was done as an afterthought, to allow access and to provide the drama of open and closing views. Near the house the planting of trees and shrubs underpinned with groundcovering creates abstract rather than geometric patterns of shadow and sunlight, conjuring an air of mystery and anticipation. It can be called a 'careless ordered garden', a phrase used by Miriam Rothschild in her preface to his book *Planting the Country Way*. Indeed, it is hard to discover the 'correct' path to the house or into the garden: making your way is an exploration.

Many of the trees, shrubs and flowers are native, linking garden and countryside together in that rhythm which is essential to all

John's work. But exotics suitable to the terrain and not too foreign-looking have their place too, although at the fringes of the site natives become predominant, so that the garden becomes an expression of its natural surroundings. John's interest in choosing plants suitable to the site goes beyond simple awareness of soil pH and local climatic conditions. To achieve his sort of naturalism he needs to understand the different nuances his garden offers. He exploits existing microclimates, recognizing that every tree, bush or plant he puts in will create new microclimatic situations for neighbouring plants – some favourable and others not; and he also appreciates that these conditions will change as plants grow, their roots stealing water from those adjacent, and casting shade on plants previously in full or partial sunlight. Although as gardeners we work within fairly stringent climatic limitations, dictated by external factors such as altitude, weather, topography and soil, nevertheless the plants in our gardens – especially the larger trees and shrubs – are themselves dynamic and over a period will

radically alter the planting nuances of a garden environment. Trees can turn a hot, dry site into a cool and sheltered oasis, a haven for wildlife as well as a comfortable garden retreat. In choosing plants it is not necessary to make a strict dividing line between natives and exotics. Plants with similar requirements and a similar appearance will look good together even if they come from different parts of the world. Matching plants of broadly similar physiognomy into harmonious groupings may be as important in a rural setting in England as in a 'lunar' landscape such as that of the dry garden of succulents at Huntington in California.

(Above left) Herbs are dominant in the central part of the garden, with aromatic sages and lavenders spilling contentedly out over pavement and gravel with alliums, *Alchemilla mollis* and giant euphorbias, evergreen plants which keep the show going through the winter. Heat-loving plants and herbs from Mediterranean or Californian regions, all requiring relatively poor infertile soil and adequate drainage, associate well together.

(Left) Fennel (*Foeniculum vulgare*), the common cooking fennel, with its feathery leaves and readiness to seed, enjoys the same sort of site as the biennial evening primrose (*Oenothera biennis*), an equally prolific seeder. It and its bronze-leaved form *F.v.* 'Purpureum' are good garden plants. Both give an attractive informal air to the Denmans walled garden and can be weeded out when young if occurring too frequently. The aspect of each small microclimatic site in the garden is in a permanently changing mode, as plants come and go, competing for water, casting new shadows and, in general, giving the garden a dynamic feel.

(Above) Glimpses of the tall soaring verbascums, from open stony ground in the Mediterranean regions and central Asia, are a dominant theme in John's garden, redolent of summer heat, and creating a definite ambiance, as well as contributing the spiky architecture that provides dramatic contrast to more rounded forms of bushes. Although looking carelessly and randomly planted, verbascums, biennials or short-lived perennials, are often grown from seed and planted out before their taproots grow too long. Although natural gardening should seem spontaneous, in actual fact, the gardener ceaselessly manipulates nature's efforts to create desirable pictures and plant associations.

The planting in the beds on the west front of Gravetye Manor, restored and replanted by Peter Herbert over the last thirty years, but following Robinson's lead through his writings and descriptions of the Gravetye garden, demonstrates how natural Robinson's border styles were. Lady's mantle, silver-leaved *Stachys byzantina* and black-leaved *Ophiopogon planiscapus* 'Nigrescens' edge the bed with gentle sweeps, while taller *Cephalaria gigantea*, roses, grey artichokes and a dramatic planting of *Eremurus robustus* give height and interest. Both Robinson and Gertrude Jekyll knew their plants intimately and liked to place them where they would thrive, in association with appropriate neighbours.

to thirty centimetres, to plant in groups. It and bearskin (*Festuca scoparia*, syn. *F. gautieri*), a hummock grass with prickly bright green foliage spreading to make tight mats, thrive in well-drained soil in full sun (or in half-shade in a hot climate). These grasses, planted in sweeps, can be intermixed with drifts of another drought-resistant poor-soil lover such as ordinary sea-thrift (forms of *Armeria maritima*), luxuriating in full sun. An article in *The Garden* in 1995 showed how with careful consideration of growth rates and plant habits these plants grew together to give substantially the effect of lawn within a couple of years. This sort of scheme needs cutting with a strimmer once or twice in the season. If the 'green' effect is not all-important, other plants could be added: some of the acaenas (*Acaena buchananii* and *A. microphylla*) from New Zealand, with grey-green or brownish leaflets respectively, are striking in the winter and able to spread under taller plants and grasses, and grey-leaved ground-huggers such as *Stachys byzantina* 'Silver Carpet' and sedums make abstract flowing patterns.

There are variations on both the water-saving gravel garden idea and the meadow garden, which depart more radically from a lawn atmosphere, with taller plants including drought-tolerant shrubs from appropriate habitats. Once the effect is no longer that of an open space you can see (and walk) across like a lawn, we begin to treat its planting more like that of a border.

The Naturalistic Traditional Border

The twice-yearly bedding-out practices of the Victorian era were the object of William Robinson's criticism when he advocated that 'The true way to make gardens yield a return of beauty for the labour and skill given them is the permanent one. Choose some beautiful class of plants and select a place for them that will suit them, even as to their effect in the garden landscape. Let the beds be planted as permanently and as well as possible, so that there will remain little to do for years.'

Robinson's journal *The Garden*, founded in 1871, aimed at discouraging bedding out in favour of growing hardy herbaceous plants. His advice perfectly expresses the more modern ecological approach in which plants are selected for their appropriateness for the site rather than merely for their appearance and flowering time. In promoting the hardy herbaceous border Robinson was a disciple of the writer Shirley Hibberd, who had been preaching the same doctrine since the 1860s and in the *Amateur's Flower Garden* in 1871 published his own recommendations: 'The bedding system is an embellishment added to the garden; the herbaceous border is a necessary fundamental feature.'

The English temperate climate, with ample moisture and mild seasons, provided the perfect growing conditions for the multitude of herbaceous perennials available to Robinson and Gertrude Jekyll in the last years of the nineteenth century. It is no wonder that the traditional border has evolved in a peculiarly English way, and the English perennial border has become the epitome of how foreigners view the 'English Garden'. The herbaceous border was not the invention of Robinson and Jekyll – it had existed in one form or another for more than a century, and began to gather momentum in the mid-nineteenth century, when borders became elements of the larger ornamental garden, rather than being confined to beds for cutting flowers in the walled kitchen garden. As early as the 1840s ornamental double borders had been incorporated in an overall garden design at Arley Hall in Cheshire. In 1864 Shirley Hibberd, pressing for the return of hardy plants, wrote: 'Prohibit … using bedding plants, and forthwith … begin to restore to the neglected borders the noble clumps of fragrant white lilies, the patches of Christmas rose, winter aconite, double daisy, polyanthus, primula, Solomon's seal, Indian pink, potentilla, and the thousand other interesting subjects, which make no blaze at any season, but are constantly presenting beautiful forms and cheerful colours.' But it was Robinson and Jekyll who brought the concept of the border into the foreground of fashion – he by promoting the border of hardy plants in his gardening journals and books, and she in her sophisticated colour borders, in which she used a mixture of plants to create special effects for a two-month period.

Today most borders of flowering perennials are forms of compromise between the highly artificial scheme in which plants are arranged in labour-intensive stiff blocks, lines or groups, with taller plants at the back carefully graded down to the smaller plants along the front edge – all planned for a two-month summer display – and the Robinsonian/Jekyllesque cottage-style idea of drifts of perennials (and often biennials, annuals and bulbs with the addition of some shrubs to give winter interest) interweaving to look 'natural'. These, while retaining a 'natural' cottage style, could be planned for a summer peak between early July and the end of September, or could give a much longer season of general interest, incorporating spring bulbs and early-flowering herbaceous plants such as aquilegias, peonies and oriental poppies, and extending into the early months of winter with aconitums, kniphofias, salvias, eupatoriums and vernonias.

In both types of border plants need staking, dead-heading and the removal of dying foliage through the season, with feeding, mulching and periodic division taking place in spring and/or autumn. But the amount of time spent on these routine tasks can be reduced from the outset if plants suitable for the soil and aspect are selected – plants that associate well with each other and require infrequent division. In the Robinsonian border, plants are encouraged to lean against and through each other and to spread and seed so that the border develops over the years, achieving a dynamic feeling of growth and change impossible in the more strictly controlled flowerbed, in which every plant has an allotted place and a definite performance expectation. On the other hand, careful editing and manipulation of plants to create natural-looking effects implies some considerable skill. The plants that naturally spread and

seed allow evolution and development, but must also be prevented from making any disruptive overall change in the purpose or aesthetics of the border. The designer and ecologist can work hand in hand.

A third type of perennial border can be even more naturalistic, with patterns of growth determined by the existing ecological conditions, which are interfered with as little as possible. The plants used are a mixture of native and almost 'wild' plants, perennials with a natural look, rather than highly bred modern varieties, which need elaborate maintenance and feeding. In this natural planting scheme, maintenance will be 'extensive' rather than intensive; manipulation by digging, dividing, cutting back and transplanting will be at an absolute minimum. These borders can be largely self-regulatory, although it will occasionally be necessary to protect slow-growing species from more aggressive neighbours.

However, there is another consideration. Although the labour required to look after the largely self-regulatory beds is less, the skill required to do so is much greater. The more natural gardener needs to combine a deep knowledge of plants and their requirements, as well as being able to make policy decisions about which plants to retain or remove. This is the antithesis of what people expect – or perhaps were led by their interpretation of the Robinsonian school to believe: that more natural gardening was simple and almost labour-free. To get the best effects in the Robinson/Jekyll-type border the gardener must have both skill and a keen aesthetic sense for fine-tuning the arrangements, although routine tasks can still be done by the relatively unskilled.

As gardens have become smaller, the 'mixed' cottage style has become more usual. Often one border, planned for an extended season of interest, is the only place in the garden for shrubs and flowers. Except in public parks or the occasional old kitchen garden, the grand old borders, magnificent in season but almost bare through the winter months, have mainly disappeared, and are replaced by tightly packed beds with special emphasis on foliage plants such as giant crambes,

In Dan Hinkley's garden at Heronswood west of Seattle – where he runs a successful nursery – he has made various naturalistic borders. These are raised to improve the drainage among the tall Douglas firs (*Pseudotsuga menziesii*). The tall tree trunks framing the colourful borders remind the gardener of how acid the soil is. The Seattle climate (Zones 7–8) is almost maritime, although with greater extremes of cold and heat than in the British Isles, dry hot summers from May to September and moist winters. All borders are mulched annually with well-rotted manure. Woody plants such as *Acer pseudoplatanus* 'Puget Pink' (raised from seed by Dan Hinkley) give form to the borders of dark red phlox, *Persicaria affinis* 'Superba', heleniums, *Salvia officinalis* Purpurascens Group, and bronze-leaved sedums.

Euphorbia wulfenii, hostas and macleayas, which provide interesting colour and texture out of the flowering season. Whichever type of border is chosen, the conventional approach has been to select plants for their height, colour and time of flowering rather than for their own requirements and suitability for the place. The ground is then prepared, and if necessary amended, to provide the plants with the soil texture and level of fertility required.

As in all garden planning, the success of a border mainly composed of perennials depends on many environmental factors and their combinations: soil type, condition and drainage, nutrients, climate and microclimate, light and shade, and the orientation of the bed, shelter and its topography. Many perennials fail because the plants selected are not suitable for the site. But for an ornamental border, rather than 'wild' planting, it is often possible to improve soil conditions radically to suit the selected plants, and by doing so eliminate excessive use of fertilizers and pesticides to keep the plants healthy. Heavy clay soils can be lightened with grit, sand and an organic compost, and drainage can be provided if the soil is waterlogged: sandy soils can be made more moisture-retentive with organic compost, mulched in summer and enriched with nutrients. Whether to choose native or exotic plants is best solved pragmatically. In the British Isles or even in northern and central Europe the conventional border would be dull if only truly native plants were used. In the United States a border of all-American perennials can be magnificent, although those most 'showy' and popular may well be those hybridized and 'improved' in Europe and sent back across the Atlantic to thrive in garden sites, approximately similar to their original habitats, instead of the original natives.

Most perennials can be assigned to a particular garden habitat depending on their native requirements, but some, once introduced to any sort of artificial garden condition, can change their needs. Faced with severe competition and marginal conditions in the wild, many

Nature's Colour Artistry in the Border

An exquisite colour border, planned for peaks of co-ordinated colour in the best Jekyll style, might seem the antithesis of naturalistic gardening. Yet, if plants have been chosen for their suitability to the site and for their suitability as neighbours, there is nothing against adding the extra colour dimension to the equation. Natural planting does not mean excluding artistry. In fact many of the flowers of good border plants follow a sequence of colour performance very close to that found in nature. In northern temperate regions blues and yellows predominate in spring, while the green of leaves is still young and fresh; pinks and purple are early summer colours, glowing against silver and glaucous foliage; and deep yellows, browns and oranges and crimsons, mainly found in the Compositae family, are associated with autumn both in the garden and in the landscape. Of course, the actual colour of flower petals and their elaborate markings, and their scent, are all related to the necessity of enticing pollinators to ensure seed fertilization and reproduction. Some insects hasten towards blue plants – with bees seeing 'blues' and 'violet' in a different spectrum from that perceived by humans; humming birds from the Americas pick out dazzling red flowers, night-flying moths seek out pale petals that glow in the dark. Some gardeners choose flowers for their attractiveness to bees and butterflies, showing a concern for the environment. In natural conditions plants flower when the natural pollinator is at hand, with petals and leaves often fading quickly as soon as pollination has taken place. (One of the reasons double-flowered cultivars are so popular in conventional borders is that their sterility makes them less transient.) Red and orange berries in the autumn ensure distribution by the birds to whom this part of the spectrum is conspicuous. Wind-pollinated flowers such as catkins and tall grass plumes have a more subtle colour allure to human taste, but one which, like the greens and greys of foliage, serves as a foil to brighter flower colours, linking garden plants to the surrounding colours of nature. Perceptions of beauty begin to alter as the mind and eye become more attuned to ecology – just as natural gardeners find delight in the browns and buffs of fading leaves and seedheads and in their stark, dramatic outlines, so also do they feel quite as strong a revulsion for a 'wrong' and unnatural plant association as for any more traditional colour clash in the border. Light intensity varies in different climates. In maritime regions such as Britain, humidity 'greys' the atmosphere and most native flower colours are muted, while brightly coloured exotics from hot countries appear garish. In very hot countries the pale 'good taste' English colours so often seen in borders can seem insipid in the bright light.

Natural colour gradations and markings in flower petals are due to the distribution of pigments, some of them soluble in cell sap, and their chemical interaction. The colour of flowers and leaves that we perceive also depends on surface texture, which reflects light differently depending on whether it is smooth and glossy, waxy, matt or velvet – all of which particular qualities often indicate from what sort of habitat a plant comes. Anthocyanins and anthoxanthins are the main flower pigments affecting reddish tints; they are influenced by soil acidity and alkalinity, flowers tending to become bluer in acid soil, redder in alkaline. Anthoxanthins produce a range of yellows, and white flowers seem white because of refraction in the plant tissue.

In colour borders natural colour harmonies are achieved by planting flowers with shared pigment colour in close association – yellows, reds, crimsons following in progression in different tones, tints and shades. Contrasts are more shocking to the eye, with complementary opposite colours making each other seem brighter: paired groups of bright blues and yellows, or deeper violet plus orange. In naturalistic schemes more emphasis is placed on the quality of the whole plant; its form, shape, habit and the beauty and texture of its leaves.

(Opposite) At Hidcote the silvery-leaved thistle-like Miss Willmott's ghost (*Eryngium giganteum*), a prolific biennial self-seeder, flowers between clumps of established red *Phlox paniculata*. The eryngium will grow and thrive in much poorer soils than phlox, which needs rich feeding, but, in conventional border situations, they thrive together. Miss Willmott's ghost looks particularly appropriate when allowed to seed in gravel. The leaf rosette is green at first and 'silvers' as the stem grows, but leaves quickly become dull as the flowers fade and set seed. Seed can be germinated in a greenhouse in autumn to encourage flowering in the next season.

(Above) Variegated Japanese silver grass (*Miscanthus sinensis* 'Variegatus') is a graceful clump-forming grass, flowering in hot sunny climates, late in the season. Here it provides a background to sedums, dark pink phlox, pink *Allium cernuum*, catmint (*Nepeta sibirica*) and lilies, with a large-flowered clematis clambering up a pole behind. This sort of unselfconscious border planting conveys colour themes without introducing dogmatic colour-associated plant choices, keeping the whole scheme in a natural mode. Purples, pinks and purplish-blues all have a shared blue pigment, which unites the planting.

(Top) At Tintinhull the colour schemes are self-consciously formal and attempts at naturalism come from encouraging self-seeding in the borders. The 'hot' border in the Pool Garden, designed by Phyllis Reiss in the late 1940s, has always had vibrant colours – red, scarlet, orange and yellow – sparked off to glow more brightly by accompanying silver and grey-foliaged plants. A large smoke bush (*Cotinus coggygria*), 'Frensham' roses, achilleas and golden tiger lilies (*Lilium lancifolium fortunei*), underplanted with *Brachyglottis* 'Sunshine', self-seeding *Alchemilla mollis* and coreopsis, create the desired Jekyllian effects.

(Above) In Peter Wooster's garden near Lichfield in Connecticut, teazels (*Dipsacus fullonum*) are encouraged to seed through the border, with the delicate *Thalictrum rochebruneanum* 'Lavender Mist', creamy regal lilies (*Lilium regale*), *Valeriana officinalis* with white seedheads, *Cephalaria gigantea*, and sanguisorba leaves – it will produce white flowers later – and pink *Lythrum virgatum* making a splash of vibrant colour in the foreground. In the Wooster garden colour schemes are so subtle that the eye takes them in almost without registering their message, avoiding the 'unnaturalness' of more formal colour schemes.

perennials perform and flower better in any sort of open site and in prepared soil. The garden aspect, including latitude and altitude, shade and sun, moisture or dry conditions, all affects how the plants grow. Some plants that occur naturally on wet ground do better in our gardens on soil that is only just moist and intermittently dry. (*Iris sibirica*, although coming from northern swamps, does not object to being dry in summer, as long as there is enough moisture in spring.) Others such as *Astrantia major* and martagon lilies, found wild on open mountain slopes, need shade in gardens in regions of lower altitude. Many perennials and bulbs that grow in full sun in the temperate British climate will thrive in shade in hot sunny countries. Acanthus, agapanthus, some asters, boltonias, clivias and *Eupatorium purpureum* require some hours of daily shade in continental summers. Growing perennials successfully in climates with very hot summers can necessitate some form of automatic irrigation. The gardener will also play a significant role in protecting plants against unseasonable cold spells or premature emergence in spring – one of the most frequent causes of loss in a temperate climate such as the British Isles.

The style of maintenance of a border will partly depend on the plants that have been selected. The more informal and 'wild' the plants are, the less need there is for constant manicuring and division, but in general, free-flowering border plants need an intensively maintained flowerbed with open, well-cultivated soil and a free root-run. This habitat will also change as small trees, shrubs and perennials themselves encroach on an area, introducing some shade and making the soil drier. In a densely planted flowering border perennials face intense competition from neighbouring plants and may need dividing within a few seasons, even before they mature to their full beauty.

There are enormous numbers of perennials suitable for the ornamental border from which to choose. Many are the result of many years' breeding: peonies, delphiniums and irises are among the showiest summer flowers.

Asters and eupatoriums from America, aconitums and campanulas from Europe will all respond to good garden conditions. They can be categorized into groups, according to their requirements of soil type, warmth and moisture. Those that require a well-maintained border with moist to damp nutrient-rich soil in light shade include plants of woodland origin. Japanese anemones, astilbes, aconitums, *Dicentra spectabilis*, hemerocallis and various lilies such as European Turk's-cap (*Lilium martagon*) and, in acid soil, *L. auratum*. Other good perennials originally from woodland-edge habitats also need a well-prepared bed, but one in a warm sunny place with a moist-to-dry soil in summer: crown imperials, peonies (both *Paeonia lactiflora* from China and European *P. officinalis* and *P. peregrina*, with tuberous roots containing reserves of nutrients and moisture, which allow survival during a long dry season), trumpet-flowered lilies such as *Lilium regale*, *L. henryi* and many hybrids. Many perennials will perform quite well, but differently, on soils unlike their own native habitat. Ideally peonies, pyrethrums, globe flowers and hepaticas need a heavy loam in order to succeed, while *Aster amellus* and gypsophila prefer a well-drained sandy soil. Rhizomatous perennials, such as macleaya and perovskia, need relatively little space on heavy ground, but spread rapidly in sandy soil. These are all facts familiar to the gardener. Plants originally from more open habitats include iris, lilies, poppies and sedums for warm sunny situations with dry soil. For damper (but well-drained) soil in a sunny situation there are *Aster amellus*, erigeron, heleniums, lupins, phlox, rudbeckias, scabious, solidago, and many North American perennials such as asters, *Baptisia australis*, *Boltonia asteroides*, *Coreopsis verticillata*, *Liatris spicata*, *Oenothera tetragona* and *Veronicastrum virginicum*.

The appearance of a border depends on groupings of plants. Just as a few small trees or shrubs create a framework for the border scheme, also some key plant groups give an architectural quality to the scheme and, by establishing a rhythm, unify the whole design. The look of

In another area of Dan Hinkley's garden sunny double borders are filled with plants such as the tall *Verbena bonariensis*, *Echinacea purpurea*, common fennel, heleniums, peach-coloured diascias, pink phlox, *Salvia sclarea* and red penstemons. *Clematis tangutica* grows on the pergola behind. The self-seeding verbenas give the whole scheme an informal relaxed air, and Dan encourages plants to spread to make their own patterns, as long as they do not overwhelm each other.

(Top left) On the perimeter of the garden verbascums (*Verbascum densiflorum* and *V. chaixii*) with mauve-flowered *Thalictrum rochebruneanum* 'Lavender Mist' and astilbe grow informally with soft waving grasses, panicum, calamagrostis and the annual self-seeding *Briza maxima*. Even if Ton ter Linden keeps his eye on colour combinations, the grasses add an informal spontaneous air to the whole scheme, and link the garden to the surrounding landscape, an important factor. His painting with plants reflects his love and knowledge of his own countryside, and he leaves flowerheads and seedheads to contribute beauty through the winter months, only cutting down soft-stemmed plants in March.

(Bottom left) In the garden at Ruinen rather than having separate garden colour areas, colour schemes fade into each other giving more natural effects, with shapes of plants and their foliage as important as flowers, which last such a short time. Here pastel colours combine with white roses and silvery leaves. Tall spiky perennials – *Verbascum chaixii*, *Veronicastrum virginicum* and *Sanguisorba canadensis* – dominate over more rounded sprawling plants such as *Anaphalis magaritacea* and *Artemisia ludoviciana*. The narrow grass path over which the plants tumble adds to the air of informality, giving the whole planting scheme a meadow-like feel.

(Opposite) The weeping pear (*Pyrus salicifolia* 'Pendula'), although pale with silvery grey leaves, provides solidity as a backdrop to some of the woven tapestry of plants in the borders. Quite weedy plants, usually found in the outer edges of the garden, combine informally to create a naturalistic atmosphere. Day-lilies (the early *Hemerocallis fulva*), which emerge with pale, almost golden, foliage in spring, red-flowered valerian (*Centranthus ruber*), which seeds between the other plants, and peonies weave together behind the invasive yellow loosestrife (*Lysimachia punctata*), with teazels and *Miscanthus sinensis* 'Gracillimus'.

PLANTING A PICTURE: A PAINTER COMPOSES HIS BORDERS

In Ruinen in the Drenthe region of northern Holland, the artist Ton ter Linden's garden combines an air of naturalism with his intense appreciation of colour nuances and compositions. His borders with many diverse colour schemes are not put together with solid blocks of plants graduated in height from tall at the back to smaller in the front, but have an unplanned, natural air, conveyed by intensifying feelings of depth and woven transparency: you look *through* plants and *beyond* them rather than *at* a bright colour block that attracts and holds the eye. Careful plant selection made possible by ter Linden's knowledge of plants, their behaviour and requirements, makes it possible to achieve a naturalistic look – although in fact his compositions are as carefully orchestrated for effect as his own paintings. His plans are never prepared on paper; spaces in the beds get filled as if he was doing freehand painting. His love of nature and of the countryside means that his flowerbed 'painting' reflects the landscape and changing seasons, both in shapes and colours. Rob Leopold has described how 'this approach of semi-spontaneous, semi-conscious composition ... leads to alternating patterns which astound us again and again – and which are different with each coming year.'

From an early age, sketching as a child, Ton ter Linden developed an interest in the form of plants and in the shapes and textures of leaves and flowers, as much as in their colours, and it is the strong structural qualities of the plants he chooses – as well as their suitability to his site – that help combine nature and art in his designs. Perennials with strong vertical stems – veronicastrums and *Veronica hastata* – contrast with more gentle, blurred forms of artemisias and catmints against a background of dark upright hedges and mown lawns. His borders, often on quite a small scale, are not just colour schemes but essays in much more subtle colour weavings and nuances, in which contrasting colours in shades and tints, linked by silvery foliage and toned down by swaying grasses, convey a distinct feeling of naturalism. This is enhanced by ter Linden's policy of encouraging seedlings, both of annuals and perennials, to volunteer to break any preconceived patterning. A natural garden has its own dynamic and spontaneously produces its own changes. Flower- and seedheads and buff foliage and stems of lasting artistic value are kept in the garden through the winter as they would be in nature. As a young man he became familiar with the nature gardens being developed at Amstelveen near Amsterdam

(see page 54), where he visited and painted pastels. He learnt there how wild flowers could be arranged artistically without losing the ecological balance of natural plant communities. His garden, over twenty-five years, has been developed from the house outwards. Each of his garden compartments is a picture in itself, but viewed from different angles assumes new subtleties of shape, colour and form, constantly changing through a season and in the following years. Unlike his paintings, which are finished with the last application of paint, the garden continues to provide anew a series of ever-changing 'pictures'.

New-style Borders in Europe Thrive on Extensive Maintenance

At Westpark in Munich a curving path is edged with pink and red groups of phlox (*Phlox paniculata*) and perovskias with some orange dahlias and the tall stems of flowering yuccas in the distance. The greatest difference between this style and more conventional uses of perennials and grasses lies in the maintenance which is 'extensive' rather than 'intensive'. As Richard Hansen points out, if distributed according to their natural patterns of growth and then allowed to grow unchecked over relatively large areas, the different forms of plants 'will gradually harmonise to make a picture of balanced natural beauty' without requiring much looking after. The wilder look does not focus on individual plants, which in the past would have had dead blooms removed and constant titivation, but rather on the total overall vision, which should have a naturalistic appearance but not be in 'wild disorder'.

The so-called 'new style' of perennial gardening, emerging as a concept primarily from both Germany and Holland, evolves from the idea that perennials and grasses can be 'naturalized' in plant communities that, if appropriately selected for climate and soil, will be self-sustaining and maintained with minimum labour. They will be most easily established where conditions resemble those of a dry meadow or open rocky steppe, with perennials and grasses from similar habitats growing in natural-looking free-form drifts and reappearing again and again throughout the scheme, as might be expected in the wild. Spreading in waves across large open areas, these new plantings require (and get) little seasonal or daily maintenance. They are a cross between the real meadow, rich in wild flowers mixed with a matrix of grasses, and more traditional borders where large masses of different plants are grown in patterns created by the gardener.

Although particularly successful in public spaces rather than in smaller, more manicured private gardens, these schemes satisfy gardeners' increasing craving for ecologically sound planting as well as for the romantic disarray of 'wild' planting. A distinct novelty contributing to the soft, natural look is the meadow grasses – calamagrostis, festucas, pennisetums and stipas interspersed throughout the schemes, with occasional more robust architectural grasses such as miscanthus used instead of shrubs. Greater emphasis is put on ecology than on purely aesthetic principles. In meadow-type communities associated perennials and grasses have their own constantly changing dynamic stimulated by the suitability of the conditions of soil and climate.

Credit for the development of this sort of planting must go to Richard Hansen for his experimental work on plant habitats at Weihenstephan and for his 1981 book (published in English as *Perennials and their Garden Habitats* only in 1993), which provided detailed ecological origins and requirements of plants in a way that had not been attempted before. These ideas were not new, but represent Robinsonian principles carried out in a more environmental way to please a more ecologically informed modern audience. This development corresponds with Robinson's goals as well as those of other distinguished garden philosophers and writers – Willy Lange, Karl Foerster, J. P. Thijsse and many others (see

(Above) At Weihenstephan the site has a continental climate and a rich soil. Strong-growing perennials flower towards the end of summer. *Rudbeckia laciniata* 'Goldquelle' and *R.* 'Herbstonne' have yellow flowers,; *Helenium* 'Moerheim Beauty' is tawny; *H.* 'Septemberfuchs' is more golden. All plants in gardens need some arranging, but these meadow-like plantings have a wildness about them which makes them look natural. Robinson warned about the frequent distortion of his views on naturalistic gardening: 'Some have thought of it – the wild garden – as of sowing annuals in a muddle – whereas it does not interfere with the regulation flower garden at all'. In fact this sort of gardening requires a huge amount of planning and skill before stable plant communities can be created.

(Top right) At Westpark Rosemary Weisse has planted up an old gravel quarry, a site open to the sun and with good drainage perfect for experimenting with some of the new ideas. Grasses and day-lilies are established in naturally self-perpetuating groups that need little regular attention. Plants spread in broad drifts across the space in a cross between the wild-flower meadow where flowers intermingle with grasses and the more conventional herbaceous border where blocks of different plants are deployed with repetitive rhythms decided by the gardener, who keeps them to their allotted place in the overall scheme, and will create pockets of amended soil for desired plants rather than selecting those appropriate to existing conditions.

(Bottom right) At Weihenstephan the continental climate is unbalanced, with frequent changes through what should be predictable periods of extreme cold and heat, and with only a very short two months of no frost incidence. Nevertheless it has predictably hot sun in summer. Perennials survive well if snow-covered but may suffer if snow is not regular but alternates with milder periods. The soil is naturally a rich loam with a pH between 6.5 and 7.2. Any soil preparation is by rotary or hand hoe, and slow-acting fertilizers and a deep organic mulch of cow manure or old bark are applied to the beds each spring. In the picture *Monarda* 'Croftway Pink', *Lythrum salicaria* and *Veronica spicata* 'Icicle' grow in harmonious association.

Chapter One). Since around 1900, regimented blocks of graded plants in borders had increasingly been supplanted by more informal mixed cottage-styles, in which plants were arranged to 'look' natural and uncontrolled but where, in practice, soil and circumstances were amended to make the effect possible. The new German ideas extend this naturalism using ecological principles.

The greatest difference between this style and more conventional gardening practice lies in the 'extensive' rather than intensive maintenance. Robinson warned against confusing his views on naturalistic gardening with 'sowing annuals in a muddle', and Hansen predicted that plant forms would 'gradually harmonize to make a picture of balanced natural beauty'. In practice this apparently gardening needs forethought, plant knowledge and appropriate selection to achieve stable plant communities.

The schemes work best in climates with hot summers and crisp autumns, where weed germination ceases after early summer. The new garden-plant communities, growing in situations where perennial weeds have been eradicated and the soil sterilized to prevent germination of annual weeds at least in the first year, will soon suppress undesirable neighbours, although hand-weeding is essential for a few seasons until plants knit together.

Another factor clearly influencing this sort of environmental gardening, reversing the trend towards standardized garden-centre plants of limited range, is the new availability of plants for every sort of situation. Neglected and overlooked native plants and old cultivars from Germany, Holland and the English countryside have been searched out by innovative nurserymen, the growers who sell directly to the public.

the planting will be more natural when many of the groups are repeated, whereas a design including a large number of diverse plants will look like a botanical collection. The stronger of these key plants, such as soaring verbascums, tall grasses, broad-leaved crambes, galegas, eryngiums, echinops, eupatoriums and kniphofias, can be in small groups – perhaps one to three in number; the weaker and less imposing plants, achilleas, phlox, scabious and veronicas (which may strike just as strong a note when assembled), can be in larger associations of five or seven. Discard the idea of grading plants from tall at the back to low-growing at the front for its boring 'unnatural' effects: there are countless ways of arrangement.

Gertrude Jekyll became a regular contributor to Robinson's *The Garden* and wrote a chapter on 'Colour in the Flower Garden' for *The English Flower Garden* (1883), his most important work. Although diverging from him in that she appreciated the usefulness of annuals and other temporary plants in border schemes, she concurred with his emphasis on giving plants the sort of situations they would enjoy and liked to use native plants in her woodland designs and on the perimeter of the garden, linking it firmly with the countryside beyond. Trained as an artist, however, she liked to 'paint' pictures with her plants, framing them with the strong architecture of terrace, steps, pergolas and summerhouses typical of the Edwardian age. In fact Robinson too needed and allowed architectural themes and features near the house, and at Gravetye Manor had terraces linked with steps and pergolas and even a rose garden.

Both Robinson and Jekyll disliked the crude colour schemes of the bedding-out period, in which hues with greatest contrasts were juxtaposed and graduated tones sharing a pigment were avoided. Instead they recommended using related colours adjacent to each other in the spectrum to create harmonies. Introducing Miss Jekyll's colour chapter in *The English Flower Garden*, Robinson wrote: 'Nature is a good colourist, and if we trust to her guidance we never find wrong colour in wood, meadow, or on mountain. "Laws" have been laid down by chemists and decorators about colours which artists laugh at, and to consider them is a waste of time. If we have to make coloured cottons, or to "garden" in coloured gravels, then it is well to think what ugly things will shock us least; but dealing with living plants in their infinitely varied hues, and with their beautiful flowers, is a different thing.' Although stylistically Miss Jekyll favoured an architectural organization as a framework for her planting schemes, and in her own work and in her own garden used many plants besides hardy perennials to create her effects, the overall 'look' of schemes themselves were those advocated by Robinson with an emphasis on the natural.

Jekyll is best remembered and revered for her designs for the hardy flower border. In this she not only exercised her artist's vision of colour combinations but also showed the depth of her knowledge of plant behaviour and needs. But although she achieved a natural look, her borders were very labour-intensive. Her plants, instead of being in defined blocks, were arranged in pseudo-naturalistic drifts to give a casual appearance, but in reality depended on very carefully contrived effects. She handled plants in such a way as to ensure both comfortable associations and flowering and colour succession, cutting back some plants to ensure later flowering, intricately training late-flowering plants and scramblers such as gypsophila and small-flowered clematis over the earlier flowerers (aquilegias, doronicums, dicentras, oriental poppies and corydalis) as they faded, while ensuring that the plants lived happily together.

The whole idea of a 'perennials-only' flower border, geared up for a distinct summer performance, is quite unnatural, but by a judicious addition of carefully selected small trees and shrubs, this sort of planting can be transformed so that the combinations reflect how herbaceous and woody plants live together and complement each other as they might in the wild. The trees and shrubs in the 'mixed' planting give structure and frame the planting of the more seasonal soft-stemmed plants. With their permanent infrastructure, they create the pockets of light and shade that would be found in a natural situation, provide shelter from wind and cold to emerging leaves in spring and fill in the picture with winter shapes of leaves, seedheads, fruit and bark after the herbaceous plants begin to fade, as well as flowering in their own season. In many cases shrubs are mainly spring-flowering, underplanted with snowdrops, crocus and scillas, with later colours coming from summer and autumn perennials. Although the design of a border is often unified by a continuous background hedge, more free-growing assorted flowering shrubs underplanted with low-growing perennials and bulbs can be just as effective. Unlike the shrubbery in which shrubs predominate, separated by lower valleys of flowering plants, in the flower border, the mixtures of perennials, biennials, annuals and bulbs provide most of their own architectural or more gently flowing shapes, flower and leaf colour, with just a few trees or shrubs to complement them, looking as much as possible as they would look in the wild. Smaller plants flow in and out between the taller specimens colonizing any bare earth. In the 'mixed' border, areas of planting are adjusted each year if stronger plants threaten to overwhelm the weaker upsetting the balance. There is no need to divide, cultivate and replant the whole border every few years; many of the best plants, grown in conditions they enjoy, continue to improve over much longer periods. Peonies, kniphofias, Japanese anemones and many others flower best if seldom disturbed.

Plant groups reflect plants' needs and flowering sequences reflect different seasonal peaks, with deciduous shrubs sheltering the earliest spring bulbs, roses growing in rich soil complemented by aquilegias, peonies and giant crambes. While *Iris sibirica* flourishes in damp soil, German irises like their rhizomes exposed to the baking sun, in well-drained, nutrient-poorer conditions. Prairie plants from the American Midwest and asters from New England flower later, needing moisture in spring but able to flourish in drier soil in summer. Lilies for sun and shade need good drainage but have definite preferences for alkaline or acid soil, depending on their origins. Taller perennials shade and shelter lower-growing plants and, as summer proceeds, provide important architectural shapes and hide the fading leaves and stems of the earlier flowerers. Giant onopordons, cardoons, verbascums and evening primroses with some of the large ornamental grasses are as important as shrub shapes, with late-flowering annuals – tobacco plants and the striking *Verbena bonariensis*, both vigorous self-seeders, filling in the gaps. The ultimate success of the border as an entity depends on giving plants the conditions they enjoy so that each season they become better established, forming and extending natural-looking garden communities that need relatively little attention.

William Robinson's own views on making 'mixed' borders reflected his mission to encourage hardy-plant growing and give plants the rich conditions they need in order to grow tall and flower in a few months. 'Select only good plants; throw away weedy kinds; there is no scarcity of the best ... Make the choicest borders where they cannot be robbed by the roots of trees; see that the ground is good, and that it is at least two and a half feet deep, so deep that in a dry season, the roots can seek their supplies far below the surface ... Do not graduate the plants in height from the front to the back, as is generally done, but sometimes let a bold plant come to the edge; and, on the other hand, let a little carpet of a dwarf plant pass in here and there to the back, so as to give a varied instead of a monotonous surface. Have no patience with bare ground.'

Even more naturalistic border effects are achieved by using a number of perennials, biennials and annuals that self-seed in the beds between plant groups, giving an unplanned natural look to the design, yet ensuring unified repetition and helping to cover all the bare earth. Seeding plants can also, by spreading into other areas of the garden, beyond the actual border, unite different

In Australia sun-loving plants such as shrubby lavender from the Mediterranean and rhizomatous *Sisyrinchium striatum* from Chile and the Argentine are lovers of stony, gravelly well-drained soil, in which they (but especially the latter) will seed and spread. Neither is long-lived. At Heronswood in Victoria they have been planted in quite formal repetitive swathes with the sisyrinchium seeding and overflowing to make an uneven relaxed edging instead of being contained by box, paving or some other material. Their obvious suitability to the site confirms the naturalistic theme.

garden elements, often germinating and flourishing in pavement cracks or other inhospitable corners where planting individual plants would be almost impossible. Most of the self-seeders will be species that come true from seed, but some, such as aquilegia hybrids, may produce interesting new flower types and colours. Seedlings are easily edited out if germinating in the wrong place. Most of the suitable plants do not require a richly prepared site, but do best in a well-drained gravelly soil, germinating wherever there is light and space. The most suitable plants are annuals that flower in the same season as they germinate; opium poppy (*Papaver somniferum*), love-in-the-mist (*Nigella hispanica* and *N. damascena* 'Miss Jekyll') or tender perennials treated as annuals, such as *Verbena bonariensis*, which make perfect infillers, coming rapidly to maturity. Biennial honesty, white- or mauve-flowered or with variegated leaves, thrives in the shade of overhanging branches, while Byzantine gladiolus and *Nectaroscordum siculum* from hot, dry, stony habitats like full sun. Valerian (pink- or white-flowered *Centranthus*) will seed to cover a corner of a border between groups of more sophisticated perennials. Biennials seeding *in situ* include sweet rocket (*Hesperis matronalis*), which flowers early as spring bulbs fade, and tap-rooted plants such as Miss Willmott's ghost (*Eryngium giganteum*), *Onopordum acanthium*, *Galactites tomentosa* and verbascums for well-drained stony soil, and *Silybum marianum* for richer conditions, all with attractive foliage in their first year. Verbascums may be short-lived perennials, biennials or annuals, but usually prolific seeders – although only species seed true. Perennials such as the prolific *Alchemilla mollis* and forms of *Aquilegia vulgaris* will seed and flourish in half shade or full sun, perfect plants to make drifts fading from sunlight into shadow. Success with seeders depends on careful editing at the germination stage. It also means making certain that more permanent plants, still coming to their maturity, are not crowded out by the more thrusting volunteers.

OEHME–VAN SWEDEN'S NEW-STYLE GARDENING

The Robinsons' garden, designed by Oehme and van Sweden, is in the rolling foothills of the Blue Ridge Mountains of Virginia, with undulating pasture in the foreground backed by thick woods. Silver grass (*Miscanthus sinensis* 'Malepartus') is used as architecture to flank the swimming pool and to frame the distant landscape. *Pennisetum alopecuroides*, fountain grass and sedum (*Sedum telephium* 'Autumn Joy') grow in swathes on the far side of the water. The Oehme–van Sweden style depends on massing suitable plants together, matching plants to the conditions and to changing aspects.

Working from Washington, DC, the landscape architects Oehme and van Sweden have evolved their own style of gardening in both public and private spaces, which has swept America. This is based on broad swathes of flowering perennials, good foliage plants and grasses (the tallest grasses giving an architectural quality in place of small trees and shrubs), and arranged with spring bulbs to encompass all the seasons. The style is broadly naturalistic in feel (although not restricted to native plants), with flowing lines rather than restrictive geometry.

Wolfgang Oehme, the plantsman of the partnership, and James van Sweden, the designer, were influenced by parallel exponents of various 'natural' styles. Gertrude Jekyll (1834–1933), although often remembered for her highly orchestrated drifts of colour in borders in England at the turn of the century, was also responsible for the 'natural' look and the cottage-style simplicity of her plant associations. Her contemporary, the great Midwestern landscape architect Jens Jensen (1860–1951) developed his Prairie Style schemes emphasizing the use of regional native plants and conservation and

Behind the house other planting scrolls are revealed. Scarlet-flowered common rose mallow (*Hibiscus moscheutos*) from swampy ground in the south-east states of North America, a sweep of Russian sage (*Perovskia atriplicifolia*) and switch grass (*Panicum virgatum*), the latter in the distance with *Calamagrostis* x *acutiflora stricta* making an almost horizontal line in the distance, are all fitted together like a jigsaw. *Pennisetum alopecuroides* provides the low spikes in the foreground. Although not all the plants and grasses are native, and the style is too controlled to be called 'natural', the curving abstract shapes have a very relaxed and free form, especially when they are carefully selected for the site as they have been here in Virginia.

reinstatement of any remaining prairie land. The German nursery-man and writer Karl Foerster (1874–1970) stressed the importance of perennials and tall-stemmed grasses used in natural associations in organic abstract designs spreading out from the house, rather than in separate and distinctive beds and borders; the grasses carried interest through the autumn and winter, when perennials were dormant. Since the 1960s champions of the native American landscape such as Darrel Morrison have renewed Jensen's ecological appeal for prairie restorations, emphasizing also the aesthetic appeal of the gently moving prairie tallgrasses. Perhaps most influential of all were the broad brush-strokes of the nature-inspired patterns of Brazilian Roberto Burle Marx (1909–95), artist, gardener and conservationist.

The Oehme–van Sweden partnership – most often associated rather too narrowly with grasses – inspires American gardeners to banish the stiff evergreen shrubs hitherto used as foundation plant-ing around the house and the environmentally unfriendly communal clipped lawn, and to substitute waving grasses and perennials (Robinson himself condemned regular lawn cutting as long ago as 1881: 'who would not rather see the waving grass with countless flowers than a close surface without a blossom...?').

Jensen used nature as his theme in all his plantings. He recognized that though 'copying' nature is impossible, by observation its 'motives' can be translated into garden spaces in aesthetic terms. This new-style American gardening *imitates* natural scenes, rather than slavishly following its detail by using only native plants. In sun, in the Oehme–van Sweden schemes, great sweeps of native rudbeckias or eupatoriums edge drifts of European calamagrostis or Asiatic miscanthus grass, flanked by a wide strip of blue-flowered ceratostigma or fleshy-leaved sedums. All these plants have flowers and stalks fading to browns and buffs to carry the garden through the autumn and early winter, with the late-flowering grasses main-taining their skeleton crispness until spring. In shade, bergenias, astilbes, heuchera, epimediums, hostas and ferns, and native trilli-ums and May-apples, drift and trail under trees. In spring, after the grasses are cut down, tulips and alliums fill time and space between emerging perennial and grass foliage. In summer, perennials are backed by waving fronds of grass: rudbeckias, coreopsis, perovskia flower in turn. The grasses, with their natural swaying and rustling beauty, come into flower last, their ripening seedheads and foliage colours turning from greens and feathery whites to autumn golds.

CHAPTER SIX

WATER, ROCK AND GRAVEL

*T*HE TWO apparently quite different elements of rock and water merit being treated together for several reasons. Both in nature are configurations of landscape: they are to do with contours, slopes and the way water runs downwards to find ever-lower levels, shaping the ground as it does so. Garden writers, plantsmen and philosophers tend to treat them in the same breath. William Robinson's subject in *Alpine Flowers for Gardeners* was the culture of alpines, but he was emphatic that in 'suitably naturalistic sites' these might be accompanied by ferns, water plants and other perennials as well as small shrubs from lower slopes of mountain ranges. The rock garden could also be associated with water, since many of the mountain plants also came from swampy marshes and from beside mountain torrents on alpine slopes.

The elements of natural water and rock tend to be absent in the 'average garden', because houses are generally put up in more-or-less level building plots, usually on conveniently flat, well-drained land designated for residential development. Thus for most gardeners creating a rock feature or bringing water into the garden becomes something of a 'project', to be deliberately designed. To make what is in effect a complicated, sophisticated new habitat is quite an achievement, and to do it so that it looks natural is a particular challenge. Key factors are that plants from these two broad categories of habitat tend to be particularly tempting to the plantsman as well as extremely demanding or even fussy as to

In Beth Chatto's gardens, by excavating heavy clay and building dams, she has provided shallow but gently moving water, which gives homes to 'emergents' while allowing lush growers, needing heavy retentive soil, to grow on the banks. She can use plants from a wide range of countries and with a range of growing requirements between aquatics and the marginal plants, which actually like to have their roots in water, and those which, although needing moisture during the growing period in spring, cannot be waterlogged all year. Some need shade and have large handsome leaves, with open pores accustomed to humidity in the air, and even if their roots are kept moist will still droop if placed in full sun.

In Catherine Hull's garden in Manchester on the North Shore at Boston, the little acid-demanding *Gentiana acaulis* from the European Alps and the Carpathians, with deep blue trumpets in spring, grows in a specially prepared tufa wall. Although not exactly 'natural' gardening, as Mrs Hull, like Beth Chatto, takes a lot of trouble to provide plants with sites specially prepared to ensure their successful cultivation, nevertheless, inside their own context, these adaptations demonstrate knowledge and regard for appropriate planting. Planting to please plants is a form of natural planting, in which native and exotic plants, selected for their similar cultural needs, are given sites in the garden where they will thrive as neighbours.

requirements. In this 'plant-led' gardening, understanding what the plant needs for growth is all-important.

The fascination and beauty of the plants that collectors were bringing home from increasingly remote places spurred gardeners to find ways of accommodating them. For more than two centuries people have been creating rock gardens, rockeries and a range of water features with varying degrees of artifice, and varying degrees of success. The movement acquired new impetus towards the end of the nineteenth century with the wave of new plants, many moisture-loving, from the Far East. Gardeners in search of naturalism combined water and rock features in new ways.

There are, of course, in-between situations more easily achieved in the average garden. Instead of open water, boggy or moist areas can be artificially created. Instead of building a rock or alpine garden, self-seeding plants requiring an open situation and excellent drainage can grow in gravel or even dry walls. Any change in level, and *any* garden vertical surface, is potentially a 'rock garden': when you allow aubrieta to tumble down a terrace wall, have cushions of mossy saxifrage sitting on a retaining wall, encourage ferns in a cool shady corner by a wall-fountain, or let *Erigeron karvinskianus* seed in a flight of steps – you are practising a form of 'rock-gardening'.

Ponds and Wetland

As a garden theme the water and bog garden, where hardy and exotic perennials grow together in harmonious drifts beside natural water features, fits as perfectly with Robinson's advocation of 'wild' gardening as does woodland gardening. As he points out in *The Wild Garden*, what makes the natural water garden so appealing is the possible 'juxtaposition of plants inhabiting different situations – water-plants, water-side plants, and land-plants thriving in moist ground'. The plants he recommended, 'of course, should be such as to grow freely among Grass and take care of themselves ... groups of free hardy things, different in each place, as one passed ...' The waterside plants, many of which grow on land and with their roots pushing out into shallow water, visually bind the two groups together to make an harmonious design, so that distinctions between land and water planting become obscured.

By the last half of the nineteenth century, with Japan and China fully open to the plant explorers, a vast number of new plants suitable for bog or marsh became available for gardens in the West. Unlike many of the bog and woodland plants from north-east America, many of these Asiatics, if provided with the right amount of moisture, were able to grow in open situations. A new kind of gardening feature, the 'water garden' came into existence. The surroundings of a

The garden for John and Susan Ulfelder in a hidden wooded ravine in northern Virginia was designed by the Oehme–van Sweden partnership. The pond is entirely artificial and the roots of sedum at its edge will not be in moist soil. Tall purple moorgrass, the Eurasian *Molinia caerulea arundinacea*, one of the best ornamental grasses for American gardens (but shedding its dying foliage stems in winter), grows with pennisetum and miscanthus, which have buff foliage and flowerheads through the winter months. The emergent water plant, *Thalia dealbata*, from the southern states of America and Mexico, has violet flower spikes and decorative seed-heads.

natural pond or lake, places where the ground is naturally wet, provide perfect planting sites for a superb range of hardy moisture-loving and bog perennials and for an array of shrubs, many of which have distinctive winter bark. Indeed, even without a natural water surface, a swamp area in a garden presents an opportunity to use these sort of plants, although the gardener needs to be aware of the distinction between bog plants, which can be waterlogged all year, and moisture-loving plants, which need sufficient water during the growing season but cannot survive if their roots and crowns are permanently wet.

It is not enough to choose plants to suit the soil type and aspect; many have quite specific requirements about the degree of moisture they need to succeed. Some plants actually thrive in the shallow water at the pond-edge; others, although needing a lot of moisture during growing periods, can survive (and sometimes need) dry periods at the end of summer and in winter. For the latter, moisture-retentive soil must be combined with adequate drainage, and plants requiring similar amounts of moisture must be grown in groups together, chosen to match the site. In fact the transitional zone between higher and better-drained ground and the shallow waters of the stream, pond or lake-side may have fluctuating degrees of moisture through the seasons, although fortunately, during the maximum growing period in spring, sites tend to be waterlogged.

Most of the plants suitable for bog gardening come from similar wet habitats, growing wild in marshes, in moorland, in rich deep soil in damp woodland, as well as in open sunny water-meadows. Some even come from mountain slopes, getting their moisture in summer from melting snows. Many suitable perennials have lush broad leaves and fleshy stems; others – irises, grasses and reeds – grow vertically providing contrasting shapes. Among shrubs, dogwoods and willows can be stooled back each spring to encourage production of new coloured stems for the following winter, strong vertical outlines rivalling the rustling reeds and rushes of summer. Given the right climatic conditions, and the right soil and moisture, these plants can grow in great naturalistic sheets by pond or lakeside in the open or in open forests, competing with grass and weeds and rapidly increasing their own garden plant communities with very little interference from the gardener. Many of these plants have spreading roots, which jut out into the water, so that as well as increasing the 'natural' look by uniting land and water, the banks are protected from erosion (the common Norfolk reed (*Phragmites australis*, syn. *P. communis*), with purple plumes in autumn, is particularly effective for this, but only suitable for large-scale planting). Many moisture-loving irises like *Iris pseudacorus* are similarly adaptable, often even extending roots or rhizomes right out into water as well as into higher, drier soil.

Many of the best strong-growing perennials, however, need to placed just beyond – and raised a little from – the wettest areas, where layers of grit providing under-soil drainage allow roots to draw up water through capillary action. All types of soil can be enriched with plenty of organic compost, and mulched each spring to retain the moisture. Clay soils – hardest to prepare and work initially, needing to be lightened and made more workable with both grit and humus – are most water-retentive; adding a thick summer mulch will prevent the soil surface from setting to cement-hardness. Gravelly soil needs less drainage, but more soil-enriching humus.

Naturally flowing water can be an existing stream or a broader stretch of quieter water or lake-side, made by damming a stream or a meandering river. (Though expert advice should be sought on both the technical and the legal implications before undertaking steps involving altering watercourses.) Water gardens can be in open meadows or in sheltered woodland. The combination of sufficient moisture and the usually nutrient-rich silts found at the edge of natural water (or left on the soil as water retreats in early summer) provides perfect growing sites for many suitable plants. In fact many plants originating in damp woodlands or open forest, such as the willow gentian (the European *Gentiana asclepiadea*), rodgersias and hostas, will grow happily in open sunny situations if the soil is sufficiently moist. Plants from open meadows and full sun will not always adapt to or tolerate shade, although in gardens at lower elevations or in hotter climates than their own habitats, many moisture-loving plants require it.

Many vigorous perennials and rhizomatous plants, mainly from the nutrient-rich margins of lakes and ponds or the fringes of slow-moving streams, can thrive in shallow water or in the very moist soil immediately adjoining the 'shallows'. Known as emergents, they have roots that need to be in water or waterlogged all year. The acid-loving skunk cabbages (*Lysichiton americanus* from western North America, also known as bog arum, and its relative *Symplocarpus foetidus* from the eastern USA) need a lot of moisture and grow most successfully in water a few inches deep. With large leaves appearing after the strange arum-like yellow spathes, these have a very similar appearance to true water plants – the aquatics, waterlily-type plants whose flat leaves float on the water or are held just above the surface, and plants with tall reed-like structures soaring out of the horizontal water surface. Among other plants best suited to this transitional area are water forget-me-not (*Myosotis palustris*), arrowhead (*Sagittaria sagittifolia*), yellow flag

Zantedeschia aethiopica, from
swamps in South Africa, grows
as a marginal aquatic in Beth
Chatto's garden, beside the
variegated form of the native
flag, *Iris pseudacorus*. If grown
in moist soil to experience frost
below 50°F/10°C, these calla
lilies must be protected with
mulch or potted up and given
greenhouse protection. If their
crowns are submerged in
water they will survive quite low
temperatures, in the same way
as the cardinal flower of North
America, African Kaffir lilies
(*Schizostylis*), and *Senecio
smithii* from the Falkland Isles.
Most of these plants from
damp places disappear
completely during the winter,
transforming the lush scenes
of summer into bare beds,
although these, covered with
a cosmetic mulch, have their
own sort of beauty.

161

(*Iris pseudacorus*), Japanese water iris (*Iris laevigata*), reedmace (*Typha latifolia*), cardinal flower (*Lobelia cardinalis*) and tender arum lilies (*Zantedeschia aethiopica* from South Africa) which will survive low temperatures if submerged in winter. To all or any of these possibilities in varying climates, many moisture-loving reeds, rushes, sedges, grasses and bamboos are indispensable natural-looking additions. With their grassy or spear-like leaves of different textures, they create a setting for softer broad-leaved flowering plants and stand out in contrast to rocks and pebbles beside a stream bed. A few actually grow in shallow water, rooting in mud but putting up with water-level fluctuations and often surviving quite dry situations during the summer months after water has retreated. In temperate climates many survive best if their roots are totally submerged in winter. Reeds and rushes include tender grass-like *Cyperus vegetus* (syn. *C. eragrostis*) and *Arundo donax*, the invasive *Phragmites australis* and flowering rush (*Butomus umbellatus*).

Sedges, including the European native *Carex riparia*, will flourish in moisture-retentive soil or submerged in water, but most also have surprising tolerance of drought and heat. Some are clump-formers, while others spread by underground runners, aiding erosion control on pond banks. Those with bright or variegated leaves must be out of full sun, or the foliage will burn. The cultivar *C.r.* 'Variegata' has arching leaves striped with white. Much lower-growing *C. elata* 'Aurea', Bowles' golden sedge, is a European native, exotic in shade with golden tufts among duller green masses. *C. buchananii* from New Zealand has wispy, slender soft brown leaves, happy in full sun in temperate climates, but requiring shade where summers are hotter. Also in shade, a golden-leaved form of Japanese hakone grass, *Hakonechloa macra* 'Aureola', with bright yellow foliage streaked with white lines which turn pinkish-red during the winter, makes a startling splash of colour. Calamagrostis grasses from marshland and deep woodland in the northern hemisphere also tolerate part shade.

Actual aquatics live *in* water, their leaves and flowers floating on the surface or rising as spears above the surface. Many have specific requirements as to depth. The most exciting development for British and European gardeners at the end of the nineteenth century was the hybridization of waterlilies, the European yellow *Nymphaea alba* with an assortment of tropical species, normally too tender for open gardens, by Marliac-Latour in France. Until then the most decorative waterlilies, with flowers in reds and pinks, flourished only in warm climates. Marliac-Latour's new hardy plants, with a range able to survive in depths of water above their roots from as little as four inches/ten centimetres to over two yards or metres, greatly extended the showy possibilities of natural water gardening. They rapidly became the stars of the new-style gardens, growing equally happily in informal or formal pools, as long as there was full sun and the water was still. Before this waterlilies possible to grow in Britain had been confined to the yellow waterlily and the brandy bottle (*Nuphar lutea*) – which had the advantage of growing in shade and running water – and white-flowered *Nymphaea tuberosa* and *N. odorata*, introduced earlier from North America. Although many of the existing lakes were naturally too deep for the new Marliac hybrids, these waterlilies could be planted in troughs or boxes raised to just the recommended height in the water, or most frequently new ponds were created especially for them, so that, combined with the recently introduced bog and emergent plants from Asia which fringed the water, whole schemes could be extended with floral beauty. Of course, in the natural water garden, leaves alone have their own beauty and other aquatics, such as the quite common South African Cape pondweed or water hawthorn (*Aponogeton distachyos*), are tolerant of some shade; this has scented white flowers that rest on the surface between the floating leaves. Arrowhead (*Sagittaria sagittifolia*) with handsome arrow-shaped leaves grows in a water depth of about two feet/sixty centimetres. Golden club (*Orontium aquaticum*), with attractive waxy leaves, from the south-east states of North America, is an aroid with white and yellow spadices in early summer.

Many bog plants grow wild in habitats that are permanently wet or marshy, often in an open sunny situation or in half-shade, combining to make natural pictures with water plants and other meadow-like plants that require plenty of moisture. An attractive natural water garden in Great Britain or in an equivalent temperate climate may be composed of European 'natives' only. These could include plants found in east Europe and spreading into west Asia (and often repeated in North America but not in western Europe, where, due to east–west mountain ranges, many plants originally indigenous failed to return after the last Ice Age). The rush known as sweet flag (*Acorus calamus*) grows wild from south-eastern Europe to Japan and in North America, but 'looks' and behaves like a native in Britain. Among the strongest growing 'natives' are invasive sedges (*Carex pendula*), yellow flag iris (*Iris pseudacorus*) and water forget-me-not (*Myosotis palustris*); creeping marsh marigold (*Caltha palustris*), ubiquitous in Europe and North America, does not actually grow in shallow water but requires a soil that does not dry out during the year. Lady's smock (*Cardamine pratensis*), meadowsweet (*Filipendula*), loosestrife (*Lythrum salicaria*) – a menace in the United States, thriving in shallow water and dominating native wetlands – invasive water mint (*Mentha aquatica*), bistort (*Persicaria bistorta*), globe flowers (*Trollius europaeus*) and ferns, in shade or sun, such as the handsome native *Osmunda regalis* and ostrich plume fern (*Matteuccia struthiopteris*) – the last introduced to Britain in the eighteenth century, but with temperate zone requirements and a distinctively native appearance – these are the sorts of plant that best associate with a large-scale lake set in a natural landscape where groups of exotics with larger, more lush foliage would show their 'foreign' origins and look inappropriate. Common or Norfolk reed (*Phragmites australis*, found everywhere in the northern hemisphere), the reed used for thatch-

ing, reedmace (*Typha latifolia*), with tall grey leaves and brown stems, and bullrushes (*Scirpus lacustris*) massed in great spreading clumps along a lakeside, given the exact conditions in which they revel, will also enhance a 'wild' scene with their movement and whispering sound, as well as their appearance. On this large scale the natural look will not be spoiled if some exotics are used, such as the bolder plants from Asia like large-leaved *Petasites japonicus giganteus* (in sun or shade). These, and other thugs mentioned above, would not be welcome in more restricted garden spaces. In winter, dark red, scarlet, golden and green stems of suckering dogwood (variations of Asiatic and Siberian *Cornus alba* and North American *C. stolonifera*) and shining willow bark (forms of *Salix alba* such as *S.a. vitellina* 'Britzensis', and the more tender *S. sachalinensis* 'Sekka', syn. *S. udensis* 'Sekka'), with attractive foliage in summer, enliven the scene, giving vertical sculptural accents to replace the summer appearance of iris, reeds and rushes.

By the end of the nineteenth century, after the introduction to Europe of many more moisture-loving perennials with typically exotic larger leaves, from the Far East and the western states of North America, and very large-leaved exotics such as the more tender *Gunnera manicata* from South America (which needs some winter protection in Great Britain), the range of possibilities was greatly extended. By the turn of the century – encouraged by Robinsonian enthusiasm for a more natural approach to garden design – much more elaborate water or bog gardens became fashionable features in gardens in which there was suitably moist soil and the right climatic conditions for the wide range of these new plants, which combined floral and foliage beauty. Water gardens, naturalistic in concept, were quite elaborate exercises in design, with contrast of flower colours and foliage colours, shapes and textures, with large-leaved plants and flowers from spring to autumn. They were as highly orchestrated as the contemporary Edwardian borders, and with bronze and buff foliage, especially of

moisture-loving grasses, lasting through most of the winter months. In an almost wild situation, the beauty of dying foliage becomes a distinct winter asset, although not always acceptable around a pond in the more sophisticated parts of the garden.

Of course, these water-gardens, with distinct Japanese overtones, were highly artificial creations needing expert management, often with water supplies and drainage carefully controlled to keep plants moist or relatively dry according to their requirements, and with specially prepared soils to suit the plant range, as well as a fine degree of aesthetic tuning. The actual gardening maintenance depends on adequate soil preparation and suitability, the choice of plants and their diversity; an elaborate scheme with many competing groups of plants (and weeds) could be quite high-maintenance, requiring considerable knowledge and skill from the gardener, while by massing of a few different but carefully selected

Japanese iris, *Iris ensata*, grow luxuriantly along the stream at Ninfa in Italy, revelling in the cool rushing water. Although occurring naturally in dry areas where there is periodic flooding, this iris is often grown as an emergent water plant and removed from the water for the winter. At Ninfa, south of Rome, winters are not severe and it thrives on the stream bank. The original species is lime-hating, but American plant breeders have produced cultivars that are much more tolerant.

sorts in suitably prepared soil or natural sites, work can be simplified and carried out by relatively unskilled helpers. As William Robinson writes: 'One of the great charms of the bog garden is that everything thrives and multiplies in it, and nothing droops or dies, but the real difficulty is to prevent the stronger plants from overgrowing, and eventually destroying, the weaker.' In the rich silty soil plants grow quickly, competing with each other (and with equally luxuriant weeds) for dominance. The natural-looking water garden as a theme seems a particularly happy interpretation of Robinson's wild gardening. The temperate climate of Great Britain has proved very favourable for many of the new bog plants, which became excellent garden substitutes for the more invasive natives, less suitable for the more intimate water garden as opposed to wilder lake shore. Trickling streams in woodland or in open meadows can be lined with drifts of natives and exotics, and can be dammed to give more solid open stretches of flower- and leaf-fringed water.

In areas where water shortages are not a problem, gardeners have perfected many ways of creating such water features artificially, from still-water ponds, through a range of trickling rills and fountains using recycled water, to bog-gardens with ground moistened to taste by buried irrigation systems. A lined pond (as opposed to one occurring naturally in damp ground) may be surrounded by perfectly ordinary garden soil, and if moisture-loving plants are to be accommodated to create the desirable transitional effects, the soil may need amendment. Of course, if the water has been artificially created and is isolated from the ground around it, an adequate irrigation and drainage system can still provide many of these plants with the moisture necessary for their growing requirements. In fact an entirely 'unnatural' water garden provides exciting opportunities for growing an extra range of plants, with appropriate green and textured leaves, which look so good beside water, but do not necessarily come from damp regions. Specially prepared pockets of soil and adjustable irriga-

tion systems for specific plants can still give a natural feel. In all naturalistic gardening, while giving plants the conditions that they most enjoy, the aim is to copy nature's 'look', not to imitate slavishly the actual planting. In water gardening luxuriant growth is an important visual aspect of the overall scheme.

The Japanese iris, *Iris ensata* (syn. *I. kaempferi*), although occurring naturally in dry areas where there is periodic flooding – the old-fashioned English watermeadow systems should suit it well – is generally thought of as a marsh plant, and only thrives if a moist soil can be provided in spring and summer. In late autumn and during winter the soil must be relatively dry. If grown in a pond, it should be in a container that can be removed after flowering, allowed to dry off and then plunged into a flowerbed until the following spring. The original species from Japan requires a lime-free soil, but extensive breeding in the United States has produced cultivars that flourish in any normal moisture-retentive soil, and will even grow with roots just below waterlevel. When the water-garden planting surrounds an artificial pond, without contact with the water, these irises can be planted in a polythene-lined hole, kept very moist while flowering and drier when flowering is over.

Besides plants from naturally boggy ground, Robinson suggested adding to the waterside some herbaceous plants of the wilder type, those which thrive in moist or heavy soil but which need well-drained conditions. Writing in *The Wild Garden* in 1870, before the great influx of moisture-loving Asiatic plants that came in during the next twenty years, he expressed his views: 'The margins of lakes and streams are happily not upturned by the spade in winter; and hereabouts, just away from the water line, many a vigorous and hardy flower (among the thousands now in our gardens) may be grown and will afterwards take care of themselves'.

Besides suggesting British native perennials 'from Iris to Meadow-sweet', for the drier places away from the water's edge, Robinson recommended the best of the foreigners: 'Day Lilies; Iris, many; Gunnera; Starwort

PRECIOUS PIEDMONT FLORA PRESERVED IN THE BRANDYWINE

The gardens of Mount Cuba in Delaware are among the more recent creations of a member of the horticulturally distinguished Du Pont family in the Brandywine valley. Pamela Cunningham Copeland and her husband Lammot Du Pont Copeland moved there from Connecticut in the mid-1930s. The house was built in the late 1930s and the '40s and the garden and terraces immediately around it were laid out then. A further twenty and a half acres/over eight hectares were acquired in the 1950s and this, after landscaping to create three ponds, has become a naturalistic garden – the Mount Cuba Center. Although not entirely excluding exotic plants, it has been developed as a refuge and research centre for the Piedmont flora, with the definite purpose of educating the public to the urgent problem of conservation of wild flowers and the prevention of wild-flower-collecting for commercial sale. This is

followed up by research into developing cultural methods of propagation for the more difficult plants (or those that are slow to increase, such as trilliums, hepaticas, actaeas, lilies and cimicifugas). Mount Cuba also encourages the production of outstanding cultivars and promotes their propagation in suitable nurseries, increasing their availability to gardeners. Three herbaceous perennials have been selected over recent years, *Aster novae-angliae* 'Purple Dome', *Solidago spathulata* 'Golden Fleece' and *Heuchera americana* 'Garnet', as well as two new shrub cultivars, *Cornus stolonifera* 'Silver and Gold' and *Leucothoe axillaris* 'Greensprite'.

Piedmont is the area through the foothills of the Appalachians in eastern North America, extending from a narrow strip in southern Virginia, widening through northern Virginia to the uplands of south-eastern Pennsylvania and the coastal plains of Maryland, Delaware and New Jersey. Typical forest trees in the woods surrounding Mount Cuba are yellow poplar, white and red oak, beech, chestnut, shagbark hickory, red maple, white ash, wild black cherry, American hornbeam and flowering dogwood, with lower shrub layers of Pinxter azaleas, mountain laurel, dwarf blueberry,

aromatic wintergreen and spotted pipsissewa. With very acid soil, hot and wet summers and wet winters, more than three thousand species have been identified, many of which are now on the threatened or endangered list.

As at Winterthur (see page 90), only three miles/five kilometres away, a high canopy of tulip trees gave shelter to development in the woods, with other trees such as hickories, oaks, American walnut and American beech. Colonies of native woodlanders such as Dutchman's breeches (*Dicentra cucullaria*), bloodroot (*Sanguinaria canadensis*) and rue-anemone (*Anemonella thalictroides*) are joined by more than a hundred species of Piedmont flora to grow in the woods. *Phlox divaricata* and both blue and white forms of the creeping *Phlox stolonifera*, foamflower (*Tiarella cordifolia*), *Hepatica americana*, trailing arbutus (*Epigaea repens*) and wintergreen (*Gaultheria procumbens*) are woven in large drifts between native shrubs. Drifts of *Aquilegia canadensis* line the woodland edge and the native *Pachysandra procumbens* is encouraged to spread in light shade. *Shortia galacifolia*, once rare in native habitats, now makes large spreading colonies. The yellow lady's slipper (*Cypripedium calceolus*) is difficult to keep going. Shrubs, besides the native flowering dogwood (*Cornus florida*), which paints the woods white in spring, include evergreen inkberry (*Ilex glabra*) and deciduous *Ilex verticillata*, red-stemmed dogwoods from Europe and Asia (forms of *Cornus alba* and *C. sibirica*) as well as the native *C. stolonifera* with dark red winter shoots and its golden-stemmed variety *C.s.* 'Flaviramea'. Native rhododendrons such as *R. prunifolium* flower in July.

(Above) Plants growing around the naturalistic cascades at Mount Cuba include a few primulas from Asia, and mainly native shade- and moisture-loving ferns, the native creeping white phlox (*Phlox stolonifera* 'Alba') and the upright native evergreen shrub *Leucothoe fontanesiana*. Mount Cuba specializes in conservation and research into local Piedmont flora, and gardening styles there complement the ecological theme, with native plant communities encouraged to grow into satisfying groups.

(Above) In the woods at Mount Cuba, where a series of ponds drops down the slope, not all plants are native, but the overall look is very natural, and any 'alien' plants are chosen for their suitability to the region and to water gardening. Skunk cabbages, with a musky smell, primulas from Asia, and stoloniferous phlox from woods in North Carolina to New York (and thriving best in acid soil in half-shade), grow around one of the man-made ponds. The true skunk cabbage, *Symplocarpus foetidus*, from north-east America and north-east Asia, as opposed to *Lysichiton americanus*, the bog arum, from the Pacific north-west, grows at the water edge. Another lysichiton, *L. camtschatcensis*, with white spathes, also comes from north-east Asia.

(Left) The spring-flowering daisy, golden groundsel (*Senecio aureus* syn. *Packera aurea*), grows in profusion around the lower pond at Mount Cuba, making a spectacular show in late spring with its yellow flowers held on dark smooth stems. It comes from boggy regions in eastern and central areas of the United States, and will thrive in damp, even wet, garden soil and is perfectly adapted to the acid soil conditions and climate of Mount Cuba.

[*Aster*] ... the deep rose variety of the Loosestrife; Golden Rods; the taller and stouter Bell-flowers (Campanula); the Compass plants (Silphium); Monkshoods...' To Robinson's list we can add fine foliage plants from northern America such as boltonias, eupatoriums, *Lysimachia ciliata*, goat's beard (*Aruncus dioicus*), Oswego tea (*Monarda didyma* and more drought-tolerant hybrids with *M. fistulosa*) and queen of the prairie (*Filipendula rubra* 'Venusta'). From Asia came *Astilbe rivularis*, Japanese filipendula (*F. kamtschatika*), hemerocallis, and the biennial giant hogweed (*Heracleum mantegazzianum*), now a potentially dangerous weed. Some of the tough *Miscanthus* grasses enjoy nutrient-rich moist soils but will not tolerate being waterlogged in winter and need open situations, as do the fountain grasses, forms of *Pennisetum*. Others such as feather reed grass (*Calamagrostis* x *acutiflora*, syn. *C. arundinacea*), tolerate some shade and in hot summer climates flower late in shady situations, with leaves bleaching to shades of orange and buff after the first frosts. *C.* x *a.* 'Karl Foerster' is very similar and will be more likely to bloom in cool climates. All thrive in heavy rich soil, surviving hot sun if there is plenty of moisture.

Many of the 'new' species came from semi-woodland (open forest with sunlit areas), from deep damp valleys in the Himalayas among birch and scrubby rhododendrons, as well as from the eastern foothills soaked by the south-west monsoon. Many are acid-soil perennials which will tolerate alkalinity if the climate is sufficiently wet and the soil is damp and rich with humus. *Artemisia lactiflora*, *Astilbe rivularis*, *Ligularia dentata* – fringe plants for the drier parts of the ornamental water garden – are found on rocky stream edges rather than in boggy swamps. Tolerant of marshier conditions are various large-leaved rodgersias (*Rodgersia aesculifolia* and *R. pinnata*). The high lush meadows on the great plateaux east of the highest mountain ranges into northern Yunnan in western China, kept damp by melting snow, are the home of the greater part of Asiatic primulas and rhododendrons, among which the giant cowslip *Primula*

florindae, growing by stream-beds washed by water from the limestone mountains, with giant rhubarbs (*Rheum* species), are tolerant of alkaline conditions. The mountains of Japan are mostly granite and many Japanese plants, especially deep-rooting trees and shrubs, demand acidic conditions, but moisture-loving Japanese perennials are often more tolerant, although preferring and doing best in soils more like those in their native habitat. Many suitable for wet temperate climates come from the colder northern part.

In gardens most of these plants, introduced to European and American gardens by the turn of the century, can be grown in shade or in sun provided they have enough moisture. Astilbes, *Astilboides tabularis* (syn. *Rodgersia tabularis*), hostas (hybrids or sports from original Japanese clones, the larger-leaved forms from woodland), shade-tolerant *Houttuynia cordata* (introduced in 1820), *Kirengeshoma palmata*, endemic to some Japanese islands but now rare in the wild, ligularias, candelabra primulas, rheums and rodgersias, all became available for gardeners towards the end of the nineteenth century, with moisture-loving American introductions, including monkey musks (forms of *Mimulus guttatus*) and the umbrella plant (*Darmeria peltata*, syn. *Peltiphyllum peltatum*) from the west, the latter with creeping rhizomes excellent for preventing soil erosion on stream or pond banks. Many moisture-loving perennials from North America had been introduced earlier, most needing acid soil. *Lysichiton americanus* arrived in 1901 but the white *L. camtschatcensis* from the Far East came earlier, in 1886. In the British Atlantic climate there are the usual setbacks. Although temperatures are never extreme, wetland plants accustomed to much lower temperatures in regions where they occur naturally do not always survive fluctuating periods of warmth and cold during the winter. Both scarlet cardinal flower (*Lobelia cardinalis*) with its 'vivid spikes ... springing from the wet peaty hollows' viewed by Robinson from his American train windows, which is hardy to severe Zone 3 temperatures

Swamp pink, the evergreen rhizomatous *Helonias bullata*, from acidic bogs and swamps from southern New York to North Carolina, thrives in a favourable microclimate created in The Garden in the Woods in Massachusetts. The fragrant flowers are carried in dense cylindrical heads on erect stems. Listed as a Zone 8 plant, hardy to at least 5°F/−15°C, but obviously capable of growing in New England Zone 5, the swamp pink demonstrates how gardeners can take advantage of favourable sites for plants from warmer regions, by growing them next to expanses of water, manipulating neighbouring planting or creating windbreaks and other ameliorating features and circumstances. The Garden in the Woods, with sheltered open glades in the forest, provides a wide range of habitats.

in the snow-covered native bogs of North America and Canada (in the east and in the Rockies) and pickerel weed (*Pontederia cordata*) from shallow pond-edges in New England will 'freeze' in the British climate, if tempted into premature growth during a warm spell. In Britain they are grown where water covers their crowns in winter. Other introduced plants originating in damp meadows require more open sunny situations: moisture-loving iris (*Iris ensata*, *I. laevigata*) from Japan and daisy-flowered *Senecio smithii* from the Falkland Isles (like the cardinal flower, hardy in temperate climates if submerged in water during winter), and the white arum or calla lily, *Zantedeschia aethiopica*, from streamsides and marshy places in South Africa.

The appearance of some plants, not natural moisture-lovers, makes them equally suitable for planting in the vicinity of artificial water, where moisture from the tank or basin does not directly reach the soil but where soil can be kept appropriately dry or damp. Robinson added some plants requiring drier conditions to his water-garden list. Pampas grass (*Cortaderia sellowiana*) comes from temperate South America and requires dry sandy soil. Willow-leaved sunflower (*Helianthus salicifolius*), 'though a small-flowered plant, is yet one of the best for the picturesque garden,' William Robinson thought; it is a native of dry plains in Nebraska and Texas. To these a further addition could be forms of both *Iris sibirica* and *I. spuria*. The former grows naturally in reed-swamps or water meadows (where in spring annual river flood-water leaves a rich deposit of silt in its native habitat), but thrives in enriched soil in a dry garden; the latter, from European damp meadows, likes moist soil in spring but will survive dry soils in summer.

Although in north-east America there is in general a far greater wealth of native plants from which to choose, the climate is too severe for many lush large-foliage plants, such as those from Asia, and for some of the European natives listed above. But it is often appropriate to use only indigenous plantings to fringe water in natural settings. Exotics can look wonderful around ponds contained on one property but, when planted beside moving stream-water, roots and seed can be washed downstream into a neighbour's property, and in the warmer summer climates multiply dangerously fast. Plants such as European loosestrife (*Lythrum salicaria*) and the indomitable Japanese knotweed (*Fallopia japonica*) can clog up waterways, disrupt ecologically based plant communities and become an environmental hazard. In New England the regional moisture-loving bog plants, such as are found in local wetlands, nearly all acid-lovers, are often the best choice. Acid-loving American bog arums and skunk cabbages (*Lysichiton americanus* and *Symplocarpus foetidus*) are a familiar sight in open meadows and in light woodland, growing half-submerged beside natural ponds and by quite fast-moving streams. Pickerel weed (*Pontederia cordata*) also grows in shallow water. Baneberry (*Actaea* species) with red or white berries, marsh marigolds (see above), dog's tooth violets (*Erythronium americanum*), boneset (*Eupatorium* species), celandine poppy (*Stylophorum diphyllum*), cardinal flower and bugbane (*Cimicifuga racemosa*) grow in woodland and cool moist sites, thriving in British gardens in moist acid soils. Stately goat's beard (*Aruncus dioicus*, also indigenous elsewhere in the northern hemisphere), bee balms (*Monarda* species) and *Iris versicolor* need sun and moisture but do not grow in water. Many Compositae found in marshy places are less intolerant of alkaline soil. Aster species, *Eupatorium purpureum*, golden rods (*Solidago* species), *Helenium autumnale*, cone-flower (*Rudbeckia laciniata*), the garden hybrids and cultivars that are the principal adornments of late-flowering borders in Britain are abundant in marshy places, although most sunflowers, forms of *Helianthus*, come from damp areas in the Midwestern prairies (see Chapter Five). All need a rich garden soil that will not dry out in periods of drought. Most transfer to Europe, as long as the soil is right, but many of the Asiatic bog- and moisture-loving plants, some from open situations in their own regions, require shade as well as moisture in North American gardens, the hot sun burning their lush foliage. Feathery astilbes and hostas, with elegant furrowed leaves and white or lavender flowers, have become indispensable perennials for shady water surrounds, as they have throughout all western gardens. *Kirengeshoma palmata*, rodgersias and rheums are hardy if mulched generously in winter. Some of the best primulas find New England too cold, but thrive further south in eastern Pennsylvania, Delaware and Maryland.

Many moisture-loving ferns, suitable for the 'wild' water garden, from acid-soil regions in north-east America, thrive in shade, planted in sweeps to provide leafy interludes between flowering perennials. Coming from acid-soil regions they require similar garden soil in order to thrive, but will succeed if the top layer of soil is sufficiently loamy. Cinnamon fern (*Osmunda cinnamomea*) and royal fern (*O. regalis*) make great peaty roots in boggy areas with sensitive fern (*Onoclea sensibilis*) and the similar netted chain fern (*Woodwardia areolata*), narrow swamp fern (*Dryopteris cristata*) and marsh fern (*Thelypteris palustris*). The summer-performing perennials and ferns can be joined by groups of shrubs, their shapes and barks adding winter interest but also making attractive summer thickets contrasting with the softer wilder look of more ephemeral soft-stemmed plants. Many from New England and Canadian bogs and swamps are confirmed acid-lovers. Exceptions are lime-tolerant suckering dogwood (*Cornus stolonifera* and especially *C.s.* 'Flaviramea' with greenish-yellow bark) and black-fruited *Aronia melanocarpa*. Acid-soil shrubs are sweet pepperbush (*Clethra alnifolia*), from fresh-water swamps and damp woods suckering to make thickets, and bright-berried cultivars of deciduous holly (*Ilex verticillata*) from swamps in Newfoundland west to Minnesota and south to Georgia and Tennessee. Evergreen sheep laurel (*Kalmia angustifolia*) and rhodora (*Rhododendron canadense*), both Ericaceae, are found in moist open places, in bogs, swamps and pastures and on rocky slopes in very cold areas.

Many of these plants spread further south, especially in the Appalachian Mountain ranges, but cannot survive the hot days and nights of regions in the deeper south. Obviously most of the native 'southerners' will not survive the extreme winter temperatures of the north-east. Plants such as herbaceous swamp mallow (*Hibiscus moscheutus*) flower in open marsh (and in rich cultivated protected borders as far north as Massachusetts and west to Michigan where summers are hot) – but are unwilling to flower in Britain. Acid-soil lovers include wandflower (*Galax aphylla*), *Iris cristata*, Louisiana iris (*I. hexagona*), bulbous *Hymenocallis* lilies and pitcher plants (*Sarracenia*). Hay-scented ferns (*Dennstaedtia punctiloba*), shield fern (*Dryopteris carthusiana*), cinnamon fern (*Osmunda cinnamomea*) and northern maidenhair fern (*Adiantum pedatum*) all thrive in damp woodland in the mountains, with shrubs such as evergreen *Leucothoe fontanesiana* and *L. axillaris* (see Chapter Three). Cannas, mainly grown as exotic annuals in Britain's temperate climate, their rhizomes stored and protected during winter, are perennials in the warmer southern US states, fringing the edge of swamps where orontiums decorate the water surface.

The Pacific north-west, with a moist temperate climate not so very different from that in Britain (mainly Zone 7), but with higher rainfall and a constant acid soil, provides moisture-lovers for the English water garden, and many of the moisture-loving plants from Asia are at home in west-coast gardens. Natives suitable for the bog garden include the umbrella plant (*Darmeria peltata*, syn. *Peltiphyllum peltatum*), monkey flowers (*Mimulus* species), bog buckbean (*Menyanthes trifoliata*) and deer cabbage (*Nephrophyllidium faurei*), found further north towards Alaska. In shade sword fern (*Polystichum munitum*) and giant chain fern (*Woodwardia fimbriata*) spread through the dark moist woods. Native shrubs from moist spots include sweet gale (*Myrica gale*) with scented leaves, and more Ericaceae: red huckleberry (*Vaccinium parvifolium*) and shade-loving but invasive salal (*Gaultheria shallon*), suitable for moist and coastal gardens with deep peaty soil in Britain.

Gardening with Rock and Gravel

Gardens do not have to be composed of a series of separate features, in which different sorts of plants are grown. In a naturalistic garden there may well be sections of woodland, shrubbery, a water garden and a rock garden – the latter, with excellent drainage, having many similarities to the open gravel-based Mediterranean garden – which can all blend together, without any abrupt transition, to make an integrated whole. An expanse of water, surrounded by boulders, with pockets of deep well-drained soil between the rocks, provides suitable planting spots for the large-leaved bog plants, emergents growing in shallow water and aquatics as well as for the rock plants, which if given the necessary drainage and their crowns kept dry, will benefit from the coolness of neighbouring water during the hotter months.

Few owners have suitable sites for a natural rock garden, to be seen as a feature on its own. More usually, successful rock gardens, in the temperate British climate, contain a wide range of plants besides the many low-growing alpines – mainly perennials and bulbs –

(Top left) The view west from Isleboro Island towards Camden and the west coast of Maine. Inland Maine is Zone 4 but coastal areas and islands are in Zone 5. The surrounding ocean prevents winter temperatures from falling or remaining low for long periods, and keeps summers relatively cool, especially the nights, prolonging the flowering periods of perennials. Spruce, pine, birch and maple grow with an understorey of native honeysuckle, sweet gale and *Ilex verticillata*, with typical acid-loving forest floor plants, reliable indicators of which plants from exotic regions, with similar climates and environments, will thrive in the garden. Mrs Homans is a dedicated plantswoman continually pushing the range of plants she grows to the limit, but without losing the 'naturalism' and beauty of the wild site.

(Far left) Creeping Jenny, (*Lysimachia nummularia* 'Aurea'), from Europe but naturalized in north-east America, carpets a raised bed under native birch (*Betula papyrifera*), a perfect foil to the elegant peeling bark. Many other European flowers have colonized New England woods since settlers first introduced them to their gardens. Not all do ecological damage like Japanese honeysuckle, Kudzu vine, Japanese knotweed and purple loosestrife, spreading to eliminate native flora. Some, such as creeping Jenny and sweet rocket (*Hesperis matronalis*) from Europe, seed on wood edge and on road sides and creeping speedwell (*Veronica filiformis*), turning lawns blue in spring, can hardly be called dangerous.

(Left) The native meadow lily, *Lilium canadense*, found from Nova Scotia to Minnesota and Nebraska and south to Alabama and Georgia, flowering in mid- to late summer, has faintly scented trumpet-shaped normally yellow flowers with recurved tips – some varieties have orange or deep red petals – and grows in open clearings in the wood, at wood edge or in moist meadows. It is generally more abundant in the wild than the larger-flowered Turk's cap lily, (*Lilium superbum*), from similar regions.

MAINE ISLAND IMITATES HIMALAYAN MICROCLIMATES

Isleboro Island, fourteen miles long and four miles wide/some twenty-two by six kilometres, lies in Penobscot Bay in mid-coast Maine. Although inland temperatures in Maine are much colder, the island is tempered by the ocean and falls into Zone 5 (USDA). Winter temperatures can drop to −20° Fahrenheit/−28° Celsius, but when this occurs the cold seldom lasts for long periods. Summer highs reach to 90°F/34°C, but nights are always cool. The soil is acid, with ledges and rocks mainly shale and very little granite or sandstone. Principal native tree cover consists of spruce, pine, birch and maple, with mousewood (*Acer pensylvanicum*) making a windshield for lower plants and a lovely understorey. Shrubby plants include sweet gale (*Myrica gale*), honeysuckle (*Lonicera sempervirens*), vacciniums and winterberry (*Ilex verticillata*). Bunchberries (*Cornus canadensis*) grow in swathes with twinflower (*Linnaea borealis*), *Clintonia borealis* and *Maianthemum bifolium* under the shrubs. In the damp air mosses and lichens make patterns on the exposed rock ledges.

Mary Homans's garden, a natural rock face with south-west sloping meadows, lies at the southern end of the island, exposed to south-westerly gales from the ocean. Mrs Homans says wind is her worst enemy, more devastating in its effects than low temperatures. In the early 1980s spindly spruce trees and some beech and ash were cleared, retaining existing native birch (*Betulus papyrifera*) on the rocky eastern corner of the property, and leaving clean, exposed ledges. Mugo pines were planted as a windbreak behind boulders placed on the northern edge and imported topsoil (a mixture of natural soil, peat, compost and pea gravel) filled in to make planting beds and pockets in the sunniest areas. Here mountain plants such as *Lewisia cotyledon* (in several forms), from the Pacific north-west, will flourish. In the natural woodland, soil was left undisturbed and only amended at planting times.

Each year new planting enriches the range of plants, creating microclimatic pockets for species almost outside the normal range for this garden. Azaleas and *Cornus kousa* shelter sweeps of native *Phlox divaricata*, *Jeffersonia diphylla* and *Pachysandra procumbens* (from further south) and Asiatic hostas and astilbes. A small pond creates the cool humidity necessary for success with Himalayan poppies (*Meconopsis betonicifolia*) – a rare or perhaps even unique sight in Maine – and for rodgersias and primulas (both *P. japonica* and *P. ioessa* from southern Tibet). On the rock faces the rosette-

Mrs Homans introduced suitable new shrubs and perennials, native and exotic, among the tall trunks of spruce, clearing glades and thinning overhead canopies to allow light to penetrate, linking areas with winding paths surfaced with soft pine needles. Enkianthus, azaleas, *Cornus kousa*, hostas and the creeping native *Pachysandra procumbens* and ferns, all not only well-adapted to the environment but 'looking' right, their physiognomy enhancing the natural ambience of the original planting. Gardening is an art form in the practice of which nature can be manipulated to allow plants, both native and exotic, to be arranged in beautiful ways, but the gardener needs highly specialized skill and knowledge to keep the natural look.

forming *Ramonda myconi* from the Pyrenees and small saxifrages spread and sow themselves in the moss.

Mrs Homans is very much an expert 'hands-on' gardener, growing new plants from seed and studying microclimatic possibilities for extending her range, continually experimenting with both native and exotic plants. Her achievements have been recognized by an award from the New England Wild Flower Society.

which can thrive if given adequate drainage and soil depth. Other plants that can take advantage of this sort of terrain can include trees, small mountain shrubs, ferns and, if water is nearby, a selection of marsh plants or aquatics. The natural rock garden, in providing well-drained soil in an open situation, becomes an ideal adjunct to other forms of naturalistic gardening. Strictly speaking true alpines, small and compact plants, living on high mountain slopes above the treeline, dormant and covered with snow for much of the year, emerge to flower and make seed as the snow melts (sometimes only emerging from the snow every few years). With roots pushing down deep to find moisture between the rocks, they endure hot sun and harsh winds – what Robinson called 'the contending forces of heat and cold' – for a few weeks or months. They survive, partly because they are adapted for these conditions, but also because there is no competition from other taller or more thrusting plants. Many of the same alpine species also grow among a mixed vegetation on lower slopes and in the cold valleys, but in these circumstances, with neighbouring plants encroaching on their territories, grow in small isolated pockets rather than in the drifts found on the open pastures or rock and gravel mountain sides.

In rock gardening, dealing with high mountain plants from variable terrains and therefore with very different requirements means creating specific planting conditions. Some come from open alpine meadows clothing the lower slopes just above the treeline. Others come from steeper screes and moraines (with subterranean water) where they are the only vegetation, flowering as the snow melts. Others originate from deep valley clefts or from mountain bogs, growing in places with silted soil or in almost soil-less depressions between rocks. Many will not survive unless given the right soil and conditions.

The vast number of rock plants, the mountain flora which can adapt to garden situations, come from mountains in all corners of the world. They come from the Swiss Alps and the mountains of Greece, from high valleys in the Himalayas and Tibetan plateaux, from Tierra del Fuego and from the Andes, as well as from the American Rockies and the Kamchatka Peninsula. Above all, mountains are their natural homes and they need good drainage and cool summers. In the face of such different and specialized demands from the plants, many alpine gardeners abandon the whole 'naturalistic' idea from the start. They concentrate on growing their plants in controlled environments mimicking native habitats, rather than trying to integrate them in the garden. In the alpine house, plants can be given the right soil, drainage, sunlight and heat, dry conditions in winter and a cool summer. Other enthusiasts, rather than making a 'landscaped' rock garden, will construct dry stone walls and raised beds with soil mixes and sites in sun or shade to suit the plants. Gardeners can often take advantage of changes in level by exploiting the planting possibilities of stone steps, retaining walls and terracing, or scree-like gravelly areas, to create a man-made but viable well-drained, stony habitat.

In rock gardening, perhaps more than any other ornamental gardening, it is essential to know the sort of conditions that plants enjoy in their native regions, to know in detail the actual 'properties' that a plant derives from its native soil and aspect so that the plants' immediate and future needs can be anticipated. Depending on their origin, some of these plants are acid-lovers, others demand an alkaline soil. To be successful the rockery as a garden feature has to combine providing suitable conditions for growth so that plants are kept dry during freezing temperatures in winter (they would be snow-covered in their own habitats) with excellent drainage, with crowns remaining dry in winter, and deep pockets of soil so that roots can find moisture and keep cool during hot summers – the smallest alpine perhaps a few inches high may have roots radiating to three feet/one metre in search of moisture, and the creeping plant that appears to cling to bare rock has, in reality, forced its hairlike roots deep into microscopic fissures. The cool English summers are not so different from summer

(Far left) In one of the gardens designed by Isabelle Greene in coastal south California, the perennial yellow daisy-flowered *Gazania rigens leucolaena*, with grey-green linear leaves, from South Africa, needing hot sun and a well-drained soil, trails among the heat-reflecting rocks, thriving where temperatures remain above 25°F/–4°C. South African plants usually adapt to Californian conditions, sharing in their places of origin a warm Mediterranean-type climate. Newer trailing hybrids are being introduced with larger orange, yellow and white flowers.

(Left) William Robinson advised G. F. Wilson at Wisley, before the gardens were acquired by the Royal Horticultural Society in 1904, playing a considerable part in the development of the wilder areas in what was originally oak woodland *Crocus tommasinianus*, growing in the 'botanic scale' rockery, first laid out in 1911 but recently restored, adds to the carefully orchestrated kaleidoscope of habitats, but as detail could be a feature of anyone's sloping garden. Here the crocus grows and flowers between the corms and foliage of ivy-leaved *Cyclamen hederifolium*.

conditions on a Swiss alpine slope but, in hot climates, alpines need cool shade, and may thrive best on a northern slope. Each species must also have the correct soil type, sufficient sun and wind, with shade coming from overhanging rock rather than from tree canopies. These saxatile plants – plants that live and grow among rocks – do not require rich feeding. All soil is basically worndown stone and these plants are dependent on some sort of stone for their survival, whether it is rocks, scree, gravel or sand, but will not thrive in wet, sticky, waterlogged heavy clay soils made up of the smallest particles of ground-up soil. A mulch of gravel over a whole bed or around the crown of a plant will prevent rotting.

Ideally, in a garden situation, the best natural rock gardens are made where high mountain conditions can be simulated: well-drained ground with a high level of gravel and shingle or (as in Reginald Farrer's garden at Ingleborough in Yorkshire) natural outcrops of local limestone where Farrer could, without much artifice, give his precious plants the conditions they needed. Natural rock gardening is just an extension of the whole conception of providing plants with a suitable environment. Rock-garden perennials, although united in their dependency on rocks, shingle, scree or gravel for their well-being, have very varied other requirements. Rock gardens do not have to have large difficult-to-arrange

175

boulders, imported from other regions; the most suitable growing places can be just sloping screes of well-drained soil, exactly the same sort of conditions as those required by Mediterranean sun-lovers – ensuring summer heat (increased by the heat-reflecting gravel surface) and excellent drainage, with suitable adjustment for soil preferences.

Some gardeners are fortunate to possess at least some of the 'natural' conditions required for growing the easier alpines and associated plants: rock outcropping such as the sandstone in Sussex or Kent, limestone in the north, glacial rocks in New England, screes or a gravelly or sandy soil, generally low in nutrients, with deep and sharp drainage, in which these sorts of plants will thrive. In hilly districts people's gardens often include quarry-like cuttings, banks or terracing with rock-garden potential. Rock gardening becomes a compensatory and 'natural' source of pleasure in garden terrain unsuitable for rich organic-filled beds for more conventional border plants.

As a style the natural rock garden is also one of the more recent gardening features to have been developed. The large-scale rockery or rock garden, where special conditions are created for plants from all over the world, many with slightly varying demands, is the most difficult of all the 'natural' styles to make pleasing. Rocks brought from other geological districts, however carefully arranged to resemble a natural stratification, may well look out of place (and today taking natural stone from regional sites, as the Edwardians did, is strongly discouraged). Nowadays it is a project to be left to the professionals in botanical gardens or theme parks. While in the Far East, in China and Japan, rocks themselves – rather than rock-garden plants – had been essential features of design for many centuries, the first modern rock gardens in the west were often bungled attempts to emulate the naturalistic (but far from haphazard) oriental arrangements, and at the same time give the alpines the conditions necessary for growth. Early rock gardens made no concessions to naturalism. The first recorded rock garden in England designed for growing specialist plants from alpine regions was made under glass at the Chelsea Physic Garden in 1772, where old stone (mainly Portland) from the Tower of London was combined with a large quantity of flints and chalk, and basaltic lava from a volcano in Iceland, presented by Sir Joseph Banks. Others followed, at Glasnevin in Dublin, at Liverpool, Cambridge and at Kew in 1867 built from Reigate sandstone, and the first version of the rock garden in the Edinburgh Botanic Gardens in about 1870, a very stiff affair divided up into uniform growing sections providing different conditions according to need. By 1882 Kew, having being given a collection of 2,500 alpines, began the construction of a 'rock' valley, more naturalistic in style, and dedicated to creating the right conditions for the plants. In 1893 the famous nursery firm of James Backhouse of York put up a rock garden of millstone grit in the Birmingham Botanic Gardens. Other rock gardens were constructed in simulated stone – a sort of superior cement – by the firm of Pulham, arranged very naturalistically to look as if it was natural outcrop, often especially adapted to the district a garden was in. Sir Frank Crisp's garden, Friar Park near Henley, was the most famous and elaborate rock garden, built like model 'alps', with 'mountains of greater and lesser height, valleys, mountain passes ... rustic alpine bridges overlooking quite formidable precipices, a waterfall... The rockery has a range of height from 30 to 40 feet', partly made by Backhouse; by 1909 it was extended by a scale model of the Matterhorn, its top covered with alabaster to resemble snow.

In William Robinson's day it was still permissible to bring stone from other areas. In his *Alpine Flowers for Gardeners*, he recommended arranging the rocks to look as if they were natural outcrops among selected shrubs and plants, or at the least stratified, as they would be in nature. But he was actually more interested in the planting possibilities, and was concerned for the natural rock garden to seem to form part of a larger natural garden. The planting of small shrubs that would be found on the

Iris setosa canadensis from North America – the type species has a wide range from eastern Russia to Alaska – enjoys conditions in the Edinburgh Botanic Garden, flowering in early summer. The climate in Edinburgh (at latitude 56° the same as Labrador) ensures a shorter growing season than the coastal areas of the west or of southern Britain. Basically the effects on climate of increasing latitude and of increasing altitude are similar; the temperature falls until, at the permanent snowline in any latitude, the climate resembles that of high altitude, with long cold winters and brief summers. Of course this sort of generalization is always modified by other topographical circumstances such as the closeness of absence of large expanses or water, tending to produce maritime conditions.

lower slopes of the mountain ranges – rhododendrons, daphnes, heaths, dwarf kalmias (*Kalmia angustifolia*) – placed in groups at the edge of the rock garden would help the rockery itself to blend into the garden scene without shading the smaller plants. Robinson also suggested that many more alpines could be grown in English gardens if more attention was paid to their specific needs. He continually reminded his readers that plants associated with rock gardens are not only the alpines from the high mountain snowlines, but also any plants that, living naturally among rocks, gravel and sand, need rapid and efficient drainage. Plants for rock-garden situations include true alpines (named for the European Alps) as well as mountain flora that adapt well to garden situations, and do not have to be grown in so-called rock gardens.

By 1913 in *The English Rock Garden* Reginald Farrer (1880–1920) was able to write with confidence: 'Times have wholly changed for the rock-garden. Fifty years ago it was merely the appanage of the large pleasure ground. In some odd corner or in some dank, tree haunted hollow, you rigged up a dump of broken cement blocks, and added bits of stone and fragments of statuary. You called this "the Rockery", and proudly led your friends to see it and planted it all over with periwinkle to hide the hollows in which your Alpines had died.' A specialist in alpines and in rock gardens and a plant collector in both Europe and the wilds of north-west Kansu and Burma, Reginald Farrer's influence has been more lasting and more important than Robinson's, in the world of rock gardening. *The English Rock Garden* still remains a classic for the aspiring rock-plant expert, although basically (like most alpine specialists) Farrer was less interested in scenic effects and naturalism than in making certain that plants had the sort of terrain they could enjoy. Born at a time when the Victorian rock garden lacked any semblance of a natural look and usually little ecological foundation for encouraging these fussy 'specialist' plants, he stamped his own decided views not only on how they should be grown but also on

THE FLOWERING OF A FORMER CAR-PARK

Beth Chatto turned her existing car-park of three-quarters of an acre/one-third hectare, sheltered by a tall hedge of Leyland cypress, into a Gravel Garden in 1991. Her soil is basically gravel and the rainfall in this part of Essex one of the lowest in the British Isles, averaging twenty inches/500 millimetres. She wanted a colourful display which, after soil preparation, planting and mulching with a topcoat of gravel – the same as used on the paths – would need no supplementary summer watering. Plants completely adapted to her fast-draining gravelly soil would be perfect for spreading out over the edges of beds, but would need to be augmented by groups of plants from richer habitats to make a satisfying visual display. Some of these would need planting pockets of amended humus-rich soil to get them through the first seasons.

The years as a car-park meant that the ground was badly compacted and had first to be broken up with a mechanical subsoiler, drawn behind a tractor. The subsoil was yellow sand and gravel, many feet deep, but such that plants – especially those with tap-roots – would be able to find moisture once they were established. The island beds, their shapes marked out in pleasing contours with curving hosepipes, were enriched with humus-making organics including home-made compost, bonfire waste and well-rotted manure. The first foundation planting was of mound-forming

(Above left) In autumn buff-coloured Mexican feather grass (*Stipa tenuissima*), sedums, silver-leaved *Artemisia stelleriana*, *Nicotiana langsdorffii* and a pale yellow kniphofia with a dark-flowered caryopteris are backed by the tall shrubby pink-flowered *Lavatera* 'Barnsley'. Although flower colour is important, plants are also chosen for foliage effects, which last through many months, and for their appearance in winter when seedheads and fading leaves shade down the colour scene to browns, beige and tawny golds to match the landscape rather than brighter flower hues. Beth Chatto has been influential in changing other gardeners' definition of beauty, encouraging them to appreciate the low-toned colours of dying flower stems.

(Above) The gravel on the paths is also used as a mulch on the beds, uniting the surfaces to make the garden look like a 'meadow' with a matrix of pale gravel. Beds and paths almost merge together, with flowerbed shapes changing yearly as some plants grow and spread more quickly than their neighbours. *Euphorbia polychroma*, a clump-forming perennial with greenish-gold surrounds to central yellow flowers, and golden-leaved aromatic marjoram (*Origanum vulgare* 'Aureum') make a splash of colour.

(Above) Beth Chatto prepared the compacted soil carefully and provided quite fertile moisture-retentive conditions in the beds in the Gravel Garden to start her plants off. Now, well mulched annually with gravel, the plants get no extra feeding and are seldom watered even in the driest summers. Eremurus thrive in the well-drained gravel with pale yellow achillea and various elegant grasses, which, waving in the wind, give a meadow-like quality to the planting schemes.

(Above) Beth Chatto's old car park, turned into a Gravel Garden, is an example of a garden where great horticultural skill and plant knowledge have been combined with an eye for beauty. Sheltered by tall trees and a Leylandii hedge, the garden has sprawling beds of first-rate perennials, spreading in gently curving abstract shapes, containing plants that thrive in the naturally well-drained gravelly soil and in the normal summer droughts of East Anglia. Beth has been known for her appropriate use of plants in other parts of her garden, where she cultivates dry-loving plants separate from those requiring moisture. She is also famous for her equally discerning Gold Medal exhibitions at Chelsea, in which she demonstrated to the public – who would later flock to her nursery – how, by providing associated plants with conditions they would enjoy, pleasure from their gardens could be maximized.

shrubs: *Salvia officinalis*, santolinas, ballota, lavenders, with creeping thymes, helianthemums, stachys and phuopsis – a mixture of deciduous with evergreens – to furnish the edges and disguise bulb foliage. Plants were chosen with contrasting forms, arching and spiky grasses contrasting with airy *Anthemis cupaniana* or leathery-leaved bergenias, giant sea-kale (*Crambe cordifolia*) with tall eremurus and kniphofias. Tall kniphofias, verbascums, *Verbena bonariensis*, alliums and some flowering grasses create an airy screen through which lower plants are viewed. Plants are grouped together for specific conditions rather than for Jekyllian colour schemes. Mediterranean-type plants with evergreen foliage combine and contrast with the parchment colours of flowering grasses to furnish the garden even in winter. The long undulating borders look meadow-like in their natural simplicity, but both conditions and plant choices have been carefully calculated to produce that artlessness. This is sustained by judicious maintenance: plants are cut down as they become unsightly, and in spring germinating seedlings are 'edited' as required.

the look of the thing. Farrer's famous criticism on contemporary rock gardens can still be appreciated today. He abhorred 'almond puddings' made with spikes and pinnacles (as at Friar Park), 'dogs' graves' (puddings with stones laid flat) and the 'devil's lapful', where cartloads of bald square-faced boulders were dropped about anywhere with no deference to either suitability or usefulness in culture – 'The chaotic hideousness of the result is to be remembered with shudders ever after.'

Farrer and Robinson influenced the making of many new natural-style rock gardens – often rocks combined with water and water-side plants. At Rowallane in Northern Ireland, glacier-smooth natural outcroppings of hard whinstone became the site for a naturalistic rock garden. Loads of peaty acid soil filled in the crevices to make homes for Asiatic primulas, gentians and meconopsis, with American erythroniums and silver-leaved celmisias from New Zealand. Lincoln Foster made a famous rock garden in Connecticut. His woods, featuring natural outcrops of glacial rock with a steep gorge and running stream opening into sunlight, made the perfect site. Boulders and rocky ledges by the stream provided sites for both native and exotic rock and water plants, while an open meadow became a field of native *Anemone canadensis*, thriving in the damp conditions, and a few feet away the sun-loving *Euphorbia cyparissias* flourished on a rocky outcrop.

At Sizergh Castle in Cumbria a rock and water garden laid out in the 1920s with water-worn local limestone from the region, surrounding a bowl of water fed by streams and pools from a natural lake above, was planted with rock plants, water plants, ferns and Japanese maples, and prostrate and dwarf conifers, planted among the rocks and overhanging the water. Gradually the high-mountain alpines have been elbowed or shaded out, while bog, aquatic and woodland plants fill the space with light and shadow. Ferns have become a speciality and today Sizergh holds an extensive fern collection, including shield and sword ferns (*Polystichum*), bladder ferns (*Cystopteris*), maidenhair (*Adiantum*), sensitive fern (*Onoclea sensibilis*) and the royal fern (*Osmunda regalis*).

The Victorian fern craze, in which collectors went mad for every possible fern, had little to do with the natural fern garden, in which ferns, for sun or shade, for dry soil or damp, for acid or alkaline soils, flourish in drifts with other plants of similar requirements. In fact in the natural garden there should be no rigid segregation and ferns, like all other plants, given the conditions they prefer, will look natural and appropriate in all the different garden habitats discussed earlier. Most, in fact, prefer damp shade, but some (like hart's tongue) seem to survive and flourish with little moisture or sustenance.

Ferns are at their most beautiful as their fronds unfold in spring but, given some attention to the requirements of each variety, they look good all through the season. In Britain there is a good assortment of natives, almost all shade-lovers or only surviving in the open if given plenty of moisture. But ferns are more adaptable than is thought. Some of the ferns from North American woodland need less shade in Britain's cooler summers and can be grown in open borders. Some are clump-formers, extending their roots rapidly into boggy, peaty soil. In Britain a few hardy ferns mix well in woodland or in woodland glades with other plants. The royal fern is one of the handsomest of Britain's native hardy ferns, able to hold up the bank of stream or pond with thick matted roots. The ostrich plume fern (*Matteuccia struthiopteris*) spreads more slowly to occupy adjacent soil and push out competitive neighbours, while the sensitive fern from North America colonizes quickly in marshy ground, and although a shade-lover in its native regions, will adapt to an open site in Britain's temperate climate.

Today it is rarely possible to transform garden terrain, even with the help of a professional contractor, into a miniature but naturalistic imitation of nature suitable for fussy rock plants, in the style of the great nineteenth-century displays such as at Hoole House in Lancashire or Friar Park, or to transform natural rock outcrops into a mountain gorge or Japanese garden. Most alpine enthusiasts make themselves content with modified forms of rock gardens, with alpines given specially appropriate spots between drifts of similar-looking plants.

Another possibility is the scree or gravel garden, with natural or prepared drainage. This form of natural rock garden is akin to meadows in its visual appeal, with mainly hardy plants (together with annuals and biennials) all chosen for their ability to seed and spread. The word 'scree' is generally used by gardeners to imply a specially prepared bed, very similar to the shingle slopes on which some of the high 'alpine' and saxatile plants are found, very often in blazing sun but watered from below by melting snow from the mountain peaks above. Gardeners, of course, cannot reproduce similar underground water supplies, but have found that on sunny slopes with adequate drainage and a reasonably moisture-retentive soil mulched with gravel, great progress can be made in triumphing with difficult alpines. To make a moraine or scree, excavations involve providing drainage to two feet/sixty centimetres or more, and new soil (a standard mix for alpines of one-third each of loam, sharp washed sand and leafmould or peat) added in proportions of roughly one-fifth to four-fifths shingle or gravel.

Gravel or dry gardens are an extension of scree to flatter areas where larger plants can be grown. Gravel is dug into the soil and beds are heavily mulched with a layer of similar washed shingle about three inches/eight centimetres deep, providing a dry bed for plant rosettes. (Many high alpines have grey leaves that are under snow during winter months in their native habitat but absorb moisture in a damp temperate climate. The gravel mulch also inhibits weed germination, while making uprooting unwanted weeds and seedlings easy. One firm advantage of a gravel bed is ease of maintenance: it is possible to walk on the surface without compacting soil or leaving footprints.

Gravel gardens may also be composed of plants from Mediterranean-type areas, which require stony poor soil.

These are given sites approximating to their native habitats, the soil mulched with gravel to retain moisture through the hottest part of the summer. In general lime-tolerant plants, many from the Mediterranean basin, cope better with dry conditions than the calcifuge ones, which normally come from areas of high rainfall. Many of these plants are prolific self-seeders, or plants with long taproots that can penetrate down to moisture (shallow-rooted plants succumb earlier to drought). Plants with small leaves, often silvery, grey or coated by waxy cuticle, adapt well to drought, and enjoy the extra heat reflected from the gravel surface. The most vulnerable plants have large thin soft leaves with no protection from the sun.

Rather than simulating a true sloping scree, the more modest gravel garden can include more low-growing plants to keep an almost flat, open surface. A different adaptation of the gravel-garden principle gives an effect more like a border by using other taller, more meadow-like perennials, the stalwarts of any sunny border, all with low water demands. Low-growing plants hugging the ground will limit water evaporation from the soil but the taller plants will need a thick gravel mulch around their stems. In the former case quick-spreading low-growing sun-loving dianthus, erodiums, euphorbias (*Euphorbia cyparissias*, self-seeding *E. myrsinites* and *E. dulcis*), rock roses, prostrate rosemaries, santolinas, *Hypericum olympicum*, dwarf-sized *Salvia taraxacifolia*, silvery-foliaged *Stachys byzantina* and creeping thymes provide a groundwork for taller plants. Those appropriately include agapanthus, angelica (*Angelica archangelica*), asphodels, asphodelines and cerinthes from Greece, *Cynara cardunculus*, mulleins, kniphofias, phormiums, alliums, Mediterranean euphorbias, and shrubs such as grey-leaved *Brachyglottis* 'Sunshine', myrtle, phlomis, rosemary, different leaf forms of *Salvia officinalis*, the curry plant (*Helichrysum italicum*) and yuccas.

Most gravel gardens made in naturally free-draining gravelly soil need some soil amendment, with organic

In the African section of the Alpine Garden of the University of British Columbia Botanic Garden in Vancouver, looking towards the North American section, scarlet *Crocosmia* x *crocosmiiflora*, summer hyacinth (*Galtonia candicans*) and *Gladiolus psittacinus* grow in front of *Spartium junceum* (from North Africa and Mediterranean regions) and the American native Colorado spruce (*Picea pungens*). The Alpine Garden at Vancouver is a skilfully prepared artificial environment in which as many alpines as possible from all parts of the world are grown. These 'alpines' include dwarf conifers, trees and shrubs. The natural site of the garden, on a promontory almost at sea-level, differs greatly from the ideal alpine habitat. Snow protection in winter is absent, and one of the features of the climate is its unpredictability, with widely varying rainfall incidence and temperatures. The growing season is long, with ample summer rain and sunshine.

composts dug in to help retain moisture and nutrients. When Beth Chatto converted a new part of her Essex garden to a gravel garden she found subsoil of yellow sand and gravel to provide plants with long taproots with moisture. She planned a colourful display that would have no supplementary summer watering in this area of low-rainfall. Plants completely adapted to her fast-draining soil were augmented by groups of plants from richer habitats, needing pockets of amended humus-rich soil to get them through the first seasons, and she included the contrasting forms of mound-forming shrubs, soaring and spiky leaves, feathery grasses and more substantial large-leaved foliage plants

Other gravel gardens, such as my own at Bettiscombe in Dorset, depend more on self-seeders, which give single and group spots of colour between evergreen shrubs such as myrtles, lavenders, *Salvia officinalis* and its different seed types, and creeping evergreens, such as *Veronica* 'Georgia Blue', thymes and sedums, which help the garden's winter appearance. A basic well-drained alkaline soil will bring best results. Seeds germinate happily and haphazardly in a pea-gravel mulch and results, after the first season, have more of a natural meadow effect, with plants choosing their own spot: salvias, poppies, *Galactites tomentosa*, a thistle with veined leaves, Scotch thistle, cerinthes, Miss Willmott's ghost, verbascums, *Reseda alba*, lychnis, the airy *Verbena bonariensis* with violas and erodiums at low level and bulbs. Many characteristic dry grassland species make good contrast, such as *Briza media* and stipas, with sedges such as New Zealand *Carex comans* and *C. flagelifera*, as well as European carnation sedge (*C. flacca*) and mat-forming *C. humilis*. Seedlings can all be edited in spring as they germinate, easily pulled out of the thick gravel surface, as also are undesirable weed seedlings. This sort of gardening, somewhere between a meadow and the conventional border, can be intensive with constant attention to plant detail, grouping and tidiness: achieving that spontaneous, natural look involves considerable care.

BIBLIOGRAPHY

Allan, Mea *William Robinson* Faber & Faber, London, 1982.

Archer-Wills, Anthony *The Water Garden* Frances Lincoln, London, 1993.

Art, Henry W. *The Wildflower Gardener's Guide* Garden Way Publishing, Vermont, 1987.

Beveridge, Charles E. and Rocheleau, Paul *Frederick Law Olmsted* Rizzoli, New York, 1995.

Brickell, Christopher (Ed.) *The RHS A–Z Encyclopaedia of Garden Plants* Dorling Kindersley, London, 1996.

Chadwick, George *The Park and the Town* Praeger, New York, 1996.

Chatto, Beth *The Damp Garden* Dent, London, 1982.

Chatto, Beth *The Dry Garden* Dent, London, 1978.

Chatto, Beth *The Green Tapestry* Collins, London, 1989.

Clausen, Ruth Rogers and Ekstrom, Nicolas H. *Perennials for American Gardens*, Random House, New York, 1989.

Collier, Gordon *Titoki Point* Moa Beckett, Auckland NZ, 1993.

Connor, Sheila *New England Natives* Harvard University Press, Cambridge, Massachusetts, 1994.

Druse, Ken *The Natural Garden* Clarkson Potter, New York, 1989.

Dwelley, Marilyn J. *Tress and Shrubs of New England* Down East Books, Camden, Maine, 1980.

Elliott, Brent *The Country House Garden* Mitchell Beazley, London 1995.

Farrer, Reginald *The English Rock Garden* T.C. & E.C. Jack Ltd, London, (2nd ed.), 1922.

Flint, Harrison L. *Landscape Plants for Eastern North America* John Wiley and Sons, Chichester, New York, 1983.

Poster, H. Lincoln *Rock Gardening* Timber Press, Portland, Oregon, 1982.

Gorer, Richard *The Flower Garden in England* B. T. Batsford, London, 1975.

Gorer, Richard *Living Tradition in the Garden* David & Charles, Newton Abbot, 1974.

Greenlee, John *The Encyclopaedia of Ornamental Grasses* Rodale Press, Emmaus, Pennsylvania, 1992.

Grese, Robert E. *Jens Jensen* John Hopkins University Press, Baltimore, 1992.

Hansen, Richard and Stahl, Friedrich *Perennials and their Garden Habitats* Cambridge University Press, English translation, Cambridge, 1993.

Hobhouse, Penelope *Plants in Garden History* Pavilion, London, 1992.

Hertrich, William *The Huntingdon Botanical Gardens 1905–1949* Huntington Library, San Marino, California, (reprint), 1988.

Jensen, Jens *Siftings* John Hopkins University Press, Baltimore, 1990.

Johnson, Hugh *The Principles of Gardening* Mitchell Beazley, London, 1979.

Justice William S. and Bell, Ritchie *Wild Flowers of North Carolina* University of North Carolina Press, Chapel Hill, 1968.

Klein, William M. *Gardens of Philadelphia and the Delaware Valley* Temple University Press, Philadelphia, 1995.

Kruckeberg, Arthur R. *Gardening with Native Plants of the Pacific Northwest* Douglas & McIntyre Vancouver, 1982.

Ladd, Doug *Tall Grass Prairie Wildflowers* London, 1995.

Lloyd, Christopher *The Flower Garden* Dorling Kindersley, London, 1993.

Lloyd, Christopher *The Well-Tempered Garden* Collins, London, 1970.

Magnani, Denise *The Winterthur Garden* Abrams, New York, 1995.

Mickel, John *Ferns for American Gardens* Macmillan, New York, 1994.

The New Royal Horticultural Society Dictionary of Gardening Macmillan, London, 1992.

Newton, Norman T. *Design on the Land* Belknap Press, Cambridge, Massachusetts, 1971.

Oehme, Wolfgang and Van Sweden, James *Bold Romantic Gardens* Acropolis Books, Washington DC, 1990.

Ottewill, David *The Edwardian Garden* Yale University Press, New Haven, Connecticut, 1989.

Perry, Bob *Landscape Plants for Western Regions* Land Design Publishing, Claremont, 1992.

Pollan, Michael *Second Nature* Laurel, Vancouver, 1991.

The RHS Plant Finder Moorland, Derbyshire, 1996.

Robinson, William *Alpine Flowers for English Gardens* John Murray, London, 1870.

Robinson, William *The English Flower Garden* Hamlyn, Twickenham, 1984.

Robinson, William *The Wild Garden* Century, London 1983.

Smith, J. Robert *The Prairie Garden* University of Wisconsin Press, Madison, Wisconsin, 1980.

Spongberg, Stephen A. *A Reunion of Trees* Harvard University Press, Cambridge, Massachusetts, 1990.

Streatfield, David C. *Californian Gardens* Abbeville Press, New York, 1994.

Stuart Thomas, Graham *Ornamental Shrubs, Climbers and Bamboos* John Murray, London, 1992.

Stuart Thomas, Graham *The Rock Garden and its Plants* Dent, London, 1989.

Taylor, Jane *Weather in the Garden* John Murray, London, 1996.

van Sweden, James *Gardening with Water* Random House, New York, 1995.

Journals

Country Life in America (1906)
Journal of Garden History
Garden History Society Journal
Gardens Illustrated
Horticulture
Pacific Horticulture
The Garden

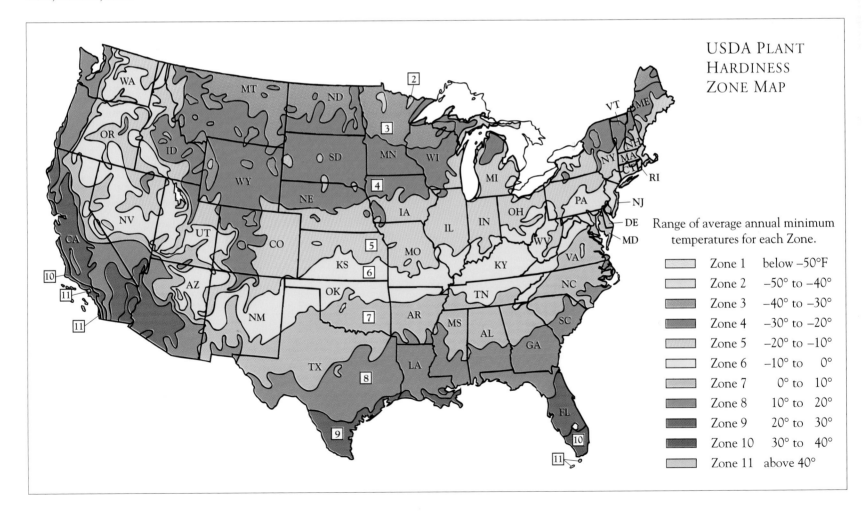

USDA PLANT HARDINESS ZONE MAP

Range of average annual minimum temperatures for each Zone.

Zone 1 below −50°F
Zone 2 −50° to −40°
Zone 3 −40° to −30°
Zone 4 −30° to −20°
Zone 5 −20° to −10°
Zone 6 −10° to 0°
Zone 7 0° to 10°
Zone 8 10° to 20°
Zone 9 20° to 30°
Zone 10 30° to 40°
Zone 11 above 40°

INDEX

Page references in italics indicate illustration captions

Abelia 105; *A.* x *grandiflora* 105
Abies balsamea (balsam fir) 46
abutilon 98, 105
acacia 105
Acaena 133; *A. buchananii* 139;
  A. microphylla 139
Acanthus 39, 64, 145; *A. mollis* 63, 86, 127
Acer (maple) 62, *172*; *A. ginnala* (amur
  maple) 47; *A. palmatum* (Japanese maple)
  52, *101*; *A. pensylvanicum* (mousewood)
  173; *A. platanoides* (Norway maple) 30,
  68, 73; *A. pseudoplatanus* (sycamore) 30;
  A.p. 'Puget Pink' *140*; *A. rubrum* (red
  maple) *19*, 90, 166; *A. saccharum* (sugar
  maple) 70; *A. spicatum* (mountain
  maple) *34*
Achillea 143, 150, *178*;
  A. millefolium (yarrow) 97, 127
Achnatherum calamagrotis 127
acid soil 52, 53, 57, 60, 99
Aconitum (monkshood) 69, 98, 111, 140, 145;
  A. carmichaelii 98
Acorus calamus (sweet flag) 163
Actaea (baneberry) 69, 74, 80, 86, 97, 170
adaptability of plants 53–61
Adiantum (maidenhair fern) 69, *181*;
  A. pedatum 71, 171
Adonis 90;
  A. amurensis (amur adonis) 89, *91*
aeonium 134
Aesculus hippocastanum (horse chestnut) 68
agapanthus 145, 183
Agave 17, 30, 40, *115*, 134;
  A. americana 16, 42; *A. attenuata* 42
Agrostemma githago (corncockle) *124*, 132
Ailanthus altissima (tree of heaven) 73, 82
Ajuga (bugle) 121; *A. reptans* 85, 112
Alchemilla (lady's mantle) 111, 128, *136, 138*;
  A. mollis 101, *137, 143*, 152
alder *see Alnus*
Alexandrian laurel *see Danae racemosa*
alkaline soil 52, 53, 86, *98*, 183
Allegheny spurge *see Pachysandra procumbens*
Allium 103, 127, *137*, 155, 179, 183;
  A. cernuum 143; *A. christophii 136*;
  A. neapolitanum 107
Alnus (alder) 68
aloe 30, 40, 134
alpine plants *44*, 51, *157*;
  rock gardens 174–5, 176, 177, *182*, 182
altitude 38
aluminium 53
Amelanchier 82, 98;
  A. canadensis (shadbush) *34*
America *see* North America

'American Gardens' 15, 57
Amomyrtus luma 73
Amorpha: A. canescens (lead plant) 131;
  A. fruticosa (indigo bush) 131
Ampelopsis glandulosa brevipedunculata 73
Amsonia tabernaemontana 71
Amstelveen, Holland 25, 54, 147
amur adonis *see Adonis amurensis*
amur maple *see Acer ginnala*
Anaphalis 55, 97; *A. margaritacea* 146
andromeda 15, 106
Anemone 88, 100; *A. apennina* (apennine
  anemone) 13, 69, 81, 87, 88, 90, 108, 122;
  A. blanda 68, 69, 80, 81; *A. candensis* 180;
  A. hupehensis 13; *A. japonica* 13, 80, 97,
  145, 151; *A. nemorosa* (wood anemone)
  68, 69, 80, 87, 88, *115*; *A. ranunculoides*
  69, 80
Anemonella thalictroides (rue anemone) 166
Angelica archangelica 183
Anigozanthus pulcherrimus (kangeroo
  paw) 27
annuals 39, 56, 128, 152; annual flower
  meadows 132–3
Anthemis cupaniana 179
Anthyllis vulneraria (kidney vetch) 127
apennine anemone *see Anemone apennina*
Aponogeton distachyos (Cape pondweed,
  water hawthorn) 162
aquatic plants 162, 174
Aquilegia (columbine) 69, 128, 140, 151;
  A. canadensis 86, 166; *A. vulgaris* 111, 152
Arabis procurrens 134
arbor-vitae *see Thuja occidentalis*
Arbutus 70, *103*; *A. menziesii* (madrone) 32,
  74; *A. unedo* 75, 78, 86, 102
arbutus, trailing *see Epigaea repens*
Arctostaphylos (manzanita) 40, 80, 86;
  A. patula 80; *A. uva-ursi* (bearberry,
  kinnikinnick) 74, 80, 102, 112
Arctotheca calendula 42
Argyll, Duke of 15
Arisaema 66, 81; *A. sikkokianum* 66
Arley Hall, Cheshire 139
Armeria maritima (seathrift) 139
Aronia melanocarpa 171
arrowhead *see Sagittaria sagittifolia*
Artemisia 30, *55*, 97, 147; *A. lactiflora* 168;
  A. ludoviciana 146; *A. stelleriana 178*
artichoke *138*
Arts and Crafts movement 11, 23, 24
Arum 62, 88; *A. italicum* 80;
  A.i. 'Marmoratum' 69, *101*
arum lily *see Zantedeschia aethiopica*
Aruncus dioicus (goat's beard) *13*, *106*, 168,
  170
Arundinaria pumila 134
Arundo donax 162

Asarum: A. canadense (American ginger)
  86, 88; *A. europaeum* (European ginger)
  68, 80, 88, 97
Asclepias tuberosa (butterfly weed) 129, 131
ash, white 90, 166
Asian dogwood *see Cornus controversa*
aspect 27, 43
aspen *see Populus tremuloides*
asphodeline 97, 127, 183
Asphodelus aestivus (asphodel) 127, 183
Aspidistra elatior 86
Asplenium scolopendrium 69
Aster 145, 165, 170; *A. amellus* 127, 145;
  A. divaricatus (woodland aster) 74, 85;
  A. laevis 'Blubird' *50*; *A. macrophyllus* 85;
  A. novae-angliae 'Purple Dome' 166;
  flowering meadows 128, *131*; shrub
  borders 94, 97, *106*, 111
Astilbe 52, 61, 85, 97, 155, 170, 173; *A.
  rivularis* 168; herbaceous borders 145, *146*
Astilboides tabularis (syn. *Rodgersia
  tabularis*) 168
Astrantia (masterwort) 81, *108*, 111, *115*;
  A. major 145; *A.* 'Shaggy' *108*
Atlas cedar *see Cedrus atlantica glauca*
atriplex *55*
aubrieta 158
Aucuba 98, 102, 103; *A. japonica* 78
azalea *see Rhododendron*
azara 105

baby blue eyes *see Nemophila menziesii*
bald cypress *see Taxodium distichum*
ballota 179
balsam fir *see Abies balsamea*
Baltic ivy *see Hedera helix* 'Baltica'
bamboos 63, 77, 102, *105*, 162
baneberry *see Actaea*
Baptisia (indigo) *B. alba* 131;
  B. australis 130, 131, 145
barrenwort *see Epimedium alpinum*
Bartram, John 57, 82
basswood *see Tilia americana*
bay laurel *see Umbellularia californica*
bearberry *see Arctostaphylos uva-ursi*
bearskin *see Festuca scoparia*
beauty bush *see Kolkwitzia amabilis*
bee balm *see Monarda didyma*
bee orchid *see Ophrys apifera*
beech *see Fagus*
Begonia evansiana (syn. *B. grandis*) 112
bellflower *see Campanula*
berberis *114, 136*
bergenia 155, 179
Bermuda grass *see Cynodon dactylon*
Betula (birch) 70; *B. alleghaniensis* (yellow
  birch) 47; *B. papyrifera* (paper birch) *19*,
  29, 34, 35, 47, *172*, 173
Biltmore Estate, North Carolina 19, 28
birch *see Betula*

Asarum: Birkenhead Park, Liverpool 18
Birmingham Botanic Gardens 176
bistort *see Persicaria bistorta*
bittersweet *see Celastrus*
black-eyed Susan *see Rudbeckia hirta*
bladder fern *see Cystopteris*
blazing star *see Liatris*
blechnum 69, 87
bleeding heart *see Dicentra spectablis*
Bloedel Reserve, Seattle *120*
bloodroot *see Sanguinaria canadensis*
blue fescue *see Festuca glauca*
blue gramma grass *see Bouteloua gracilis*
blue gum *see Eucalyptus globulus*
blue poppy *see Meconopsis*
blue-eyed Mary *see Omphalodes verna*
bluebell *see Hyacinthoides*
bluebell, Virginia *see Mertensia virginica*
blueberry 70
bog arum *see Lysichiton americanus*
bog buckbean *see Menyanthes trifoliata*
bog gardens 158–60, 163–5; plants 52,
  160–3, 165–71
Bois des Moutiers, France 69, 78
Boltonia 111, 145, 168; *B. asteroides* 145
boneset *see Eupatorium*
borders *see* herbaceous borders;
  shrubberies and shrub borders
boron 52, 53
botanic gardens 38
Bouteloua gracilis (blue gramma grass) 120
Bowles' golden grass *see Milium effusum*
  'Aureum'
Bowles' golden sedge *see Carex elata*
  'Aurea'
box *see Buxus*
Brachyglottis 61, 105; *B.* 'Sunshine' (syn.
  Senecio 'Sunshine') 61, 105, 143, 183
brandy bottle *see Nuphar lutea*
Britain: climate 27, 44, *44*, 48, 51, 52, 57;
  herbaceous borders 141; history of
  gardening styles 11–16, 23–4; native plant
  gardening 30; plants from abroad 57–61;
  shrub borders 96–7, 102; woodland
  gardens 58, 68, 72–3, 76–7, 80
Briza (quaking grass): *B. maxima* 132, *146*;
  B. media 183
bromeliad, Chilean *see Puya chilensis*
Brookes, John 93, 136
Brown, Lancelot 'Capability' 14
Brunnera 111; *B. macrophylla* 80, 108
Buchloe dactyloides (buffalo grass) 120–1
buckthorn *see Rhamnus alaternus*
buckthorn, sea *see Hippophae rhamnoides*
Buddleja 62, 97; *B. alternifolia* 95;
  B. davidii 9
buffalo grass *see Buchloe dactyloides*
bugbane *see Cimicifuga*
bugle *see Ajuga*

Buglossoides 108; *B. purpurocaerulea* (blue gromwell) 112
bulbs 39, 51, 52, 151, 183; flower meadows 122, 128; shrub borders 94, 99, 103; woodland gardens 67, 69, 75, 87–8
bullrush *see Scirpus lacustris*
bunchberry *see Cornus canadensis*
Bupleurum fruticosum 103
Burle Marx, Roberto 33, 120, 155
burning bush *see Dictamnus albus*
butcher's broom *see Ruscus aculeatus*
Butomus umbellatus 162
buttercup *see Ranunculus*
butterfly weed *see Asclepias tuberosa*
Buxus (box) 78, 80, 103, 108, 136
Bye, A. E. 23
Byzantine gladiolus 127, 152

cabbage palm *see Cordyline*
Cabot, Frank 34, 46, 47
cacti 30, 37, 40, 134
caladium 86
Calamagrostis 65, 146, 155, 162; *C.* x *acutiflora* (feather reed grass) 23, 168; *C.* x *a.* 'Karl Foerster' 168; *C.* x *a. stricta* 155
calcifuges (lime-hating plants) 52, 67, 72, 80, 105
calcium 52, 53
caliche soils 27
California 44, 57, 74–5, 104, 134
Californian lilac *see Ceanothus*
Californian poppy *see Eschscholzia californica*
Californian privet *see Ligustrum sinense*
calla lily *see Zantesdeschia aethiopica*
Callirhoe involucrata (poppy mallow) 131
Caltha palustris (marsh marigold) 163
Camassia 106, 127, 128; *C. cusickii* 123; *C. quamash* 123, 127
Camellia 44, 80, 99, 102, 103
Campanula (bellflower) 47, 111, 128, 133, 145, 168; *C. glomerata* 97, 127; *C. lactiflora* 128; *C. poscharskyana* 134; *C. rapunculoides* 112, 128; *C. trachelium* (nettle-leaved bellflower) 80, 112
campion *see Silene*
Campsis radicans (trumpet vine) 45
canary creeper *see Tropaeolum peregrinum*
candytuft *see Iberis sempervirens*
canna 171
canyon oak *see Quercus chrysolepis*
Cape pondweed *see Aponogeton distachyos*
Cardamine pratensis (lady's smock) 122, 163
cardinal flower *see Lobelia cardinalis*
Cardiocrinum giganteum (giant lily) 88
cardoon *see Cynara cardunculus*
Carex: C. buchananii 162; *C. comans* 183; *C. elata* 'Aurea' (Bowles' golden sedge) 162; *C. flacca* (carnation sedge) 183; *C. flagelifera* 183; *C. humilis* 183; *C. morrowii* (Japanese sedge) 86; *C. pendula* 86, 163; *C. riparia* 162; *C.r.* 'Variegata' 162
Carline thistle 127
carnation sedge *see Carex flacca*

Carnegia gigantea (saguaro) 37
Carpenteria californica 104
carrot, wild *see Daucus carota*
Carya (hickory) 90, 166
caryopteris 97, 178
Castanea dentata (chestnut) 82, 90
catbrier *see Smilax*
Catesby, Mark 57
catmint *see Nepeta*
Cautleya: C. lutea 113; *C. robusta* 113
Ceanothus (Californian lilac) 40, 62, 98, 104
Cedrus atlantica glauca (Atlas cedar) 16
celandine *see Chelidonium*
celandine poppy *see Stylophorum diphyllum*
Celastrus (bittersweet) 73
celmisia 44, 180
Centaurea (knapweed) 127, 132; *C. cyanus* (cornflower) 124, 132
Central Park, New York 18
Centranthus (valerian) 12, 127, 152; *C. ruber* 12, 146
Cephalaria gigantea 55, 138, 143
Ceratostigma 155; *C. plumbaginoides* 134
Cercis canadensis (redbud) 20
cerinthe 132, 183
Cetinale, Italy 14
chain fern *see Woodwardia fimbriata*
Chamaemelum nobile (chamomile) 132, 133
Chatto, Beth 9; gravel garden 178–9, 178, 179, 183; water garden 157, 161; woodland garden 76, 77
checkerberry *see Gaultheria procumbens*
Chelidonium (celandine) 122, 128
Chelone (turtle-head) 70
Chelsea Physic Garden 176
cherry laurel *see Prunus laurocerasus*
cherry, wild *see Prunus avium*
chestnut *see Castanea dentata*
Chicago Botanic Gardens 131
chicory *see Cichorium intybus*
China, plants from 51, 61, 78
Chionanthus 97; *C. retusus* 99; *C. virginicus* (fringe tree) 97, 99
chionodoxa 88, 90, 105, 115
Choisya 102, 103; *C. ternata* (Mexican orange) 103
Christmas box *see Sarcococca*
Christmas fern *see Polystichum munitum*
Chrysanthemum: C. coronarium 124; *C. leucanthemum* (moon daisy, ox-eye daisy) 94, 123, 124, 126, 127, 128; *C. segetum* (corn marigold) 132
Chusan palm *see Trachycarpus fortunei*
Cichorium intybus (chicory) 127
Cimicifuga (bugbane) 69, 85, 97; *C. racemosa* 170
cinnamon fern *see Osmunda cinnamomea*
Cistus (rock rose) 97, 115, 183
Cladastris lutea syn. *C. kentukia* (yellow wood) 20
clay soil 53, 98, 111
Clearing, The, Wisconsin 21
Clematis 113, 143, 150; *C. tangutica* 145; *C. texensis* 113; *C. viticella* 113
clerodendron 100

Clethra 100; *C. alnifolia* (sweet pepperbush) 98, 171
climate 27, 38–52, 56–7, *see also* microclimates
Clintonia borealis 173
clivia 145
clover, red *see Trifolium pratense*
coffee berry *see Rhamnus californica*
coffee tree, Kentucky *see Gymnocladus dioicus*
Collier, Gordon 61
Colorado spruce *see Picea pungens*
Columbian Exposition, Chicago (1893) 19, 28
columbine *see Aquilegia*
comfrey *see Symphytum*
compass plant *see Silphium laciniatum*
Comptonia peregrina (sweet fern) 98
coneflower *see Echinacea; Rudbeckia*
coneflower, prairie *see Ratibidia columnifera*
conifers 39, 61
continental climate 43, 45, 51, 57, 69–72, 97
Convallaria majalis (lily-of-the-valley) 28, 80, 88, 112
Copeland, Pamela & Lammot 166
Cordyline (cabbage palm): *C. australis* 24, 61; *C. indivisa* 61
Coreopsis 143, 155; *C. tinctoria* 129; *C. verticillata* 145
corn marigold *see Chrysanthemum segetum*
corncockle *see Agrostemma githago*
cornflower *see Centaurea cyanus*
Cornus (dogwood) 62, 105–9, 105, 160; *C. alba* 108, 163, 166; *C. a.* 'Spaethii' 108; *C. alternifolia* 108; *C. canadensis* (bunchberry) 68, 86, 173; *C. controversa* (Asian dogwood) 108; *C. florida* 20, 85–6, 90, 98, 105, 109, 166; *C. kousa* 105, 173; *C. k. chinensis* 105, 109; *C. nuttalli* 105, 109; *C. n.* 'Eddie's White Wonder' 109; *C. sibirica* 166; *C. stolonifera* 34, 108, 163, 166, 171; *C. s.* 'Flaviramea' 166, 171; *C. s.* 'Silver and Gold' 166
corokia 61, 105
Cortaderia sellowiana (pampas grass) 107, 169
Corydalis 80, 88, 90; *C. flexuosa* 80, 113
corylopsis 108
Corylus (hazel) 68, 114; *C. maxima* 'Purpurea' 114
Cotinus coggygria (smoke bush) 93, 96, 99, 114, 143
Cotoneaster 102, 103, 106; *C. conspicuus* 103; *C. dammeri* 121; *C.* 'Rothschildianus' 103; *C. salicifolius* 103
cotula 133
cowslip *see Primula veris*
crab apple *see Malus ioensis*
Crambe 140, 150, 151; *C. cordifolia* (giant sea-kale) 179; *C. maritima* 12
cranesbill *see Geranium*
Crataegus (hawthorn) 21, 22
cream bush *see Holodiscus discolor*
creeping Jenny *see Lysimachia nummularia*
crinodendron 105
Crisp, Sir Frank 176

Crocosmia x *crocosmiiflora* 182
Crocus 88, 88, 123, 151; *C. florida* 20; *C. tommasinianus* 89, 175
crown imperial *see Fritillaria imperialis*
Cruden Farm, Australia 30
cucumber magnolia *see Magnolia acuminata*
Cupressus (cypress): *C. macrocarpa* (Monterey cypress) 40; *C. sempervirens* 'Fastigiata' (Italian cypress) 63
curry plant *see Helichrysum italicum*
Curtis, Will 70
Cyathea (tree ferns) 86; *C. dealbata* 61, 61
cycads 16, 40
Cycas revoluta (sago palm) 16
Cyclamen 13, 68, 75, 88, 103, 105, 112; *C. coum* 85, 101; *C. hederifolium* 69, 75, 88, 101, 175; *C. repandum* 69, 101
Cynara cardunculus (cardoon) 151, 183
Cynodon dactylon (Bermuda grass) 120, 134
cypress *see Cupressus*
cypress, swamp or bald *see Taxodium distichum*
Cypripedium: C. acaule (moccasin flower) 71, 107; *C. calceolus* (lady's slipper) 70, 71, 86, 113, 166; *C. reginae* 70
Cyperus vegetus (syn. *C. eragrotis*) 162
Cyrtomium 87; *C. falcatum* (holly fern) 69, 86
Cystopteris (bladder fern) 180
Cytisus battandieri (Moroccan broom) 13, 106, 113

Dacrydium cupressinum (rimu) 61
Dactylorhiza maculata (heath spotted orchid) 123, 128
daffodil *see Narcissus*
dahlia 114, 148
daisy bush *see Olearia*
Danae racemosa (Alexandrian laurel) 78, 103
dandelion 122, 128
Daphne 102, 106, 177; *D. laureola* (spurge laurel) 78
Darmera 115; *D. peltata* (syn. *Peltiphyllum peltatum*)(umbrella plant) 168, 171
Dasyphyllum diacanthoides 86
Daucus carota (wild carrot) 126
day-lily *see Hemerocallis*
deciduous plants 39, 57, 88; shrubs for the shrub border 105–9
deer cabbage *see Nephrophyllidium faurei*
Denmans, West Sussex 93, 136–7, 136, 137
Dennstaedtia puncticloba (hay-scented ferns) 74, 171
Deschampsia cespitosa (tufted grass) 86
Desfontanea 106; *D. spinosa* 105
deutzia 108
dianthus 111, 114, 183
diascia 145
Diboll, Neil 131
Dicentra 68, 81; *D. cucullaria* (Dutchman's breeches) 166; *D. eximia* 112; *D. formosa* 112; *D. spectabilis* (bleeding heart) 98, 111, 145
dichondra 133
Dicksonia (tree ferns) 61, 87; *D. fibrosa* 61; *D. squarrosa* 61

Dictamnus albus (burning bush) 97, *111*
Digitalis (foxglove) 80, 126; *D. grandiflora*
111; *D. purpurea* 111; shrub borders 97,
106, *107*, 111, 112; woodland gardens 69,
80, 85
Dipsacus fullonum (teazel) *143*, *146*
Dodecatheon (shooting star) 113;
D. meadia 113
Doe Run, Pennsylvania *128*
dog's mercury *see Mercurialis perennis*
dog's tooth violet *see Erythronium
americanum*
dogwood *see Cornus*
Doronicum (leopard's bane) 94
Douglas, David 32, 61, 74
Douglas fir *see Pseudotsuga menziesii*
Dower House, Barnsley, Glos *85*
Downing, Andrew Jackson 18, 119
Dracaena drago 41
Drimys 98; *D. lanceolata* 86, 105;
D. winteri 105
Drosanthemum floribundum 42
Dryas octopetala 134
Dryopteris: *D. carthusiana* (shield fern) 171,
180; *D. cristata* (narrow swamp fern) 170
Du Pont family 90, 166
Du Pont, Henri 88, 90, *90*
Du Pont, Pierre 82–3
Duchesnia indica (false strawberry) 112
Durand, Herbert 31
Dutchman's breeches *see Dicentra cucullaria*

earthworms 52, 53
eastern hemlock *see Tsuga canadensis*
echeveria 134
Echinacea (coneflower): *E. pallida* 130;
E. purpurea 130, *145*
Echinocactus 37
echinops 104, 150
Edinburgh Botanic Garden 176, *176*
Edsell Ford Garden, Detroit *11*
Elaeagnus 98, 102; *E. angustifolia* (Russian
olive) 30
Elymus arenarius 127
English Flower Garden, The (Robinson) 24,
94, 103, 106, 150
Enkianthus 173
Eomecon chionantha (snow poppy) 113
Epigaea repens (trailing arbutus) 70, 112,
166
epilobium 126
Epimedium 69, 80, 81, 85, 155; *E. alpinum*
(barrenwort) 81; *E. perralderianum* 85
Eranthis 13, 88, 90, 105; *E. cilicica* 85; *E.
hyemalis* (winter aconite) 68, 85, 88, *88*,
91; *E. pinnatifida* 85; *E.* x *tubergenii* 85
Eremurus 178; *E. robustus* 13, *138*
Ericaceae 72, 80, 97
Erigeron 145; *E. karvinskianus* 123, 133, 158
erodium 183
Eryngium 104, 150; *E. giganteum* (Miss
Willmott's ghost) *143*, 152, 183
Erythea armata (Mexican blue palm) *17*
Erythronium 88, 100, 105, 108, 180; *E.
americanum* (dog's tooth violet) 170

escallonia 98, 105, 106, *111*
Eschscholzia californica (Californian poppy)
40, *41*, *57*, 128
Eucalyptus (gum) *30*, 105; *E. citriodora 30*;
E. globus (blue gum) 40
eucryphia 73, 98, 105
Euonymus 102; *E. japonicus* 78
Eupatorium (boneset) *55*, 155, 168, 170;
E. maculatum (Joe Pye weed) 131;
E. purpureum 128, 145, 170; herbaceous
borders 140, 145, 150; shrub borders 98,
111
Euphorbia 97, 111, *137*, *183*; *E.
amygdaloides* (wood spurge) 78, 97, 101;
E.a. robbiae 78; *E. cyparissias* 180, *183*;
E. dulcis 183; *E. griffithii* 111;
E. myrsinites 183; *E. polychroma 178*;
E. sikkimensis 111; *E. wulfenii* 141
evening primrose *see Oenothera*
evergreen plants 39, 57, 75; shrubs 78,
102–5, 106–7

Fagus (beech) 68, 166; *F. grandiflora* 91
Fallopia japonica (Japanese knotweed) 170,
172
false spikenard *see Smilacina racemosa*
false strawberry *see Duchesnia indica*
Fargesia nitida (fountain bamboo) 77
Farrer, Reginald 177–80
fatsia 103
feather grass *see Stipa*
feather reed grass *see Calamagrostis* x
acutiflora
fennel *see Foeniculum vulgare*
ferns *19*, 61, 155, 166, 180–1; rock gardens
173, 174; shrub borders 94, 100; water
gardens 163, 170, 171; woodland gardens
68, 69, 74, 76, 86–7, 90
Festuca 110; *F. glauca* (syn. *F. cinerea*) (blue
fescue) *16*, 134–9; *F. ovina* var. *glauca 16*;
F. scoparia (syn. *F. gautieri*) (bearskin) 139
Filipendula (meadowsweet) 97, 163;
F. kamtschatika 168; *F. rubra* (queen of the
prairie) *55*, 131; *F. r.* 'Venusta' *55*, 168
flag iris, yellow *see Iris pseudacorus*
flame flower *see Tropaeolum speciosum*
Flanders poppy *see Papaver rhoeas*
flowering meadows 116, 122–6, 129–32;
annual 132–3; maintenance 126–7;
plants for 127–9
foamflower *see Tiarella cordifolia*
Foeniculum vulgare (fennel) *93*, *137*, *145*;
F. v. 'Purpureum' *137*
Foerster, Karl 25, 155
Forde Abbey, Dorset *88*, *118*
forget-me-not *see Myosotis*
Foster, Lincoln 180
Fothergill, Dr John 57–8
Fothergilla 70, *82*; *F. gardenii* 83;
F. major 73
fountain grass *see Pennisetum*
foxglove *see Digitalis*
foxtail barley *see Hordeum jubatum*
France 16
fremontodendron 104
Friar Park, Henley 176, 180

fringe tree *see Chionanthus virginicus*
Fritillaria: *F. imperialis* (crown imperial) 145;
F. meleagris (snakeshead fritillary) *123*
frost 43, 44–5, 48, 69, 102
Fuchsia 'Koralle' *114*
fuchsia-flowered gooseberry *see Ribes
speciosum*
fumitory 80, 132

gaillardia 130
Galactites 103–4; *G. tomentosa* 152, *183*
Galanthus (snowdrop) *123*, 151; woodland
gardens 68, 69, *85*, 88, *88*, 90
Galax aphylla (wandflower) 74, 113, 171
Galega (goat's rue) 150; *G. officinalis* 97
Galium odoratum (woodruff) 68, 71, 80, 88,
97
Galtonia 99; *G. candicans* (summer
hyacinth) 99, *182*
Garden in the Woods, Massachusetts 70,
71, 73, *169*
Garrya elliptica (silk tassel bush) 61, 104;
G.e. 'James Root' 104
Gaultheria: *G. procumbens* (checkerberry)
86, 166; *G. shallon* (salal) 32, 61, 74, 171
Gaura lindheimeri 133
Gazania rigens leucolaena 175
Gentiana 180; *G. acaulis* 158; *G. asclepiadea*
(willow gentian) 85, 109, 112, 160
Geranium 76, 77, 100, *111*, 127, 128;
G. endressii 112; *G. macrorrhizum* 101,
112, 121; *G.* x *magnificum* 112;
G. nodosum 81, 112; *G. pratense* 127;
G. psilostemon 96, *106*; *G. sylvaticum* 81
Germany 18, 24, 25–6, 148
Geum x *borisii* (syn. *G. coccineum*) *114*
Gillenia trifoliata 85
Gilpin, William 16, 18
ginger, American *see Asarum canadense*
ginger, European *see Asarum european*
ginkgo 82, 83
Gladiolus 127, 152; *G. psittacinus 182*
Glass, Charles 16
Glaucidium palmatum 67, 81, 98;
G.p. 'Leucanthum' *67*
globe flower *see Trollius europaeus*
goat's beard *see Aruncus dioicus*
goat's rue *see Galega*
golden club *see Orontium aquaticum*
Golden Gate Park, San Francisco 40, *41*
golden rod *see Solidago*
gomphrena 129
grasses 86, 119, 155, *178*; flowering
meadows 127, *130*, *131*, 132;
herbaceous borders *149*, 150, 151;
lawn substitutes 134–9; lawns 119–21;
water gardens 162, 168
gravel gardens 134, *178–9*, 180–2
Gravetye Manor, Sussex *12–13*, *12*, *13*, *58*,
138, 150; shrubs 96, 106–7, *106*, *107*
Gray, Asa 70, 90
Great Dixter, Sussex 122, *123*, 128
Greene, Isabelle *42*, *175*
griselinia 61, 105

gromwell, blue *see Buglossoides
purpurocaerulea*
groundcover: alternative to lawns 121,
133–9; shrub borders 111–12
groundsel, golden *see Senecio aureus*
gum *see Eucalyptus*
Gunnera 30, 165; *G. manicata* 62, *63*, 163
Gymnocladus dioicus (Kentucky coffee tree)
20
gypsophila 145, 150

Hacquetia eqipactis 81
Hakeonechloa macra (Hakone grass) 86;
H.m. 'Aureola' 86, *162*
Hall, William Hammond 40
Hamamelis 97
Hamilton, Charles 15
Hansen, Richard 25, *25–6*, 33, 113, 148,
148
Hardesty, Nancy 86
hardy plants 10, 38, 43, 48, 50, 75; breeding
for hardiness 56, *see also* perennials
hart's tongue fern *see Phyllitis
scolopendrium*
hawksbeard *see Hieracium*
hawkweed 128
hawthorn *see Crataegus*
hay-scented fern *see Dennstaedtia
punctiloba*
hazel *see Corylus*
Heale House, Wiltshire 75
heath spotted orchid *see Dactylorhiza
maculata*
hebe 61, 105
Hedera helix (ivy) 121; *H.h.* 'Baltica' (Baltic
ivy) 68, 75; *H.h.* ssp. *hibernica* (Irish ivy)
77
Helenium 98, 140, 145, *145*; *H. autumnale*
170
Helianthemum (rock rose) 97, 179, *183*
Helianthus (sunflower) 128, 131, 170; *H.
salicifolius* (willow-leaved sunflower) 170
Helichrysum italicum (curry plant) *183*
Heliopsis helianthoides 21
Helleborus: *H. foetidus* (stinking hellebore)
80; shrub borders 97, 98, 100; woodland
gardens 69, 74, 75, 80, 81
Helonias bullata (swamp pink) 70, *169*
Hemerocallis (day lily) 56, 128, 165, 168,
172; *H. fulva* 146; 'Stafford' *86*;
herbaceous borders 145, *149*;
shrub borders 94, 97, 111, *114*
hemlock 70, 74
Hepatica 70, 80, 145; *H. americana* 166
Heracleum mantegazzianum (giant
hogweed) 168
herbaceous (perennial) borders 23, 51,
93–4, 94, 116–18, 139–55
herbaceous plants 39, 56, 72, *see also*
perennials
Herbert, Peter 12, *58*, *138*
herbs *135*, *137*
Heronswood, Seattle 86, *116*, 140, 152
Hesperis matronalis (sweet rocket) 152, *172*
Heteromeles arbutifolia (toyon) 86

Heuchera 57, 111, 114, 155; *H. americana* 83; *H.a.* 'Garnet' 166; *H. micrantha* 'Palace Purple' *50*; *H.* 'Montrose Ruby' *82*; *H. villosa* 83
Hibberd, Shirley 139
Hibiscus moscheutus (rose mallow, swamp mallow) 23, *155*, 171
hickory *see Carya*
Hidcote Manor, Glos 114, *114, 115, 143*
Hieracium (hawksbeard) 122
Highdown, Sussex 109
Hillier Arboretum, Hants 104
Himalayan plants 51, 58–61
Himalayan poppy *see Meconopsis betonicifolia*
Hinkley, Dan *87*, 140, *145*
Hippophae rhamnoides (sea buckthorn) 98, 102
hogweed, giant *see Heracleum mantegazzianum*
Hoheria 61, 105; *H. glabrata* 61; *H. lyallii* 61
Holker Hall, Cumbria *124*
Holland 25
holly *see Ilex*
holly fern *see Cyrtomium falcatum*
holm oak *see Quercus ilex*
Holodiscus discolor (cream bush, oceanspray) 32, 61, 74, 86
Homans, Mary 19, *172*, 173
honesty *see Lunaria*
honeysuckle *see Lonicera*
Hooker, Sir Joseph 73
Hoole House, Lancashire 180
hop, golden 112, *113*
Hordeum jubatum (foxtail barley) 132
horse chestnut *see Aesculus hippocastanum*
hosta *19*, 52, *61*, 141, 155, *173*; shrub borders 98, 108, 111, *115*; water gardens 160, 168, 170; woodland gardens *80*, 85, 86
Houttuynia cordata 168
Howard, Lelia and Hubert 62
huckleberry, red *see Vaccinium parvifolium*
Hull, Catherine *66, 158*
Humboldt, Alexander von 30
Huntington Botanical Gardens, California *37, 134*
hyacinth, summer *see Galtonia candicans*
Hyacinthoides (bluebell): *H. hispanica* (Spanish bluebell) 90, *90*, 122; *H. non-scripta* 13, 68, 88
Hydrangea 78, 97, 100, 102, 108–9; *115*; *H. arborescens* 74, 98, 109, *115*; *H.a.* 'Grandiflora' 109; *H. aspera villosa* 99; *H.* 'Blaumeise' (syn. 'Teller Blue') *79*; *H. involucrata* 'Hortensis' 109; *H. macrophylla* 108–9, *115*; *H.m.* 'Kluis Superba' *86*; *H. paniculata* 108–9; *H. quercifolia* 74, 83, 109; *H. sargentiana* 109; *H. serrata* 108–9; *H. villosa* 109
Hylomecon japonica 81
Hymenocallis 171
Hypericum 100; *H. calycinum* (rose of Sharon, St John's wort) 112, 121; *H. olympicum* 183

Iberis sempervirens (candytuft) 94, *107*
Iceland poppy *see Papaver nudicaule*
ice plants *42*
Ilex (holly) 68, 97, 98; *I.* x *altaclerensis* 78; *I. aquifolium* 68, 78, 103; *I. glabra* (inkberry) 78, 102, 166; *I.* x *meserveae* 102; *I. verticillata* (winterberry) 166, 171, 173; *I. vomitoria* (yaupon) 86
indigo bush *see Amorpha fruticosa*
indigo, wild *see Baptisia*
inkberry *see Ilex glabra*
Inula magnifica 97
Inverewe, Scotland *24, 44*
Iris 12, 40, 62, *80, 136*; *I. cristata* 81, 171; *I. douglasiana* 41, *101*; *I. ensata* (Japanese flag) 56, 165, *165*, 169; *I. foetidissima* (Gladwin iris) 80; *I. hexagona* (Louisiana iris) 171; *I. laevigata* (Japanese water iris) 162, 169; *I. pallida* 13; *I. pseudacorus* (yellow flag) *115*, 160, *161*, 162, 163; *I. setosa canadensis 176*; *I. sibirica* 97, 145, 151, 170; *I. spuria* 170; *I. versicolor* 170; herbaceous borders 145, 151; shrub borders *107*, 111; water gardens 160, 165
Isleboro Island, Maine *19, 172*, 173, *173*
Italian cypress *see Cupressus sempervirens* 'Fastigata'
Itea: I. ilicifolia 105; *I. virginica* 74
ivy *see Hedera helix*
ivy, poison *see Rhus radicans*

Jacaranda mimosifolia 48–9
Jacob's ladder *see Polemonium*
James Backhouse Company 176
Japanese anemone *see Anemone japonica*
Japanese honeysuckle *see Lonicera japonica*
Japanese knotweed *see Fallopia japonica*
Jefferson, Thomas 18, 74
Jeffersonia diphylla (twinleaf) 113, 173
Jekyll, Gertrude 23, 24, *79*, 139, 150, 154
Jensen, Jens 19, 20–1, 22, 23, 30, 154, 155
Jerusalem sage *see Phlomis fruticosa*
Joe Pye weed *see Eupatorium maculatum*
Johnstone, Major George 73
Juglans nigra (walnut) 57, 166
Juncus patens 41
Juniperus communis var. *depressa* 34

Kaffir lily *see Schizostylis*
Kalmia 57, 80, 98; *K. angustifolia* (sheep laurel) 15, 102, 171, 177; *K. latifolia* (mountain laurel) 74, 82, 102, 106, 166
kangeroo paw *see Anigozanthus pulcherrimus*
Kentucky bluegrass *see Poa pratensis*
Kentucky coffee tree *see Gymnocladus dioicus*
Kew Gardens 176
kidney vetch *see Anthyllis vulneraria*
Kiftsgate, Glos *111*
Kikuyu grass 134
kinnikinnick *see Arctostaphylos uva-ursi*
Kirengeshoma palmata 85, 98, 113, 168, 170
knapweed *see Centaurea*
knautia 111, 127

Knightshayes, Devon 73, 100–1, *100, 101*
kniphofia 103, 140, 150, 151, 179, 183
knotweed, Japanese *see Fallopia japonica*
Kolkwitzia 108; *K. amabilis* (beauty bush) 99
kudzu vine *see Pueraria lobata*

La Reggia, Italy 16
lady's mantle *see Alchemilla*
lady's slipper *see Cypripedium calceolus*
lady's smock *see Cardamine pratensis*
Lamium galeobdolon 68
Lampranthus 133–4
Lange, Willy 24
Langley, Batty 15
Larix laricina (larch) 46
Lathyrus: L. latifolius (perennial sweet pea) 113; *L. vernus* 80
laurel *see Prunus*
laurel, mountain *see Kalmia latifolia*
laurel, sheep *see Kalmia angustifolia*
Laurelia serrata 73
Laurustinus 78, 86, 106
Lavandula (lavender) 103, *115, 116, 137, 152*, 179, 183; *L. stoechas* 27
Lavatera 'Barnsley' *178*
lead plant *see Amorpha canescens*
lemonade berry *see Rhus integrifolia*
Lenné, Peter Josef 18
Lent lily *see Narcissus pseudonarcissus*
leopard's bane *see Doronicum*
Leopold, Aldo 23
leptospermum 61, 105
Les Quatre Vents, Canada 34–5, *34, 35*, 46–7, *46, 47*
Leucanthemum vulgare (moon daisy, ox-eye daisy) 94, 122, *123, 124*, 126, 127, 128
Leucojum (snowflake): *L. aestivum* 88; *L. vernum* 88
Leucothoe 80, 103; *L. axillaris* 74, 171; *L.a.* 'Greensprite' 166; *L. fontanesiana* 83, 166, 171
Lewisia cotyledon 173
Leymus arenarius 127
Liatris (blazing star) 70; *L. pycnostachya* 131; *L. spicata* 131, 145
libertia *101*
Ligularia 61, 65, 168; *L. dentata* 168; *L.d.* 'Desdemona' *65*; *L. przewalskii* 9
Ligustrum sinense (Californian privet) 30
lilac 102
Lilium (lily) 111, 145, 151; *L. auratum* 145; *L. canadense* (meadow lily) 46, *172*; *L. henryi* 145; *L. lancifolium fortunei* (tiger lily) *143*; *L. martagon* (martagon lily) 80, 88, 145; *L. philadelphicum* 21; *L. regale* (regal lily) *143*, 145; *L. superbum* (Turkscap lily) 70, *172*
lily, giant *see Cardiocrinum giganteum*
lily, May *see Maianthemum bifolium*
lily, toad *see Tricyrtis*
lily-of-the-valley *see Convallaria majalis*
Limnanthes douglasii (meadow foam) *41*, 132
Limonium perezzii 27

Lincoln Memorial Garden, Illinois 20, *20, 21*
Lindera: L. benzoin (spicebush) 90; *L. obtusiloba* 86
Linnaea borealis (twinflower) 173
Linum: L. grandiflorum 128; *L. perenne* 127
liquidambar 57
Liriodendron tulipifera (tulip poplar, tulip tree) *50*, 57, 88, *91*, 166
Liriope 68, 113, 121; *L. muscari 65*; *L. spicata* 86
Lloyd, Christopher 122, 128
loam 53, 97
Lobelia: L. cardinalis (cardinal flower) *9*, 70, 162, 168, 170; *L. siphilitica* 9; *L. tupa* 9
Lombardy poplar *see Populus nigra* 'Italica'
London pride *see Saxifraga urbium*
Long Hall, Stockton *96*
Longwood Gardens, Pennsylvania 82–3, *82, 83*
Lonicera (honeysuckle): *L. japonica* (Japanese honeysuckle) 73, *172*; *L.j.* 'Halliana' *30*; *L. pileata* 74, 78; *L. sempervirens* 173; *L.* x *purpusii* 108
loosestrife *see Lysimachia*
loosestrife, purple *see Lythrum*
Lotusland, California 16
Loudon, John Claudius 18, 45
love-in-the-mist *see Nigella*
Luma apiculata 105
Lunaria (honesty) 68, 106, 152; *L. rediviva* 81
lungwort *see Pulmonaria*
Lupinus (lupin) 114, 145
Lutsko, Ron 40
Lutyens, Edwin 23, *79*
Luzula sylvatica (greater woodrush) 69, 81, 86, *87*
Lychnis 183; *L. coronaria* 132
Lysichiton: L. americanus (bog arum, skunk cabbage) 61, 80, *115*, 160, *167*, 168, 170; *L. camtschatcensis* 167, 168
Lysimachia (loosestrife): *L. ciliata* 168; *L. nummularia* (creeping Jenny) 85, 112, 134; *L.n.* 'Aurea' 134, *172*; *L. punctata* 146
Lythrum (purple loosestrife): *L. salicaria* 149, 163, 170; *L. virgatum 143*

macleaya 128, 141, 145
Maclura pomifera (osage orange) 57
McQueen, Sheila *108*
madrone *see Arbutus menziesii*
Magnolia 44, 57, 62, 99; *M. acuminata* (cucumber magnolia) 20, 82, 83; *M. campbellii* 40; *M. grandiflora* 14, 58; *M.* x *soulangeana* 108; *M. tripetala* (umbrella tree) 58; shrub borders 98, 99, 100, 108; woodland gardens 73, 74, 82
Mahonia 74, 101, 103; *M. aquifolium* (Oregon grape) 61, 78; *M.* 'Buckland' 103; *M.* 'Charity' 103; *M. japonica* 103; *M.* 'Lionel Fortescue' 103; *M. lomariifolia* 103
Maianthemum bifolium (May lily) 81, 173
maidenhair fern *see Adiantum*

Malus ioensis (crab apple) *21, 22*
Malvaviscus arboreus (Turk's cap) 'Drummondii' 86
manganese 52, 53
Manning, Warren H. 28, *29*
manzanita *see Arctostaphylos*
maple *see Acer*
marigold 128
maritime climate *42, 43,* 44, 57, 61
marjoram *see Origanum vulgare*
Marliac-Latour 162
marsh fern *see Thelypteris palustris*
marsh marigold *see Caltha palustris*
martagon lily *see Lilium martagon*
masterwort *see Astrantia*
matilija poppy *see Romneya coulteri*
Matteuccia struthiopteris (ostrich plume fern, shuttlecock fern) 61, 69, *71,* 87, 163, 180
May apple *see Podophyllum peltatum*
May lily *see Maianthemum bifolium*
meadow clary *see Salvia pratensis*
meadow foam *see Limnanthes douglasii*
meadow lily *see Lilium canadense*
meadows *see flowering meadows*
meadowsweet *see Filipendula*
Meconopsis (poppy) 52, 113, 180; *M. betonicifolia* (Himalayan poppy) 88, 97, *173; M. cambrica* (Welsh poppy) 81
Mediterranean plants 51, 52, 180–1; shrubs 39, 56, 57, 97, 103, 104–5
Mentha (mint) 133, 134; *M. aquatica* (water mint) 163
Menyanthes trifoliata (bog buckbean) 171
Menzies, Arthur L. 40
Mercurialis perennis (dog's mercury) 80
Mertensia 90, 97; *M. virginica* (Virginia bluebell) *11,* 86, 113
Mexican blue palm *see Erythea armata*
Mexican feather grass *see Stipa tenuissima*
Mexican orange *see Choisya ternata*
Michaux, André 70
microclimates 38, 44, 48–50, 67, 75, 99, 105
Milium effusum 'Aureum' (Bowles' golden grass) 101
Miller, Philip 15
Miller, Wilhelm 10, 22–3
Mimulus (monkey musk) 171; *M. guttatus* 168
mint *see Mentha*
Miscanthus 65, 128, 155, *159,* 168; *M. sinensis,* 'Gracilimus' *146; M.s.,* 'Malepartus' *154; M. s.,* 'Variegatus' *143*
Miss Willmott's ghost *see Eryngium giganteum*
Mitchella repens (partridgeberry) 86
mixed borders 93–4, 94, *see also* herbaceous borders
moccasin flower *see Cypripedium acaule*
Molinia caerulea arundinacea (moorgrass) *159*
Monarda 'Croftway Pink' *149; M. didyma* (bee balm, oswego tea) 168, 170; *M. fistulosa* 168
mondo grass *see Ophiopogon japonicus*
monkey musk *see Mimulus*

monkshood *see Aconitum*
Monterey cypress *see Cupressus macrocarpa*
Monterey pine *see Pinus radiata*
moon daisy *see Leucanthemum vulgare*
moorgrass *see Molinia caerulea arundinacea*
moraine (scree) 181
Moroccan broom *see Cytisus battandieri*
Morris, William 11, 23, 24
Morrison, Darrel 26, 121, 155
mosses 100, 121
mother-of-thousands *see Saxifraga stolonifera*
Mount Cuba, Delaware 50, 166, *166, 167*
mountain ash, American *see Sorbus americana*
mountain flax *see Phormium cookianum*
mountain laurel *see Kalmia latifolia*
mountain maple *see Acer spicatum*
mousewood *see Acer pensylvanicum*
mugo pines *see Pinus mugo*
mullein *see Verbascum*
Murdoch, Dame Elizabeth *30*
muscari 88, 122, 127
Muthesius, Herman 24
Myosotis (forget-me-not) 12, 111, 132; *M. palustris* (water forget-me-not) 160, 163
Myrica (sweet gale) 106; *M. gale* 171, 173; *M. pensylvanica* 98
Myrtus (myrtle) 183; *M. communis* 103; *M.c. tarentina* 103; *M. lechleriana* 73; *M. luma* 105

Nancy Bryan Luce Herb Garden *135*
Narcissus (daffodil) 88, *88,* 90, 122, 128; *N. poeticus* 127; *N. pseudonarcissus* (Lent lily) 88, *118, 123; N.p. obvallaris* (Tenby daffodil) *118*
narrow swamp fern *see Dryopteris cristata*
nasturtium *see Tropaeolum majus*
Nectaroscordum siculum 152
Nemophila menziesii (baby blue eyes) 40
Nepeta (catmint) 127, 147; *N. sibirica* *143; N.* 'Six Hills Giant' *13*
Nephrophyllidium faurei (deer cabbage) 171
netted chain fern *see Woodwardia areolata*
New England Wild Flower Society 70
New York Botanical Garden *135*
New Zealand 61, 61, 105
New Zealand flax *see Phormium*
Newby Hall, Yorkshire *80, 109*
Nicotiana (tobacco plant) 133, 151; *N. langsdorffii 178*
Nigella (love-in-the-mist): *N. damascena* 129, 132; *N.d.* 'Miss Jekyll' 152; *N. hispanica* 129, 132, 152
Ninfa, Italy 62, *63, 165*
Norfolk reed *see Phragmites australis*
North America: climate 27, 44, 48, 51–2, 57, 61; herbaceous borders 141; history of gardening styles 18–23, 24, 26; lawns 118, 119, 120–1; native-plant gardening 30–2; shrub borders 97–8, 102; woodland gardens 68, 70–1, 72, 73–4, 85–6
Norway maple *see Acer platanoides*
Nothofagus 61; *N. procera* 73
Nuphar lutea (brandy bottle) 162

Nymphaea (waterlily): *N. alba* 162; *N. odorata* 162; *N. tuberosa* 162
Nyssa sylvatica 82

oak *see Quercus*
oceanspray *see Holodiscus discolor*
Oconee bell *see Shortia galacifolia*
Oehme, Wolfgang *23,* 65, 154, *154, 155, 159*
Oenothera (evening primrose) 111, 151; *O. biennis* 137; *O. speciosa* 131; *O. tetragona* 145
Olearia (daisy bush) 61, 105; *O. chathamica* 61; *O.* 'Henry Travis' (syn. *O. semidentata*) 61
olive, Russian *see Elaeagnus angustifolia*
Olmsted, Frederick Law 18–19, 119
Omphalodes 81, 100, 108; *O. verna* (blue-eyed Mary) 81
Onoclea sensibilis (sensitive fern) 61, 87, 170, 180
Onopordum 103, 151; *O. acanthium* (Scotch thistle) 152, 183
Ophiopogon 68, 121; *O. japonicus* (mondo grass) 86; *O. planiscapus* 'Nigrescens' *138*
Ophrys apifera (bee orchid) 128
opium poppy *see Papaver somniferum*
Opuntia (prickly pear cactus) 70
Orchis mascula 123
Oregon grape *see Mahonia aquifolium*
oriental poppy *see Papaver orientalis*
Origanum vulgare (marjoram) 'Aureum' *178*
Orontium aquaticum (golden club) 162–3
Osage orange *see Maclura pomifera*
Osmanthus 98, 103; *O. heterophyllus* 78, 103
Osmunda: O. cinnamomea (cinnamon fern) 74, 87, 170, 171; *O. regalis* (royal fern) 87, 163, 170, 180
ostrich fern *see Matteuccia struthiopteris*
Oswego tea *see Monarda didyma*
ox-eye daisy *see Leucanthemum vulgare*
Oxalis acetosela (wood sorrel) 87
ozothamnus 61, 105

Pachysandra 80, 103, 121; *P. procumbens* (Allegheny spurge) 83, 86, 166, 173; *P. terminalis* 68
Paeonia (peony) 44, 99, *123,* 128; *P. lactiflora* 145; *P. officinalis* 145; *P. peregrina* 145; herbaceous borders 140, 145, 151
pagoda tree *see Sophora japonica*
Painshill, Surrey 14, 15
pampas grass *see Cortaderia sellowiana*
Panicum 146; *P. virgatum* (switch grass) *155*
pansy 132
Papaver (poppy) 132, 145, 183; *P. nudicaule* (Iceland poppy) 12; *P. orientalis* (oriental poppy) *24, 93, 123,* 128, 140; *P. rhoeas* (field poppy, Flanders poppy) *123, 124,* 126, 128, *128; P. somniferum* (opium poppy) 152
paper birch *see Betula papyrifera*
partridgeberry *see Mitchella repens*
Paulownia 82; *P. tomentosa* 45
Paxton, Joseph 18

pear, weeping *see Pyrus salicifolia* 'Pendula'
Pennisetum (fountain grass) 159, 168; *P. alopecuroides 23,* 154, *155; P. orientale* 132; *P. setaceum* 132
penstemon 55, 114, *145*
peony *see Paeonia*
perennials 39, 50–2, 56, 61; herbaceous borders 141–5, 145; rock gardens 175; shrub borders 93, 94, 97–8, 99, 111–13, *111;* water gardens 160–2, 163, 165–71; woodland gardens 67, 69, 80–6
periwinkle *see Vinca*
Perovskia 98, 145, *148,* 155; *P. atriplicifolia* (Russian sage) *23, 155*
Persicaria 106, 128; *P. affinis* 'Superba' *140; P. amplexicaulis 24,* 128; *P. bistorta* (bistort) *101,* 163; *P. capitata* 133; *P. polystachya* 128
pesticides 121
Petasites 121; *P. japonicus 47; P.j. giganteus* 163
pH of soil 52–3, 75, 88, 133
philadelphus *47,* 56, *96,* 108
Phillyrea 86, 103; *P. latifolia* 78
Phlomis 98, 183; *P. fruticosa* (Jerusalem sage) 103
Phlox 55, 101; *P. divaricata* 50, *83,* 86, *91,* 112, *166, 173; P. paniculata* 143, *148; P. stolonifera* 83, 86, 97, 112, 166; *P.s.* 'Alba' *166; P. subulata* 134; herbaceous borders *140, 143,* 145, *145,* 150
Phormium (New Zealand flax) 61, 105, *114,* 183; *P. cookianum* (mountain flax) 61; *P. tenax* 61, *61*
phosphorus 52, 53, 133
Phragmites australis (common reed, Norfolk reed) 160, 162, *163*
phuopsis 179
Phyllitis scolopendrium (hart's tongue fern) 87
Phyllostachys bambusoides (timber bamboo) 63
Picea (spruce) 34, *172; P. abies* 46; *P. glauca* 34, 46; *P. nigra* 46; *P. pungens* (Colorado spruce) *182; P. sitchensis* (sitka spruce) 74
pick-a-back plant *see Tolmiea menziesii*
pickerel weed *see Pontederia cordata*
Pierce's Woods, Longwood 82–3, *82, 83*
pieris 74
pimpernel 132
pink-shell azalea *see Rhododendron vaseyi*
Pinus (pine) 62, *172, 173; P. banksiana* 46; *P. mugo* (mugo pine) 173; *P. pinea* (stone pine, umbrella pine) *63; P. radiata* (Monterey pine) 40; *P. resinosa* 46; *P. strobus* 46
pitcher plant *see Sarracenia*
pittosporum 61, 105
pixie moss *see Pyxidanthera barbulata*
plane tree 28
Poa pratensis (Kentucky bluegrass) 120
Podophyllum peltatum (May apple) 35, *83,* 86, 90, 155
poison ivy *see Rhus radicans*
Polemonium (Jacob's ladder) 111, 127
Pollan, Michael 119

Polygonatum (Solomon's seal) 68, 69, 80, 94, 97; *P.* x *hybridum* 111; *P. odoratum* 111, 112–13
polypodium 87
Polystichum 69, 181; *P. acrostichoides* 69; *P. munitum* (Christmas fern, sword fern) 69, 87, 171, 180; *P. setiferum* (soft shield fern) 87
ponds *see* water gardens
Pontederia cordata (pickerel weed) 169, 170
poplar *see Populus*
poppy *see Papaver*
poppy, matilija *see Romneya coulteri*
poppy, snow *see Eomecon chionantha*
poppy mallow *see Callirhoe involucrata*
Populus (poplar) 68; *P. canadensis* 35, 47; *P. nigra* 'Italica' (Lombardy poplar) 34, 47; *P. tremuloides* (quaking aspen) 34, *41*, 46
Portugal laurel *see Prunus lusitanica*
potassium 52, 133
prairie coneflower *see Ratibidia columnifera*
prairie meadows 23, 126, 128, 130–1
prairie sentinel *82*
Price, Uvedale 16, 19
prickly pear cactus *see Opuntia*
primrose *see Primula vulgaris*
Primula 52, *61*, 69, 97, *166*, 168, 170, 180; *P. florindae* 80, 168; *P. ioessa* 173; *P. japonica* 173; *P. veris* (cowslip) 111, 127; *P. vulgaris* (primrose) 18–19, 69, 81
Prunella vulgaris 127
Prunus: P. avium (wild cherry) 68; *P. laurocerasus* (cherry laurel) 78, 103; *P. lusitanica* (Portugal laurel) 78, 103; *P. spinosa* 'Purpurea' *114*
Pseudopanax crassifolius 61
Pseudotsuga menziesii (Douglas fir) 32, 74, *86*, *120*, *140*
Pückler-Muskau, Prince 16–18
Pueraria lobata (Kudzu vine) 30, 73, *172*
Pulmonaria 68, 77, 81, 100; *P. saccharata* 'Reginald Kay' 77
pulsatilla 127
Puya chilensis 41
pyrethrum 145
Pyrus salicifolia 'Pendula' (weeping pear) *146*
Pyxidanthera barbulata (pixie moss) 70

quaking aspen *see Populus tremuloides*
quaking grass *see Briza*
quamash *see Camassia quamash*
queen of the prairie *see Filipendula rubra*
Quercus (oak) *166*; *Q. agrifolia* 68, 86; *Q. alba* (white oak) 90, 166; *Q. chrysolepsis* (canyon oak) 86; *Q. douglasii* (blue oak) 86; *Q. ilex* (holm oak) 68, 75; *Q. kelloggii* 86, 90; *Q. lobata* (valley oak) 86; *Q. robur* 88; *Q. rubra* (red oak) 57, 90, 166; *Q. virginiana* 86

Ramonda myconi 173
Ranunculus (buttercup) 128, 132; *R. acris* 122; *R. bulbosus* 122; *R. repens* 122
Ratibidia columnifera (prairie coneflower) 130

redbud *see Cercis canadensis*
reedmace *see Typha latifolia*
reeds 162
regal lily *see Lilium regale*
Rehder, Alfred 44
Reiss, Phyllis *143*
Repton, Humphry 15, 16
Reseda alba 183
Rhamnus: R. alaternus (buckthorn) 103; *R.a.* 'Argenteovariegata' 103; *R. californica* (coffee berry) 86
Rhaza orientalis 71
rheum 168, 170
Rhododendron (rhododendrons and azaleas) 15, 28, 40, *50*, 52, 56, 57, 61; *R. arborescens* 83; *R. arboreum* 73; *R. atlanticum* 82; *R. austrinum* 83; *R. canadense* 171; *R. candelulaceum* 83; *R. catawbiense* 74; *R. kaempferi* (torch azalea) 91; *R. maximum* (rosebay) 74; *R. ponticum* 30; *R. prunifolium* 166; *R. serrulatum* 82; *R. vaseyi* (pink-shell azalea) *50*, 74, 83; *R. viscosum* 82; rock gardens 173, 177; shrub borders 97, 98, *100*, 102, 103, 106, *107*; water gardens 166, 168; woodland gardens 72, 74, 76, 80, 83, 88, *90*
Rhodotypos scandens 105
rhubarb 168
Rhus (sumach) 20, 98, 102; *R. integrifolia* (lemonade berry) 86; *R. radicans* (poison ivy) 73; *R. typhina* (stag's horn sumach) *34*, 102
Ribes: R. sanguineum 61; *R. speciosum* (fuchsia-flowered gooseberry) 86
rimu *see Dacrydium cupressinum*
river fern *see Thelypteris kunthii*
Robinia 68; *R. pseudoacacia* 'Frisia' *86*, *136*
Robinson, William 10–11, 23, 26, *175*; and annuals 132; on architects 24; on buckthorn 103; Gravetye Manor garden 12–13, *58*, 96; on grouping plants 67, 112; on herbaceous borders 139, 150, 151; and J. L. Olmsted 18; on lawns 121, 155; and moccasin flower 71; on Portugal laurel 103; on shrubberies 94, 102, *107*, 109, 111, 113; on shrubs 106–7, *107*; on starworts *106*; on water gardens 158, 165, 165–8; on wild gardens *75*, 149; on winter aconite *85*; on woodland gardens 68, 78, 88; *Alpine flowers for Gardeners* 157, 176–7; *The English Flower Garden* 24, 94, 102, 106, 150; *The Wild Garden* 10, 11, 19, *58*, 67
'Robinsonian' gardening 26, 30
rock gardens 157–8, 171–83
rock rose *see Cistus*; *Helianthemum*
rockfoils *see Saxifraga*
Rodgersia 30, 160, 168, 170, 173; *R. aesculifolia* 168; *R. pinnata* 168
Romneya: R. coulteri (matilija poppy) *9*, *104*
Rosa (rose) 62, 73, *130*, *136*, *138*, 151; *R.* 'Cerise Bouquet' *111*; *R.* 'Frensham' *143*; *R. glauca* 96, *115*; *R. pimpinellifolia* 102; *R. rugosa* 102, *115*; *R. virginia* 102;

Robinson growing *58*; shrub 99, 100, *106*, 108, *115*; shrub borders *93*, 97, 98, 102, *113*
roscoea 113
rose *see Rosa*
rose mallow *see Hibiscus moscheutos*
rose of Sharon *see Hypericum calycinum*
rosebay *see Rhododendron maximum*
rosemary 103, 183
Rosmini, Chris 27
Rothschild, Miriam 136
royal fern *see Osmunda regalis*
Rubus 103; *R.* 'Benenden' 105; *R. cockburnianus* 'Golden Veil' *86*; *R. pentalobus* 112; *R. tricolor* 112
Rudbeckia (coneflower) 23, 145, 155; *R. hirta* (black-eyed Susan) 130; *R. laciniata* 170
rue anemone *see Anemonella thalictroides*
Ruinen, Holland 54, *55*, *146*, 147
Ruscus aculeatus (butcher's broom) 78
rushes 162, 163
Ruskin, John 11, 23
Russian olive *see Elaeagnus angustifolia*
ryegrass 119, 128

sage *see Salvia*
sage, Russian *see Perovskia atriplicifolia*
Sagittaria sagittifolia (arrowhead) 160, 162
sago palm *see Cycas revoluta*
saguaro *see Carnegia gigantea*
St John's wort (*Hypericum calycinum*) 121
salad burnet *see Sanguisorba minor*
salal *see Gaultheria shallon*
Salix (willow) 160; *S. alba* 163; *S.a. vitellina* 'Britzensis' 163; *S. sachalinensis* 'Sekka' (syn. *S. udensis* 'Sekka') 163
Salvia 140; 'Indigo Spires' *133*; *S. farinacea* 'Victoria' 133; *S. officinalis* 12, 111, *137*, 179, 183; *S.o.* Purpurascens Group *12*, *114*, *140*; *S. patens* 133; *S. pratensis* (meadow clary) 127, 132, 133; *S. regla* 86; *S. sclarea* 145; *S.s. turkestanica* 133; *S. taraxacifolia* 133
sandy soil 53, 98, 133, 141
Sanguinaria canadensis (bloodroot) 68, 86, 112, 166; *S.c.* 'Flore Pleno' 86
Sanguisorba 55, *143*; *S. canadensis* 146; *S. minor* (salad burnet) 127
Santa Barbara Botanic Garden 57
santolina *115*, 179, 183
Sarcococca (Christmas box) 80, 103, 108
Sarracenia (pitcher plant) 70, 171
Sasa veitchii 105
Saxifraga (rockfoils) 94, 158, 173; *S. fortunei* 113; *S. stolonifera* (mother-of-thousands) 112; *S. urbium* (London pride) 'Elliot' 134
scabious 111, 127, 145, 151
Schinkel, Karl Freidrich 18
Schizostylis (Kaffir lily) 161
Schoenaich, Brita von 132
scilla 69, 88, 105, *115*, 122, 151
Scirpus lacustris (bullrush) 163
Scotch thistle *see Onopordum acanthium*
Scott, Frank J. 119
scree gardens 180–1

sea buckthorn *see Hippophae rhamnoides*
sea-kale, giant *see Crambe cordifolia*
seathrift *see Armeria maritima*
sedges 86, *130*, 162, 163, 183, *see also Carex*
Sedum 107, 139, 155, *159*, *178*, 183; *S. telephium* 127; *S.t.* 'Autumn Joy' *23*, *154*; herbaceous borders *140*, *143*, 145
self-seeding plants 54, 97, 151–2, 183
Senecio: S. aureus (syn. *Packera aurea*)(golden groundsel) *167*; *S. smithii* 161, 169
sensitive fern *see Onoclea sensibilis*
shadbush *see Amelanchier canadensis*
shade 65, 67–8, 74–5, 99, *see also* woodland gardens
sheep laurel *see Kalmia angustifolia*
shield fern *see Dryopteris carthusiana*
Shipman, Ellen Biddle 28
shooting star *see Dodecatheon*
Shortia galacifolia (Oconee bell) 70, 74, 113, 166
shrubberies and shrub borders 93, 94–6, 99; Britain 96–7, 100–1; bulbs 94, 99; North America 97–8, 102; perennials *93*, 94, 97–8, 99, 111–13; preparation and maintenance 98, 109–111; shrubs 97–8, 98–9, 102–9
shrubs 39, 56, 57, 93; deciduous 105–9; evergreen 78, 102–5, 106–7; herbaceous borders 150–1; rock gardens 174, 177; shrub borders 95, 97–8, 98–9, 102–9; water gardens 160, 170–1; woodland gardens 67, *76*, 78–80, 85–6
shuttlecock fern *see Matteuccia struthiopteris*
Sieberling, Frank & Gertrude 28
Silene (campion) 132; *S. dioica* 'Richmond' 77
silk tassel bush *see Garrya elliptica*
Silphium, S. laciniatum (compass plant) 168
silts 53
Silybum marianum 152
Simmonds, O. C. 19, 22, 23
Sisyrinchium 133; *S. striatum* 116, *152*
sitka spruce *see Picea sitchensis*
Sizergh Castle, Cumbria 180
skimmia 103
skunk cabbage *see Lysichiton americanus*
Smilacina racemosa (false spikenard, false Solomon's seal) 68, 85
Smilax (catbrier) 73
Smith, W. Gary 82, 83
smoke bush *see Cotinus coggygria*
Smyrnium perfoliatum 81
snakeshead fritillary *see Fritillaria meleagris*
snapdragon, lesser 132
snow poppy *see Eomecon chionantha*
snowberry *see Symphoricarpos albus*
snowdrop *see Galanthus*
snowflake *see Leucojum*
soft shield fern *see Polystichum setiferum*
soil 27, 52–3, 98, 99, 111, 126; pH 52–3, 75, 88, 133; in shade 68
Solidago (golden rod) 69, 130, *131*, 145, 168, 170; *S. rugosa* *50*; *S. sphathulata* 'Golden Fleece' 166

Solomon's seal see Polygonatum
Solomon's seal, false see Smilacina racemosa
Sophora japonica (pagoda tree) 82
sorbaria 105
Sorbus americana (American mountain ash) 35, 46
Southcote, Philip 15
Spanish bluebells see Hyacinthoides hispanica
Spartium junceum 182
speedwell see Veronica filiformis
Spence, Joseph 15
spicebush see Lindera benzoin
spikenard, false see Smilacina racemosa
spiraea 108
spruce see Picea
spurge laurel see Daphne laureola
Stachys 179; S. byzantina 138, 183; S.b. 'Silver Carpet' 139; S. macrantha 101
stag's horn sumach see Rhus typhina
Stan Hywet Hall, Akron, Ohio 28, 28, 29
starwort see Aster
Steele, Fletcher 66
Stenotaphrum secundatum 120
Stiles, Howard 'Dick' 70
stinking hellebore see Helleborus foetidus
Stipa 183; S. gigantea (feather grass) 127; S. tenuissima (Mexican feather grass) 178
Stone House Cottage, Kidderminster 113
stone pine see Pinus pinea
strawberry, false see Duchesnia indica
Strybing Arboretum and Botanical Gardens, San Francisco 40–1, 41
Stylophorum diphyllum (celandine poppy) 90, 113, 170
Styrax 97, 98
succulents 16–17, 39, 42, 133–4, 134
sugar maple see Acer saccharum
sumach see Rhus
summer hyacinth see Galtonia candicans
sunflower see Helianthus
swamp cypress see Taxodium distichum
swamp mallow see Hibiscus moscheutus
swamp pink see Helonias bullata
sweet fern see Comptonia peregrina
sweet flag see Acorus calamus
sweet gale see Myrica
sweet pea, perennial see Lathyrus latifolius
sweet pepperbush see Clethra alnifolia
sweet rocket see Hesperis matronalis
switch grass see Panicum virgatum
Switzer, Stephen 15
sword fern see Polystichum munitum
sycamore see Acer pseudoplatanus
Symphoricarpos 105; S. albus (snowberry) 74, 78
Symphytum (comfrey) 85, 107, 108, 121; S. caucasicum 81; S. grandiflorum 81, 112
Symplocarpus foetidus 160, 167, 170

tall grasses 130, 155
Tanacetum parthenium 112
Tasmanian plants 61, 105
Taxodium: T. ascendens 82; T. distichum (bald cypress, swamp cypress) 82
teazel see Dipsacus fullonum

Tellima grandiflora 69, 81, 101
temperate climate 27, 43, 44, 45, 51, 57, 61, 96
Tenby daffodil see Narcissus pseudonarcissus obvallaris
ter Linden, Ton 54, 55, 146, 147
Teucrium fruticans 103
Thalia dealbata 159
Thalictrum: T. dipterocarpum 97; T. rochebruneanum 'Lavender Mist' 143, 146
Thelypteris: T. kunthii (river fern) 86; T. palustris (marsh fern) 170
Thermopsis montana 128
Thijsse, Jacques P. 25, 54
Thuja occidentalis (arbor-vitae) 34, 46
thyme 133, 134, 179, 183
Tiarella cordifolia (foamflower) 35, 69, 77, 81, 82, 86, 166
tiger lily see Lilium lancifolium fortunei
Tilia americana (basswood) 20
timber bamboo see Phyllostachys bambusoides
Tintinhull, Somerset 75, 88, 143
Titoki Point, New Zealand 61
toad lily see Tricyrtis
tobacco plant see Nicotiana
Tolmiea 69; T. menziesii (pick-a-back plant) 113
torch azalea see Rhododendron kaempferi
toyon see Heteromeles arbutifolia
Trachycarpus fortunei (Chusan palm) 24
Trachystemon orientalis 108
trailing arbutus see Epigaea repens
tree ferns see Cyathea; Dicksonia
tree of heaven see Ailanthus altissima
trees 56, 68, 98, 150–1, see also shrubs; woodland gardens
Trewithen, Cornwall 73
Tricyrtis (toad lily) 69, 74, 97, 98, 109; T. formosana 112; T. hirta 112
Trifolium pratense (red clover) 122, 127
Trillium 13, 155; T. cuneatum (syn. T. sessile) 77; T. grandiflorum 21, 66; shrub borders 97, 100, 112; woodland gardens 70, 77, 86, 90
Trollius europaeus (globe flower) 145, 163
Tropaeolum: T. majus (nasturtium) 9; T. peregrinum (canary creeper) 113; T. speciosum (flame flower) 113
trumpet vine see Campsis radicans
Tsuga canadensis (eastern hemlock) 34
tubers 39, 69
tufted grass see Deschampsia cespitosa
tulip tree, tulip poplar see Liriodendron tulipifera
Tulipa 122, 123, 155; T. sylvestris 69, 88, 122
turf grasses 118, 119–120, 124
turkeybeard see Xerophyllum phodelioides
Turk's cap see Malvaviscus arboreus
Turkscap lily see Lilium superbum
turtle-head see Chelone
twinflower see Linnaea borealis
twinleaf see Jeffersonia diphylla
Typha latifolia (reedmace) 162, 163

Ulfelder, John and Susan 159
Umbellularia californica (bay laurel) 86
umbrella pine see Pinus pinea
umbrella plant see Dasyphyllum diacanthoides
umbrella tree see Magnolia tripetala
University of British Columbia Botanic Garden 182
Uvularia grandiflora 86

Vaccinium 57, 74, 80, 173; V. parvifolium (red huckleberry) 171
valerian see Centranthus
Valeriana officinalis 143
valley oak see Quercus lobata
van Sweden, James 23, 65, 154, 154, 155, 159
Vancouveria hexandra 81
Vaux, Calvert 18
Veratrum viride 97
Verbascum (mullein) 55, 137, 179, 183; V. chaixii 146; V.c. 'Album' 55; V. densiflorum 146; flowering meadows 126, 127, 128; herbaceous borders 150, 151, 152
Verbena: V. bonariensis 133, 145, 151, 152, 179, 183; V. hastata 55
vernonia 128, 140
Veronica 150; V. filiformis (creeping speedwell) 172; V. 'Georgia Blue' 183; V. hastata 147; V. spicata 97; V.s. 'Icicle' 149
Veronicastrum 55, 147; V. virginicum 145, 146
vetch 132
Viburnum 62; V. acerifolium 83; V. betulifolium 73; V. × bodnantense 'Dawn' 108; V. davidii 78, 103; V. dilatatum 98; V. farreri 108; V. nudum 'Winterthur' 82; V. plicatum 113; V. × pragense 97; V. rhytidophyllum 97; V. sargentii 98; V.s. 'Onondaga' 98; V. sieboldii 98; V. tinus 78, 103; V.t. 'Eve Price' 103; V.t. 'French White' 103; V.t. 'Gwenllian' 103; V. utile 97; shrub borders 97, 98, 99, 103, 108; woodland gardens 70, 76, 80
Vinca (periwinkle) 121; V. difformis 75, 81; V. minor (European periwinkle) 28, 29, 81, 85, 112
Viola (violet) 69, 111, 115, 183
Virginia bluebell see Mertensia virginica

Waldsteinia ternata 80
walnut see Juglans nigra
Walska, Madame Ganna 16
Walther, Eric 40
wandflower see Galax aphylla
Washington, George 18
water forget-me-not see Myosotis palustris
water gardens 157–60, 163–5; plants 52, 160–3, 165–71
water hawthorn see Aponogeton distachyos
water mint see Mentha aquatica
waterlily see Nymphaea
Weihenstephan, Holland 25, 148, 148
Weisse, Rosemary 149

Welsh poppy see Meconopsis cambrica
Westonbirt Arboretum 72–3, 78
Westpark, Munich 9, 148, 149
wetlands see water gardens
Whately, Thomas 14, 15–16
white ash 90, 166
white oak see Quercus alba
Whitton, Middlesex 15
wilderness areas/plantations 10, 15
wild flowers 54, see also flowering meadows
Wild Garden, The (Robinson) 10, 11, 19, 58, 67, 158, 165
willow see Salix
willow gentian see Gentiana asclepiadea
willow-leaved sunflower see Helianthus salicifolius
Wilson, E. H. 73, 97
Wilson, G. F. 175
winter aconite see Eranthis hyemalis
winterberry see Ilex verticillata
Winterthur Gardens, Delaware 88–9, 90, 90, 91, 127
wisteria 12
Woburn, Beds 15
Wooburn Farm 15
wood anemone see Anemone nemorosa
woodland gardens 23, 65, 66–7, 68–72, 74–8; Britain 72–3, 76–7; bulbs 87–9; ferns 86–7; grasses and sedges 86; North America 70–1, 72, 73–4, 85–6, 90–1; perennials 67, 69, 80–6; shrubs 67, 76, 78–80, 85–6
woodlands 65–6, 67–8, 76
woodruff see Galium odoratum
woodrush see Luzula sylvatica
wood sorrel see Oxalis acetosela
wood spurge see Euphorbia amygdaloides
Woodwardia: W. areolata (netted chain fern) 170; W. fimbriata (chain fern) 171; W. radicans 86
Wooster, Peter 143
worms 52, 53
Wright, Frank Lloyd 20, 22, 23

Xanthorhiza simplicissima (yellowroot) 74
xeriscape gardening 32, 133–9
Xerophyllum asphodeloides (turkeybeard) 70

yarrow see Achillea millefolium
yaupon see Ilex vomitoria
yellow birch see Betula lutea
yellowroot see Xanthorhiza simplicissima
yellowwood see Cladastris lutea
Yemm, Helen 95
yucca 40, 134, 148, 183

Zantedeschia aethiopica (arum lily, calla lily) 63, 161, 162, 169
Zinnia angustifolia 133
Zoysia japonica 120